Women's Travel Literature from Travelers' Tales

THE BEST WOMEN'S TRAVEL WRITING

Volume 9

TRUE STORIES FROM AROUND THE WORLD

TRAVELERS' TALES

THE BEST WOMEN'S TRAVEL WRITING

Volume 9

TRUE STORIES FROM AROUND THE WORLD

Edited by
LAVINIA SPALDING

Travelers' Tales
an imprint of Solas House, Inc.
Palo Alto

Travelers' Tales and *Travelers' Tales Guides* are trademarks of
Solas House, Inc.

Credits and copyright notices for the individual articles in this collection
are given starting on page 298.

Art direction: Kimberly Nelson
Cover photograph: © Solovyova Lyudmyla
Page layout and photo editing: Scribe Inc. using the fonts Granjon,
Nicolas Cochin and Ex Ponto
Interior design: Melanie Haage
Author photo: Erica Hilton
Production: Natalie Baszile

ISBN 1–60952–084–7
ISSN 1553–054X

First Edition
Printed in the United States
10 9 8 7 6 5 4 3 2 1

The purpose of life, after all, is to live it, to taste experience to the utmost, to reach out eagerly and without fear for newer and richer experiences.
—Eleanor Roosevelt

For my sister, Blake

Table of Contents

Introduction

*I*n January, I sat with six women around a table in a dimly lit restaurant in San Miguel de Allende, Mexico. And while they drank and laughed and clapped, I cried.

When we first arrived, I was fine. Really. It was a perfectly intimate room with a handful of tables; the ceilings were high, the yellow walls covered with artwork, and a small lamp with a punched tin shade threw stippled prisms of light around the room. We ordered quesadillas*, pes a la Veracruzana, tacos de nata*, chiles rellenos, margaritas, martinis, wine. We toasted and gossiped and passed iPhones, comparing photos. A week before we had been mostly strangers—just two teachers and a group of writers convening south of the border. Now we felt inexorably bound by the stories we'd shared and the colonial town we had quickly grown to love.

About ten feet from our table, two men wearing all black sat with guitars in their laps next to a pair of striking women in flamenco dresses. One was young and sexy, in a tight black dress with a flowered pattern; the other was older, elegant, in bright red with long yellow fringe.

As our laughter crowded the small room, the other diners—mostly twosomes leaning into each other—started to shoot tiny annoyed glances our way. We ignored them; it was our last night together and we felt entitled to a little noise. But when the first guitar chords struck, our attention drifted to the musicians. And when the dancers stood and began to stomp their feet and clap their hands loudly, quickly, above their heads, we fell silent.

It didn't take long for me to start crying, and once I started I couldn't stop. The musicians' fingers flurried across the strings, gently, then fiercely, occasionally rapping on the body of the guitar, sometimes muting the sound with a palm of the hand before all ten fingers fired again toward a furious crescendo. I watched and listened, and the stitches on an old hole in my heart tore open.

It was the first time I'd heard live flamenco music performed since my father—an acclaimed flamenco guitarist—died eight years before. I suddenly saw him in front of me, his lanky frame and tanned, balding head bent ever-so-slightly over his own instrument, his long slender fingers flying across the strings. I closed my eyes and listened to the notes. They were his own voice, returned to visit me in the place he once loved.

Marianne, my friend and co-teacher, sat to my left. "Are you O.K.?" she whispered.

"I miss my dad," I told her—and the music had moved me in ways I couldn't explain, ways I didn't even understand.

Before I was born, my parents spent a summer in San Miguel de Allende. I grew up hearing stories of the town where my father studied guitar, and where at dusk my mother loaned my then-two-year-old sister to the local teenage girls so they could parade her around like a doll as they strolled the main plaza—the *Jardin*—during *paseo*. And now, almost fifty years later, I was finally in the fabled town myself.

Though this was my first visit to San Miguel de Allende, I'd spent my share of time in Mexico. Growing up in Arizona, border towns were the natural choice for spring breaks, camping trips, shopping excursions, and underage tequila runs. In my teens and twenties I partied in Puerto Peñasco; in my thirties my best friend and I rented a casita in San Carlos. When I wanted to retreat alone after my father died, I chose a quiet old silver-mining town called Alamos. I collected seashells at dusk on a beach in Kino Bay, and one quiet midnight in

Puerto Vallarta, I rode on a marine biologist's ATV in search of turtles hatching eggs in the sand. I was fond of Mexico, but after spending much of my life exploring more remote countries, it didn't seem "foreign." To me, it hardly counted as travel at all.

Nevertheless, I was thrilled to spend the first two weeks of 2013 teaching there. I had arrived on New Year's Eve, and standing in the Jardin beneath an almost full moon, an enormous Christmas tree, and the magnificent gothic La Parroquía church (its doors wide open for midnight mass), it occurred to me that nearly everything I saw was illuminated from within, including the locals surrounding me. When the hands on the clock tower met and pointed to the stars, thousands of revelers cheered and twirled two-foot-long sparklers—and when I asked a little girl in pigtails if I could buy one from her, she happily handed me two, refusing my pesos. Then a giant metal *"Feliz Año Nuevo"* sign exploded in flames and scared the hell out of me, and fireworks brightened the sky. As the band played *cumbia*, grizzled cowboys danced with their daughters, and gorgeous couples made out shamelessly. Skinny little boys hurled rocket-shaped mylar balloons into the air, and grown men wore blinking plastic Minnie Mouse bows on their heads. I stayed till the end, following the cobblestone streets back to my rented casa at 3:00 A.M.

Now, two weeks later, I was crying into my margarita.

Libby, sitting on my right, rubbed my arm gently, while across the table Jen photographed the performers, sensing I would someday want to see the images. The other women in our party just held my gaze tenderly.

Eventually I stopped sniffling, ate my quesadilla, and enjoyed the show. And after dinner when the guitarists were packing up, I approached one and tried to explain what his music had meant to me. I wanted to tell him about my father—that he studied with Paco de Lucia and played for the Prince of Spain and dedicated his life to music, the very same music they played that night—but my Spanish was limited and his English was basic. He smiled and nodded, but I knew he didn't quite understand. It wasn't until later that night, walking the narrow roads home past orange walls and blue doorways, beneath icicle lights and fiesta flags strung between rooftops, that *I* finally understood. I stopped, closed my eyes, and made a belated New Year's resolution: I would start playing the dusty guitar that hung on my office wall back home—the one my father left me.

Mexico surprised me. I'd assumed I knew what the country had to offer, but I was wrong; I underestimated it. And while reading submissions for *The Best Women's Travel Writing Volume 9* this year, I found myself similarly surprised by the number of exceptional stories that came from not-so-far-away. Among the four-hundred-plus submissions I read were dazzling essays from locations that did not seem all that foreign to me—places that, like Mexico, "hardly counted as travel." There were mesmerizing tales of adventure in the United States, life lessons learned in Mexico, heartbreak in Canada.

Was it a sign of the economy, I wondered? Were people staying closer to home these days? Were travel writers running out of frequent-flier miles? Or had these places suddenly become more popular destinations?

Of course, I still read hundreds of stories that flew (and ferried and taxied and tuk-tuked) me clear across the globe—to Egypt and India and Rwanda and Afghanistan, Laos and Bangladesh and Spain and Cambodia, Jordan and Australia and Italy and Namibia—plus some places I never even knew existed.

But to my delight, this year I was transported equally far, both emotionally and culturally, by stories close to home.

I find international travel ineffably rich and profound; I believe the first taste of foreignness is one of life's greatest joys and opportunities, and that immersing oneself in another culture for an extended period of time should be required for every human being. I think listening to the words of people far away and returning to tell their stories can help make the world a more tolerant, connected place.

But I've also realized that the transformative effect of travel sometimes bears little relation to the distance of destination. That profundity and cultural diversity can be found *anywhere*. That what we take from a place is directly proportionate to what we bring to it. And that what we gain from our wanderings depends more on our mentality than our locality.

Indeed, travel is virtually limitless in its capacity to change our perspective. But then again, isn't travel itself a matter of perspective? You may someday stumble upon an isolated village on a naked stretch of map and decide it's the most exquisite, exotic place you've ever been. But the villagers, while smiling politely, will wonder what the hell you're doing there, taking pictures of their laundry and pet cow. And while you might regard your own hometown as hopelessly mundane— the drafty old church, the all-you-can-eat Chuck-a-Rama, the vacuum repair shop—someone from that isolated village on that naked stretch of map will perceive it as impossibly exciting. She will take photos of your Chuck-a-Rama.

And maybe you should, too.

Maybe we all should.

Because if we can extend our definition of travel to the point where we begin to regard our own environs with the same curiosity a foreigner would—and with the same curiosity we ourselves would carry to a foreign land—then maybe we can reproduce that unique sense of awe we feel when we're out traveling, discovering the weirdest, wildest patches of our planet. And if we practice this enough—though it may at first feel contrived—it might eventually become natural. And then we will find ourselves living each ordinary day with extraordinary wonder and gratitude.

Of the many lessons I've learned over the years from the publishers of Travelers' Tales and the women who submit their amazing-but-true stories to *the Best Women's Travel Writing* series, perhaps the most important is this: the entire world is worthy of exploration and appreciation—including the places we live, day in and day out.

Travel has the power to transform us, but it may be like the law of romantic love—to love another person, we must first love ourselves. I propose that as we go about romancing the rest of the world, we also rekindle our affair with the not-so-far-away. And this book is an excellent place to start.

In this ninth volume of *The Best Women's Travel Writing series*, you'll take a trip to the site of Wounded Knee in North Dakota with Jenna Scatena and her mother, who is heading home and hell-bent on redemption. You'll go late-night frog hunting in a southern Louisiana bayou with Natalie Baszile. Kirsten Koza will drive you (and some Chinese celebrities) on a thrill ride around the U.S., chasing tornados. And you'll join Suzanne Roberts as she kayaks one hundred fifty miles in the Gulf of Mexico and is put to the ultimate relationship test.

You'll also visit Mexico a few more times: to Morelia, where you'll experience Day of the Dead through the eyes of a curious two-year-old (and his pregnant mother, Molly Beer), and to Sarah Menkedick's Oaxaca, where you'll fall under the spell of a city caught up in a revolution. Then you'll fly to Vancouver with Rachel Levin, where you'll discover that life is never as simple as immigration officials want it to be.

And you'll travel farther, of course. Julia Cooke will take you antique shopping in Cuba, and Apricot Anderson Irving will lead you on a nostalgic tour of the Haiti of her childhood.

You'll cheer on Abbie Kozolchyk as she strives to fulfill an epic quest to Suriname, Paraguay, Guyana, and French Guiana. And in Ecuador, if you're Laura Resau, you'll pay good money to stand in your bra while alcohol is spit in your face and fireballs are thrown at your body.

You will, as you read, wind up far, far away. Perhaps in that same isolated village on a naked stretch of map, dining at someone else's version of Chuck-a-Rama, praying in someone else's drafty old church. You'll confront fears in Bangladesh with Holly Morris and in Rwanda with Marcia DeSanctis. You'll solve risotto riddles in Italy with Laura Fraser and research rhinoceros in Namibia with Blair Braverman. You'll unravel family histories with Jill Paris in Scotland and Helen Rubinstein in Moldova. And you'll witness the abiding kindness of strangers in South Africa with Amanda Jones and in India with Meera Subramanian.

As always, I hope you enjoy the trip, and that it inspires your own journeys, however far or near, foreign or familiar.

When I returned to San Francisco after my two weeks in San Miguel de Allende, I began playing guitar again, little by little. I will probably never be the musician I was at ten years old, practicing every afternoon while my father hummed along, tapping his foot to help me keep time. And I'll certainly never be as good as he was, or the musicians in that tiny restaurant. But every day I'm a little better than I was before I visited Mexico.

This is the promise of travel. It doesn't matter where we go: if we give it permission to change us, it just will. I urge you to stay open to the surprises.

—LAVINIA SPALDING
San Francisco

LAURA RESAU

ᔕ ᔕ ᔕ

Barren in the Andes

She asked herself what she really, truly wanted.

Breathless, I hurry along narrow trails between Quichua family farms, past barking dogs, squawking chickens, and curly-tailed piglets. My destination is a shaman who lives in this village on the outskirts of Otavalo, Ecuador. I'm going partly for book research, but mostly as a last-ditch hope that he can heal me. Back in Colorado, I tried everything—Eastern and Western medicine, herbs and tinctures, weird diets. And now I'm teetering on the edge of bitter despair.

I emerge from the foliage to a vista of fifteen-thousand-foot peaks rising above emerald fields dotted with red-tiled roofs and grazing sheep. Two of these mountains are said to be ancient Incan gods: the male, Imbabura, and his lover, Cotacachi. When she's covered with light frost at dawn, locals claim it's semen from a night of passion. Their offspring—smaller, baby mountains—lie scattered between them.

The very earth beneath my feet is considered the fertile body of Pachamama, the World Mother, honored in agricultural rituals and indigenous festivities across the Andes. It's easy to imagine her generous curves filling this landscape, her skirts swirling into valleys and ridges, patchworks of velvet fields and silken pastures.

Fertility is a deep and ancient craving, at once visceral and mythical, elemental and universal. This, at least, is my impression as an anthropologist, or, more to the point, as a woman who cannot seem to have a baby.

At my side is my close friend, María, who was born in a nearby indigenous village. She easily navigates the path despite her Otavaleña clothes—ankle-length skirts, flimsy sandals, delicate lace blouse, strands of coral and gold beads. Her son, Yanni, skips and circles around us with exuberant five-year-old energy, a stick swinging in his hand, a braid swinging at his back. "Laurita!" he shouts, offering me a plucked flower. "For you!"

"*Gracias*," I say, blinking back tears.

I've played with Yanni since he was a baby. Over the years, a tender fact has throbbed beneath our laughter: if my first pregnancy hadn't ended in miscarriage, my child would be Yanni's age. And if any of the next five years of fertility treatments had worked, I'd have a preschooler, or toddler, or baby. I'd be holding his pudgy hand, or idly tousling his hair, or, what I crave most, kissing his tiny feet.

A few months ago, after years of heartbreaking negatives, a miracle of sorts occurred: I got pregnant again, naturally. But anxiety eclipsed the initial moments of joy; my body felt fragile and broken. Terrified I'd lose the baby, I refused to have sex with my husband, ate only hyper-hygienically-prepared organic food, let no synthetic chemicals touch my skin. Despite my paranoid vigilance, after eleven weeks, I lost the baby. When the ultrasound showed no heartbeat, a D and C was scheduled for the next day, and my uterus was scraped raw.

Now, one month later, my heart still feels as raw and broken as my belly. If my body had functioned, a baby bump would just be showing. I place my hand over the plane of my abdomen, flat except for a smattering of recent bedbug bites.

After this second miscarriage, I mustered up my scant energy and planned a trip to Ecuador. My official reason was to do research on my book with María, whom I'd met years earlier in English classes I taught in Colorado. But at the heart of it, I needed to get out of my house, with its heavy, empty, childless silence.

The shaman's curing room is large and high-ceilinged, yet cavelike, with soot-blackened adobe walls holding the scent of candle wax and wood smoke and incense. A bare bulb dangles above the packed dirt floor, illuminating the far wall, a riot of color—an Ecuadorean flag, a flowered oilcloth, strings of lights, images of saints and Virgins. A wooden bench lines one wall, and an altar in the corner holds candles, roses, stones, a lighter, cigarettes, scissors, and a golden, laughing Buddha covered with happy babies.

Behind the altar stands the shaman, a young man—early twenties at most—with a handsome, smooth face. After María explains my desire for a baby, she translates his confident response. "Yes, *cumarita,* I can help you." *Cumarita* is an affectionate Quichua term for *comadre*, or co-mother, a term meant to inspire trust. Something that I seriously lack. I have doubts about his ability to understand my situation—his life is probably all about *not* getting anyone pregnant—but María assures me he's been healing since he was fourteen. I smile politely as he puts on an enormous feathered headdress and arranges the stones and bottles on the altar.

María settles on the bench and pulls Yanni onto her lap, nuzzling him, breathing in his scent as he breathes in hers. She wraps her arms around him, whispers in his ear, kisses his hair, all in a way that makes it clear: she is his world, his own personal Pachamama.

I swallow hard and look away, back at the young shaman who is cutting rose petals into a small pile of red, pink, and white confetti beside the baby-covered Buddha. He then positions me smack in the center of the room and gives an instruction in Quichua, translated by María with a suppressed smile. "Strip to your underwear, *cumarita*."

I stand, blinking, thinking of what hides beneath my clothing: a stretched-out, sweat-stained, grandma-style sports bra in an unflattering shade of beige. And covering my entire torso are angry, crimson bedbug bites, a downfall of traveling in rural Latin America with sensitive skin. And I don't even want to think about exposing my grubby, graying underwear. I shoot María a pleading look, and thankfully, she negotiates for me to at least keep my shorts on.

With a nervous shiver, I take stock of my body, which frankly, I've come to hate more with every month of infertility. Encased in the beige polyester are my ever-milkless breasts, six pounds of useless meat serving only to remind me of what I don't have. My gaze drops lower, to the faint surgical scar at my navel—a fruitless effort to reduce pain and restore fertility by scraping rogue endometrial cells from various reproductive organs. I take a wavery breath, trying to leave behind negativity and focus on this moment.

The young shaman is now opening a glass bottle, releasing the overpowering fragrance of cheap cologne. Feeling itchy at the mere smell of this stuff, I twitch my nose, scratch some welts on my waist. I know from anthropological research that the young shaman will probably spit this all over me. Which, of course, brings up a whole array of fertility-related anxieties like, *exposure to toxic synthetic estrogens!* These kinds of worries have transformed me into a fearful version of the woman I once was—only *slightly* anxious, but mostly carefree, traveling the world alone, leaping into adventures.

"*Lo siento,*" I say. "Sorry, but can you use something else? I just have, um, allergies." I'm fairly certain there's no ancient Incan-derived term for synthetic estrogens.

The shaman glances at María with amused confusion. After she translates, a round of laughter ensues. His eyes lively, the young shaman puffs out his cheeks and does a fat guy impression. Yanni giggles so hard he practically falls off the bench. (Later I'll discover María claimed that cologne makes me swell up like a large balloon.)

Thankfully, the young shaman is willing to accommodate. "We'll just use liquor instead," he says, grinning, and picks up a green glass bottle shaped like a woman in large skirts—reminiscent of the old Aunt Jemima syrup bottles—filled, I presume, with alcohol. He chants and whistles a meandering tune as he circles the bottle in some type of blessing, then grabs a pinch of rose petal confetti, sticks it between his lips, takes a mouthful of liquor, and, as anticipated, spits it all over me.

I shut my eyes, try not to wince. But the blast, like a shock of sea spray, is surprisingly refreshing. As the young shaman spits wave after wave, I try to imagine myself as a goddess, solid and fertile as the semen-coated mountain Cotacachi. I envision Pachamama herself, rising through the earthen floor, filling me. I visualize the gusts blowing away the dark energy clinging to me.

It does require effort, however, to ignore the saliva of a strange man covering my body, and I'm relieved when he stops spitting and begins beating me instead. Gently, I should add, with a bundle of healing *chilca* leaves. It's actually a pleasant sensation, my body turned into a drum. He pounds the leaves on my chest, over my heart, as if giving it a new rhythm, a passionate, strong one. *O.K.,* I tell myself, *picture your womb as something lush, rich with potential, your breasts spilling over with milk, your body pulsing with the timeless rhythms of life and birth, a universal heartbeat.*

But no, I can't. It's too cold; I'm too shivery. My thoughts creep instead to the distinct *lack* of heartbeat on the ultrasound last month. That night, I'd lain in bed, staring at the overhead fan in the blue half-light, tear-soaked and sob-wracked. Near dawn, when I was cried out, I found myself repeating, *fuck, fuck, fuck,* a beating like a heart, a rhythm like a drum. It went on for a long, long time. Hours, maybe. By the time morning light came, I knew I couldn't bear another month of hope and heartbreak. A few days later, in my bathrobe, with damp tissues spilling from the pockets, I searched online for adoption information. Maybe, I thought, heavy with desperation and shame, if I adopt, then I'll get pregnant.

My gloomy ruminations continue as the young shaman taps me with shell-intact raw eggs (to absorb negative energy), and then (for reasons that remain unclear) blows cheap local cigarette smoke all over me, punctuated with a kind of smoky kiss on the top of my head. He then picks up the Aunt Jemima-style bottle, which he raises to his lips, presumably, to spit on me some more. Still half-lost in mournful memories, and vaguely aware that I already reek of a seedy, late-night bar, I take a deep breath and brace myself for the next round.

But this time is different. This time the young shaman, standing about six paces away, extends a lighter at arm's length before he spits the spray of liquor. A mist of alcohol blasts through the flame and catches fire. Catches fire!

And oh my God there's a fireball heading toward me and holy crap I'm covered in flammable liquid.

Fear explodes through me. There is no time to dive out of the way. There is only time to squeeze my eyes shut and pray. A wave of heat rolls over me.

María and Yanni gasp on the sidelines.

I open my eyes, look down at my body. I am not on fire. Thank God, I'm not on fire! Chest pounding, I peer closer, at the light hairs on my arms. Unsinged. The fireball must have burned up just before reaching me. I let out a breath. *Oh, thank God, my bug-bitten flesh is intact. Thank God my broken body remains whole.*

The young shaman is already taking another mouthful. I steel myself, shut my eyes, and pray. Another wave of heat. A flash of fear. Afterward, a mental scan of my flesh. Still not on fire. *Thank you.* And on and on they go. There's nothing like fireballs blazing toward you to burn up pesky little anxieties like synthetic estrogens. By the time the flames stop, my body is quivering like a plucked string, but now thoroughly warmed. Pulse racing, sweat pouring from my armpits, I wonder what comes next.

The young shaman picks up a large, smooth, black stone from his altar. Andean shamans' stones have personalities, talents, lives of their own. He places his helper stone over my belly, and then, in a powerful voice, as if he's channeling the wind, shouts, "*Shunguuu!*" It's a *whoosh*, this word, and it *whooshes* right into me.

"*Shunguuu!*" he shouts again, with the force of a storm, and any silly thoughts that were not burned up by the fireballs are now blown away. *Shunguuu, shunguuu, shunguuu* . . . It is the perfect word for this focused power aimed straight into my center.

He then places two white stones in my palms and motions for me to rub them over my body, head to feet. I close my eyes and slide the stones across my bony elbows, my knobby knees, the curve of my hips, my breasts, my butt. And silently, I thank this body that has somehow not caught fire. This body that has actually, in most ways, served me quite well. This body that is my own familiar landscape. This body that is as sensitive as a cranky old lady. This body tied to this battered heart of mine.

The young shaman murmurs something to María, who translates, "Think about what you want, *cumarita*."

I am very practiced at wishing. For every birthday and shooting star sighting and heads-side-up penny over the past five years, I have wished for increasingly detailed versions of the same thing: *that I get pregnant with a baby in my own womb with my own egg and Ian's sperm and give birth to my healthy and beautiful and happy full-term baby.* There is no room for nasty surprises from the universe with that degree of specificity.

I now prepare to carefully whisper my wish, but then, I stop myself. I glance at Yanni, still curled on María's lap, watching me curiously, probably hoping for more fireballs. And then I surprise myself by asking, *Laura, what do you really, truly want?*

In response, something happens inside my chest. A kind of *whoosh* of sunlight into my heart. It's as if a doorway has opened, a passage I never knew existed. And on the other side, in the light, are tiny, tender feet, secret scents and whispers and kisses. There is a baby who nestles into my body, his world. A baby who is not inside my belly, but inside my heart, in this light-filled space that was here all along. This baby, these feet: This is what I want. This is the wish I whisper.

As the shaman wraps up his chanting, I finish rubbing the stones on my body, with a new gratitude now, a softness and lightness. Soon he gives me a final blessing and returns the stones to his altar, ending the ceremony. I stand, soaking wet in my shorts and sports bra, plastered with bits of rose petals, my heart still hurting, but stronger now, encased in this flawed but loved body. I bask inside my own hidden patch of light as the shaman explains that to complete the ceremony, I may not indulge in the following items for three days: chocolate, pork, fish, avocado, milk, chili, and showers.

For the next three days, I'll be living with a thin coating of alcohol and saliva and smoke and rose petal confetti on my skin and hair. But none of that matters because I'm not thinking so much about my body now, but my heart, and its surprise doorway, and the baby feet, and the glimpse of joy.

Glancing at me and nodding confidently, the young shaman tells María one more thing. She beams as she translates,

"This *mujercita*—this little woman—will have a baby very soon!"

Yes, I think, *this mujercita will.*

Back home, as my bedbug welts heal and fade and springtime blooms in Colorado, I embark on a nine-month-long adoption process, not as means to a pregnancy, but as a pathway to this baby inside my heart, *my* baby. My husband is supportive, but, as is typical in adoptions (and pregnancies), it's the woman who labors, the woman who, one way or another, delivers her child. My life quickly fills with reams of paperwork, endless trips to Kinko's, long waits in government buildings, social worker visits, background checks, huge money transfers, drives to parenting classes in Denver, obsessive email checking, anxious visits to the Department of State website, and multiple trips to Guatemala.

I deal with these tasks the way a pregnant woman deals with morning sickness and swollen feet and other annoyances that pale beside the monumental and sparkling anticipation of *the baby coming.* At the three-month mark, instead of an ultrasound, I'm rewarded with photos of the newborn whose spirit is growing inside me. As his arrival nears, something inside me thrums. Something stronger than kicks or hiccups—something inside my chest, the beating of ten thousand shimmering wings.

Just before Christmas, my nine-month-old son and I cuddle in blue afternoon light filtered through his bedroom curtains. We gaze into each other's eyes for long stretches, breathing in each other's scents, lost in our secret spaces between skin. And as his eyelids close and his breathing grows rhythmic and he drifts to sleep, I cup his little hobbit feet in my hands, raise them to my lips, and kiss the soles.

ॐ   ॐ   ॐ

*Laura Resau is the award-winning author of seven novels for young people, all set in places where she's lived or traveled, including Mexico, France, Guatemala, and Ecuador. Her most popular books with adults—*Red Glass *and* The Queen of Water—*have gained prized spots on Oprah's reading lists for teens. Resau's travel essays have appeared in anthologies by Travelers' Tales, Lonely Planet, and others. This piece won the Silver medal in the Solas Awards for Best Travel Writing. She lives in Colorado with her husband and young son and donates a portion of her royalties to indigenous rights organizations in Latin America. For more about her writing, please visit www.lauraresau.com.*

გჳ გჳ გჳ

Blot Out

O Prophet! Tell thy wives and thy daughters and the
women of the believers to draw their cloaks close round
them [when they go abroad]. That will be better, so
that they may be recognized and not annoyed.
— Koran 33:59

You can pretend you're in a tunnel. You can make believe
you have on blinders. You can stare a hundred yards
ahead of you at a random point. You can walk with urgency
or purpose. You can look prickly or preoccupied. You can
wear an iPod. You can make a cell phone call. You can fake a
cell phone call. You can write a text message to no one.

These are the ways foreign women get down the street in
Cairo. These are the tricks they teach me to "beige out," as one
woman put it, to fog up the glasses, whenever outside. Outside is the sphere of Egyptian men. Men run markets, crowd
alleys, fill every subway car but the very middle one, marked
by a huddle of headscarves. Females are scarce on Cairo's
streets, and those who do appear seem hurried, like mice suddenly exposed in the middle of a room, rushing for cover.

I'm a journalist, here for just one month. The only thing I
have to do inside is write about what I see outside. In short:
I don't have the option to coop myself up. My very first day,

unsure of Egypt's codes, I played it safe and tied a silk pink scarf around my face. In the mirror, I looked like a little girl dressed up as the Virgin Mary. Covered, I felt safe but no less overwhelmed. On too many streets, mine was the lone headscarf weaving through tight teams of men. Their stony gazes felt like scorn.

I ditched the headscarf once I met American women living in Cairo. Covering my head wasn't necessary, they told me, laughing. People knew I wasn't Muslim. I was obviously a Western woman, and, yes, that meant un-virginal here, and, sure, that aroused disapproval—all of which I should get over, quickly, and just focus on making it down the street.

I make it down Suleiman Gohar Street by staring hard at middle distance. Sometimes I practice the Arabic words for left and right—*shmal*, *yamin*—to the rhythm of my footfalls. And sometimes, in the blur of my peripheral vision, I catch sight of a black ghost—an Egyptian woman draped from head to toe in dark fabric—and wonder what it's like under there, dressed in *niqab*.

The *niqab* is a headdress that covers not just the hair, but the face, ears, and neck. Paired with a long black tunic, it leaves nothing exposed. A narrow, tight-threaded grille covers the eyes. The woman underneath can see out, but no one can see in.

Controversial in the West, the *niqab* was banned in France because it was viewed as a means of repressing Muslim women—"a walking jail," said one French politician. That was my first read on it; I felt sorry for the women in that brutally hot costume, imagining possessive husbands and overbearing fathers. But the Western objection presumes that being seen is a freedom women desire. After walking alone as a blonde, non-virginal, youngish woman in the streets of Africa's most densely populated city, where almost everyone is a boy or a man, visibility is the last thing I desire. The *niqab* begins to tempt me like a secret passage—a way to be outside without actually being seen. At the end of a month in Cairo, nothing sounds more liberating.

"I've always wanted to do that," says Maryanne, a horse rancher who raised two children in Cairo, when I ask her to venture out in *niqab* with me. Years ago, she had this idea herself—she and every American woman in Cairo, it seems. I proposition teachers and journalists and a belly dancer from Los Angeles, looking for an accomplice but also testing their reactions. How irreverent *is* this? Am I playing with fire? Nobody cringes though; instead, I discover it's a common fantasy; a few women have already done it. "You feel like you're getting away with something you shouldn't get away with," says Abby, a foreign correspondent. Egyptian women, I hear, have their own history of mischief in *niqab*. Women cheat on exams in *niqab*; women cheat on husbands in them; some prostitutes go to work in them.

Kate is the only one who tries to talk me out of my plan. The editor of *Egypt Today*—an American whose expertise is Muslim culture—Kate is worth listening to. She argues that even women in *niqab* get harassed, treated like meat, ass-grabbed. That's not the point, I tell her. I just want a break, I say, a break from being so seen. For once, I want to hold Cairo in *my* gaze.

There's a place in this city where I long to do the looking. Every Friday, there's an outdoor market teeming with antiques, junk, and exotic animals. In guidebook write-ups, there's usually a warning for Western women (e.g., "be accompanied by male friends in order to feel more at ease"). This is where I want to pass invisibly, I tell Kate. At the great Egyptian *souq*.

"But you don't speak Arabic," she says. Kate's worried that someone will try to converse with me and that my silence will give me away. And then what? What happens when a Muslim man sees through a non-Muslim woman? What, actually, is our worst case scenario? Kate doesn't give me one.

But I consider her point on my routine walk down Suleiman Gohar Street, where I'm heckled once a block on average. Erase the color of my skin and hair, screen the green from my eyes, hide my face, cover my neck, cloak my shoulders, wrap my arms, bury my chest and waist and hips, shroud my knees and calves and ankles, let the fabric fall straight down to the roofs of my plain black shoes, and it's hard to imagine what a man in the street would have to say.

Tori is the one who says yes. A young yoga instructor with flaxen hair and deep dimples, Tori has more reason than most to blot herself out of Cairo; she looks like California. The "I'm-on-a-mission-walk": that's how she makes it down the street.

To hide under *niqab*, we must first find one. We try Ataba, a shopping district that's Vegas-bright on a Tuesday night. There's no clarity in Ataba on what's a street, what's a store, what's a lot, what's a place where cars won't hit you. Finally, we find a dingy mall where a man on the third floor sells the full getup. I watch the shopkeeper's face closely as Tori tries it on, receding under layers of jet-black fabric. He's not amused. He's not bothered. He just wants to make a sale.

When the sale is made, we head to the subway, passing a woman in *niqab* who's sound asleep on the ground by her tarp of fruit. "Look at that," I say, pointing like a kid. I can't help it; the idea of feeling relaxed enough to fall asleep outside in this furious city—even when cocooned inside all those layers—is unfathomable to me. But we don't have to fathom. We have the material. We can get under there ourselves.

*   *   *

Tori presses down the camera's shutter, but nothing happens. The camera refuses: SUBJECT IS TOO DARK. I am the subject, and I am too dark. I am darkness with a slit for eyes. Only when we leave Tori's dim bedroom and stand in the kitchen will my camera cooperate. Later, looking at the photos, I won't be able to tell whether the person in them is Tori or me.

The *niqab* has one too many layers. There's the priestly tunic and then a veil that fastens right above the ears, covered by another veil with an eye screen. Our worst-case scenario— that the *niqab* will slip off in an outdoor scene crowded with men—suddenly feels quite likely; if I don't grip a handful of my long tunic it's going to trip me. Plus, my vision is confined now—a forward tunnel, subtly dimmed. Though I do notice Tori slip a water bottle under her cloak.

"I have this fainting problem," she says.

Tori and I are headed to Cairo's largest outdoor market, and she thinks maybe I should know that my companion will slip out of consciousness if she gets too parched. I decide against telling her that I, too, have a fainting problem. Mine is a new condition; all the doctors can tell me is that anticipating stress and pain may trigger it. Fear is another trigger. I fear fainting. Fear of fainting recently made me faint. I try not to think about triggers and fears as Tori and I step outside. We pass from her living room into an entryway, where the slam of an upstairs door and heavy footsteps send Tori rushing frantically down the staircase. She leaves me on the landing, grasping for a fistful of fabric and the courage to move quickly in *niqab*.

Mahmoud, my driver, has been waiting outside. He's actually the driver of an American woman who assured me, jotting down his number, "There's nothing wrong with hiring a babysitter." I dislike being babysat, both as a traveler and as a woman, but Tori and I agree that a jam-packed subway car is not the place to go in our loose-fitting disguises.

Before I disappeared inside Tori's apartment, I tried to warn Mahmoud, who speaks taxi-English, that I would not look the same when I came back out. I would be in *niqab*; I would be bringing another woman, dressed the same. Did he understand that he would soon no longer see me? I didn't think so.

It's no small relief, then, when Tori and I come down the street, clutching each other like grannies, to see Mahmoud watching. I lift my hand to wave, and he does the same. We climb without a word into his back seat.

How is the city so quiet today? Fridays are always subdued, but never like this. You could hear a scarf hit the ground in Cairo today.

"*Esmee* Tori," my friend introduces herself in a breathy whisper. "My name is Tori."

I would love to know how all this sits with our driver-babysitter. Is he drawing, in his imagination, a face to match the voice of the new presence in his car? Thankfully, there's no sign that we've spooked him. On the contrary, he tells Tori in Arabic that we forgot gloves. Women in *niqab* wear black gloves. All we can do is bunch up our sleeves now. I look over at my friend. There's only one thing to look at: her mesh eye screen. And Tori's eyelashes have poked right through it.

The hardest part is not speaking. I keep wanting to say things while we walk down a street crowded with goats and men about to shear them. But talking is the surest way to expose ourselves, so we utter just a few words, like "Hold my arm," and "I'm still nervous," and "I feel things slipping," and "Shh," adjusting gradually to the new code of silence. We are entities that waddle and watch but do not speak. We waddle carefully and watch hard. I watch the faces of the men who

pass and seem focused on goats alone. I watch them tug the
ears of goats that bleat as if they know it's shearing day. Everything about this feels precarious. I sense things slipping—and
by "things," I mean veils, both of them, neither of which I can
fix now, because the car is far behind us and Mahmoud has
opted to stay there. Still, I can't resist whispering three words
to the entity floating beside me like a steady boat:

"Nobody *sees* us."

What they see, all they see, is *niqab*. They see *niqab* move;
they see it has a twin; they see caution, co-dependence. There's
nothing more, though, to take from our image. Onlookers
quit looking. Passersby pass right by. They beige out, resume
daydreams or scan the air for other things, things with color
or curves or noses. I watch it happen over and over through
my eye slit, scrutinizing the gaze of every person we walk by.
And no matter how many people look bored of us, no matter
how many eyes gloss over, I'm paranoid about the look that
somehow gets in. I'm reading every face, ready for a mouth
to open, a finger to point. Instead, the first gasp comes from
inside my veil when Tori and I pass a full-length mirror in the
furniture mart and neither one of us appears.

It's easy to fall into reverie when you're not speaking, when
you're staring through a slit and dividing focus between your
feet (*step with care, step with Tori, do not step on the hem*) and
your head (*stay, veils; stay, veils; slide a little slower if you cannot stay*), plodding and plodding, past the aisle of toilets, the
doves in cages, the Korans on tables, bikes on train tracks, cas-
settes on dirt, heaping mountains of defunct remote controls.
This *souq* lies on the edge of a cemetery, under the shadow
of a raised highway. The market will go up in flames mere
months from now, a fire sparked by a car accident; within a
year, the entire city will be ablaze in political protest. But no
one this Friday morning knows any of this. Today is about

trade. You can buy hawks here. You can buy hedgehogs. You can buy 1970s exercise bikes. There's a man who swallows shards of glass, another who sells busted keyboards. It all blends together like a long and lovely hallucination, a market I dreamed up, letting boundaries blur, as dreamers do, letting the *souq* be two things at once, as things in dreams—behind the curtain of closed eyes—can be: squalid and splendid, treasure and trash.

If Tori speaks up, it's only to comment on the breeze. Tori loves breeze. When a rare gust of air makes it under her *niqab*, she thanks it aloud. If I speak up, it's to wish there were some way to take photos. My clunky camera—impossible to wield under *niqab*—is in the car, and this place is my photographic wonderland: antique mart meets junkyard meets unregulated zoo. The clashes are incredible. The clashes are so Cairo. And my photographer fantasy—invisibility—is all but granted here. I'm free to stare, to focus, ogle, dawdle—tortured to have all those new liberties but not my camera.

Powerless to capture the *souq*, I ask it questions—the same question I ask all public places in Cairo: where have you hidden the women? And because there are things that qualify as girly here—pink berets and floral perfumes—I feel more entitled than usual to ask. A grizzly looking man walks by with a rack of little-girl dresses slung over his shoulder, and I let the clash—lace against stubble—amuse me. And over by the table of ladies underwear, a few male buyers stand perfectly still, riddled with indecision (what color; what size; good Lord, what *cut*?). I stare at their unmoving profiles and want to freeze them, right there, in a perpetual puzzle involving women's underpants, until they agree wives should be let out of homes.

There's a kind of vortex at the Friday *souq*, where six different mud paths intersect. Bird vendors meet jean sellers meet spice men meet fish delivery boys meet two blonde imposters under *niqab* who sooner or later, like it or not, must enter. It's impossible to know how trafficked the vortex is until you're down in it—yes, "down," for the vortex is a dip. We—all of us—converge with the push of gravity. A Tweety Bird blanket hangs over the fray, too high for anyone to grab. Right when my foot has found the outer banks of the dip and I am climbing out, a hand finds my ass and squeezes hard. I wriggle, shove ahead, and nearly take Tori down.

It's the first time anyone's groped me in Cairo. Kate was right. Men don't need a figure or face to treat a woman like meat. Someone with imagination pushed right through the *niqab*. We exploit our anonymity at this *souq*, and so does this stranger's hand.

Back on level ground, it becomes clear that someone's following us. Tori veers us down an alley toward the cemetery, hoping to lose the middle-aged man, but he keeps up, asking in Arabic, over and over, "What are you doing here?"

In a whisper that she hopes hides her accent, Tori says, "Leave us alone." I don't speak Arabic. I just sweat. My *niqab* is gaining sweat weight. Tori leads us deeper into the City of the Dead, a maze of mausoleums, until finally the accoster falls away. The man must have heard our whispers, or maybe seen a veil slip, caught a glimpse of hair, skin, freckle, dimple. Regardless, he seemed ready to yank Tori's *niqab* right off. Again: Kate was right. There were reasons not to do this.

Nothing, though, can spoil this *souq* for me. Not the sweaty fabric, not my fury at men, not my indignation on behalf of women, not a veil slipping or an ass grabbed, not even a stranger who wants us shamed. There are places that feel like the answer to the question of why we travel in the first place, why we bother to trespass, sometimes crossing lines that look like fences. This place is one of my few.

We're leaving, reaching the homestretch. We see Mahmoud looking straight at us, bless him, as if he's been scanning the edge of the market for twin black blobs ever since he lost sight of us hours ago. Still, Tori can't wait to reach the finish line to say aloud what she enjoyed most. I think of the other American women who wear blinders, who beige out, who stare a hundred yards ahead at a random point. I'm sure they would all nod, as I do, when she says the best part was looking strangers square in the eye.

We collapse into the back seat of Mahmoud's car with a tremendous ruckus. We phew and sigh and breathe air like people who just crawled out of graves. We yank down veils and suck down water, making the transformation back to Westerners, blonde and green-eyed.

I watch Mahmoud watch Tori become Tori in the rear-view mirror; I catch him smile as he sees for the first time the dimpled cheeks that match the little voice. She later tells me how strange this was—not because she caught our babysitter peeping but because she wanted to introduce herself all over again, "*Esmee* Tori."

Mahmoud is ready to drive off, but I can't yet. I cannot leave without taking pictures. Tori, knowing I need a companion, offers to come. And so we head back into the *souq* without coverage, straight into what, at our approach, now sounds like a motel room full of male athletes who've just located the porn channel. I take Tori's hand. It's perfectly acceptable for people of the same gender to hold hands in Egypt, and I appreciate that fact in this moment because I need this hand. I need this hand like I might someday need a cane. Cairo is excellent at reminding me I cannot make it alone, and never more so than now: in the bright light and open air with my friend, who looks as bare as I feel, with the shadows of men like a forest just ahead.

My fingers interlock with Tori's; our knuckles can't get any closer. Many things are yelled at us. "Big dick" is yelled at us. "Sex" is yelled at us. And so is a question: "Are you lovers?" Which I find interesting. Someone in this jungle of hecklers has noticed how tightly we're holding hands. He sees something in those interlocked fingers, and rightly so. If there were a place with the power to change my sexual orientation, would it not look like this? If there were a moment when I swore off men and partnered instead with my own kind, wouldn't it be now, as I walk back naked into the Friday *souq*?

Some men stare; others hiss. Gangly boys trail us and bleat the word *sex*. But because none of this happened just moments ago, because the contrast is so stark, so ludicrous, I want to taunt back: "We were just here, fools!" If there were a way to gloat, how I'd gloat. I'd pull a veil out of my pocket, wave it overhead like a crazy lady, and let every ogler know, "You just looked right through me."

But it's my turn to look right through people. I pretend I see no ruckus, no fury, no storm. I scan the fields of junk and, before anyone can chase us away, shoot, shoot, shoot. A half-hour into this reverie, the reverie of looking through not veil but lens, I realize I have no idea whether the boys trailing Tori and me, flinging dirty words and sticking their fingers into my photos, are the same boys who began doing so thirty minutes ago. That's when I realize I've beiged back out.

I once read that camels have an extra eyelid—a translucent cap that keeps out grains of sand. There are many reasons camels survive in the desert. They have special pads on their feet and humps of sustenance to go days without food. The way they weather sandstorms, though, moving through the desert at its most furious, is this secret lid that slides right down over the open eye.

❧ ❧ ❧

Colleen Kinder has written essays and articles for The New Republic, Salon, Ninth Letter, A Public Space, The New York Times Travel Section, Ms, National Geographic Traveler, The Gettysburg Review, The Wall Street Journal, Gadling, *and* The New York Times Magazine. *She lives in Brooklyn, teaches at Yale, and collects antique globes.*

MEERA SUBRAMANIAN

ఎ ఎ ఎ

Mucking About

Stepping into the unknown on the banks of the Ganges.

Stair-stepped ghats hug the western shore of the Ganges River like a string of very old pearls, one after the other, fused together by faith and history and mud. The stairs link the mucky dung-spattered streets on land to the murky brown water of the holy river below, with riotous colors of fabric and flowers between.

I was expecting more dead bodies in Varanasi, really, burning bodies everywhere, for this is the place Hindus come to die, hoping for instant liberation from the cycle of birth and rebirth. But instead I discover that only two of the dozens of ghats are "burning ghats," stacked with wood and smoldering funeral pyres. Most everywhere else, people are just very busy living. Some do cremate their loved ones here, but most engage in more quotidian tasks.

They wash dishes, wash clothes, wash their bodies. Mothers cook, feeding twigs into compact wood cook stoves and food into hungry mouths. People sell things; they buy things. They pray and dunk themselves in the water vigorously, jumping up and down as they fulfill a lifelong Hindu requirement to bathe in the waters of the Ganges. Others light candles and incense and circumambulate the grand broad-leafed pipul trees where

I'm sure all these deliciously pagan-disguised-as-Hindu rituals originated, the idea of God and greater things tumbling from the branches like dappled sunlight.

While children string garlands of radiant marigold flowers, sadhus do yoga. Young boys fly kites and launch their lithe bodies into the river, flailing skinny arms and legs before they land with a splash. Men sit in circles playing cards. They squat and shit in not-so-discreet places and urinate anywhere. (Women find ways to be private in these matters.) Straightedge razors glide across chins and scalps, sometimes in preparation for a ritual and sometimes just to clean up. Come nightfall, bodies slumber, covered head-to-toe with thin blankets. In the past week, I have seen humans performing almost every act that fills a human life except the one that makes more life. For that, my eyes drift, just for a moment, to the stray dogs and randy bulls that roam the narrow alleyways.

I'm staying on the southern end of the series of ghats, at the Assi Ghat, named for the river that once flowed into the Ganges at this spot. The river is no longer here because city planners and civil engineers decided to move it south a few years back, part of a complex plan to Save the Ganga that has gone terribly awry at every juncture over the last twenty-five years. The Holy Ganga—the goddess whose fall from the sky was broken when Lord Shiva caught her in his locks of hair—is now thick with heavy metals, pesticides, human waste, and industrial effluent. All attempts to clean her sullied waters have failed. But to bathe in her waters is to tick a checkbox on the to-do list for achieving *moksha*, final release from the interminable cycle of *samsara* in which we humans are trapped, lives sentenced to deaths that only lead to more lives and more deaths.

Remnants of Hindu blood pass through my veins, but this river is not holy to me. My father's family, from South India, has traveled here for pilgrimage. My grandparents came once, a long while back, though they died in the South, their ashes spread in a river a thousand miles from here. Aunts and uncles and cousins have come to bathe in her waters more recently.

My father hasn't made it to the Ganges, though; his own pilgrimage was a one-way journey to the United States in 1959, a young engineer in search of a Ph.D. The only relic of Hinduism he carried was a small wood-framed image of Saraswati, the goddess of education and knowledge. He fell in love with a Midwestern woman who had outgrown the Baptist Jesus of her childhood, just as he had removed his sacred Brahmin thread. They were married in a Presbyterian Church by a Methodist minister, with Jews, Hindus, and Christians bearing witness. Together they raised me in a seaside town, where I found my own holy ways in the waters of the pond behind my house and the rivers that drained into the crashing surf of the Atlantic Ocean just a few miles away.

All that liquid life created my own desire for communion with water, which I seek out wherever I travel. Yet I feel no such pull toward these polluted waters. Last week I made one tentative dip of a finger into the river while on a boat ride (just to say I had), but that was enough contact for me. I am a science journalist traveling in India as I write a book about the environment. I have read too many bleak studies. A billion liters of raw sewage seep into the Ganges each day, causing cholera outbreaks and virulent E. coli strains. Lead, cadmium, and other heavy metals, along with PCBs and organochlorine pesticides, all swirl in her eddies. And now that I'm here, the anecdotes back up the science. One local tells me he rubs his body with mustard oil before taking his daily Hindu ablution and washes again at home afterwards, to reduce the rashes.

Yet for most Hindus, the Ganges remains inviolably sacrosanct. Vendors sell plastic water bottles to pilgrims so they can carry her water home to share with others unable to make the journey. Five years ago I watched in horror as my father, recovering from surgery in a hospital in South India, was offered a vial of the gray Gangetic water to drink, a blessing from a kind friend to aid my father's healing. (He politely refused.) One can view something as so sacred that no foul substance should ever be allowed to defile it. Or one can believe that something is so sacred that nothing, absolutely nothing, could ever desecrate it, no matter how toxic or dirty.

The moving of the river Assi has not helped clean the water one bit. Instead it left a deluge of silt on the shores. I'm told that while mud has always washed over the ghats with each monsoon season, it's even worse after the river relocation. The clay is fifteen feet deep at Assi Ghat, and every day men with fire hoses force the dirt back into the water to continue its passage downstream, along with human remains and Durga statue sacrifices and offerings of flowers still trapped in plastic bags.

It's here on this clay deposit that I've decided to take a wander one morning at dawn, as a fiery sun rises through the smoke and haze. A group of men are rolling what appears to be a dead cow toward the river when it suddenly kicks and tries to stand up, startling them all in a Monty Python moment. Broad wooden boats cluster at the shore, unloading passengers and awaiting others. I pause by two men sitting on the clay that has hardened and cracked like the surface of a desert, watching as they paint lovely soft-hued watercolors of the buildings along the shore, glowing with the dawn light. The clanging of morning puja bells emanates from a small temple under a pipul tree up by the sidewalk, where men sit drinking chai tea, and I head toward them. And then, with one step, my right foot vanishes. In retrospect, my next step should have been back, not forward—but forward I go, and the lower half of my left leg vanishes completely.

What trouble have I gotten myself into now? It was more than a morning wander that sucked me into this muck. It was a pull to roam that has greater control over me than I like to admit. Such insistent desires are why I've left my home, my garden, my love, to travel solo across India, doing research, for months on end. And while South India is a place where I have homelands of the heart, places where there is family who will welcome me and nourish my body and soul, I have not made time for such destinations in my itinerary. I have sought out the unfamiliarity of the North, where the Hindi language is nothing more than sounds whirling in my ears. I let the stories I seek take me where they will. And each time I arrive to a new place, still the urge to wander more fidgets in my feet and I am up at dawn, trying to figure out where to roam next. On prior walks in other unknown towns, I've ended up on desolate roads with leering men. I've explored hidden nooks in a fortress wall, and stumbled upon couples fully engaged in private affairs. Now, I seem to have found quicksand.

Somehow, I'm able to pull my right foot out, my sandal completely smeared with the colorless clay. But my other leg is lost. There is no bottom to press my sole against, and so I freeze and look up. Because this is India (population one billion and counting), I am not alone. The two chai-sipping men sitting under the tree (which seemed so close a moment ago and now is an achingly long fifty feet away) see my predicament. "Go back!" one calls out, while the other, waving his arms, motions me to retreat. But I can't move at all. I shrug and shake my head.

A visit to India, and Varanasi in particular, is always met with warnings of "touts," a word we seldom use back home though we, too, are besieged with advertising from every direction, imploring us to purchase something we may or may not need. Somehow we're more troubled by an individual wanting to sell us peanuts or a boat ride than a barrage of car and drug ads booming from our television sets. But the India I have often experienced is one where more people want to help than harangue. Ask one man a question and four will appear like iron filings to a magnet to proffer an answer, maybe even based in a smidgeon of truth. When one cycle rickshaw driver left me far from my destination a few days earlier, a random passerby stepped in to assist me.

So I am not surprised when the men set down their tea and rush to my rescue, traveling on the hardened path amid the quicksand, the safe passage I had missed. The two men each reach out their hands and I clasp them, abandoning the shoe as my leg slides out with a loud sucking sound. They call over a small boy who carries a wicker basket with delicate cups of marigolds and candles, which he sells for river offerings to pilgrims and tourists. Someone holds the basket while his tiny frame floats atop the clay that my weight sank into, and he sticks his thin arm down the bottomless hole to fish out my sandal.

As quickly as they came and before I can even utter *dhanyavad* in thanks, the men vanish. The boy, Raju—the only hero whose name I get—and two other children with their baskets of flowers are now leading me back down a hundred feet to the water's edge. Sticky as glue under my bare feet, the clay is the same color as the warm water of the Ganges that we use to wash away the mud, the difference merely a matter of concentration. But with enough splashing, the silt slips away into the river. I give Raju some rupees for saving my left shoe, and me, and then I squish my way back in my soggy sandals to my guesthouse, intact but for a humbling dose of humiliation. Only later do I learn that just a week ago another woman slipped into the same mire and it took a crew of people, including one man stuck up to his neck, three hours to get her out.

Belatedly, back at the guesthouse, I suddenly realize I have taken my requisite Hindu bath in the Holy Ganges. I think my grandparents would be happy, that is if their souls weren't already busy living new lives, or, perhaps, tripping the light fantastic of *moksha*. What they would think of my solo wanderings around India, I'm less certain. But just as they were dedicated to the recurring rituals of their daily faith, I am hooked to inching my toes into the unknown muck of unexplored horizons. My pilgrimage has no endpoint, no set destination ordained by the gods. The peregrinations themselves are the purpose, and the stories of the people I meet along the way carry as much weight to me as Lord Shiva must have felt when he caught the heft of the tumbling goddess Ganga.

For my grandparents and aunts and uncles and cousins, Varanasi is the place where Shiva whispers his secret "mantra of the crossing" to whisk you at death to spiritual liberation. It is where the Ganges concentrates the energy of the Great Goddess that courses through India, and through their own veins. For me, this city and this river mark the sacred site where Raju and a cohort of strangers saved me from sinking, releasing me so I could continue on my own wayward sacred journey, in search of other stories.

ॐ ॐ ॐ

Freelance journalist Meera Subramanian writes for national and international publications including Nature, The New York Times, Virginia Quarterly Review, Smithsonian, Orion, *and many others. She loves her quiet home in Cape Cod as much as the reporting that takes her far from it. She is currently working on a book about environmental issues in India. You can find her at www.meerasub.org*

෴ ෴ ෴

Frogging Quintana

Turns out they were all in the same boat.

few days before I leave for south Louisiana, Stephen calls to say he has a surprise for me. "How'd you like to go frogging?" he asks. "My friend Jay has agreed to take you if you're interested."

"I'm in," I answer, without thinking twice—because Stephen is my running buddy, my Ace Boon Coon, my concierge for all things south Louisiana. When we're together, we obsess over eighteenth-century antiques, French portraits, sushi, and Acadian architecture. We're equally miserly when it comes to clothes and couldn't give less than a damn about the cars we drive, but if a rare cypress armoire or mahogany tester bed were to come up at auction, we'd both be tempted to sell one of our children. I have a strict policy of saying yes to Stephen's invitations, no matter how crazy they sound, because he loves adventure, has a mischievous streak, and in the southern storytelling tradition, can spin a yarn like nobody's business. I've heard him tell hilarious stories of near misses and improbable encounters and figure it's about time I see where he gets his material.

Fifty years ago, our friendship wouldn't have been possible. If Louisiana law hadn't prohibited a black woman and a white man from being friends, the social pressure would have made it unbearable.

"Great," Stephen says. He sounds happy and slightly amused, as if he knows something I don't. "Be sure to pack pants, long sleeves, and some shoes you don't mind getting muddy."

It's after dark, and the sky is filled with glossy stars when Stephen and I pull up in front of a one-story brick house just off Main Street in Franklin. In the driveway, a Toyota Tundra is hitched to a goose-neck trailer on top of which sits an aluminum batteau, a modern version of the flat-bottomed wooden boats fur traders used during the colonial days. The garage door is open, so we walk in and climb steps that lead to the kitchen. That's something I've learned about south Louisiana: people rarely enter houses through the front door. Even guests go through the garage or around the side.

"Welcome to the Dog House," Jay says as we step into the kitchen. To my San Franciscan eye, he looks like a farmer—big and boyish, with a doughy face and hands to match.

The place looks strangely unused—no dishes in the sink, no pots on the stove, no appliances on the counter. No plants, no family pictures; none of the extra touches that make a house a home. A bachelor's pad, I'm guessing.

"Why do you call it the Dog House?" I ask.

"This is where I come when my wife gets mad at me and puts me out," Jay says, zipping his camouflage windbreaker. He laughs. "Actually, my father owns this house and uses it mostly for parties and storage." Turns out the Dog House is next door to Cashway, the pharmacy Jay manages. He crashes here when he works late and doesn't feel like driving forty miles to his home in Youngsville.

We load a cooler into the truck bed and set off for the Franklin Canal. The three-quarter moon follows us through the empty streets and across the railroad tracks to the back of town. A truck approaches from the opposite direction.

"Probably just got finished doing what we're about to do," Jay says. Frogging season opened in June. It's mid-July now.

I catch myself wondering what my dad would say if he knew I was riding around the Louisiana countryside with two white guys. My dad hated Louisiana, and for good reason: In the 1950s when he was a teenager and lived in a small town not far from here, he worked at a gas station after school. When he fell asleep on his breaks, the white boys slathered his bare feet with liquid rubber and set them on fire, then fell over themselves laughing as they watched him hop around trying to extinguish the flames. The night he graduated from high school, he packed his bags and left for California, which is where I was born. But as much as I consider myself a Californian, Louisiana pulls at me. I love it here. I feel rooted. The place is in my blood. There's something waiting in me, something that sits dormant when I'm in San Francisco. If my dad were still alive, that's what I'd tell him.

At the boat landing, it's a Chinese fire drill as Jay slides from behind the wheel and climbs into the batteau, and Stephen takes his place as the driver. Lots of hand motions and whistling follow as Stephen backs the whole rig down the ramp into the water.

"Not too fast," Jay calls, "or water will come up over the back."

That's another thing I've noticed about south Louisiana: everyone owns a boat, or knows someone who does. In the week I've been here, I've heard folks talk about new trawlers that can navigate the high seas, watched kids jet ski out at the Point, and caught sight of speed boats zipping up and down the bayou behind Stephen's house.

A minute later, the truck is parked and we're all situated in the batteau.

"Who wants a drink?" Jay says. "I've got Michelob Ultra, Bud Light, Coors Light, Abita Light, water, and Gatorade."

Thirty years ago we would have been chugging screwdrivers. *My God*, I think, *we've gotten old*.

Jay cracks open a Bud Light, hands us both waters, then guns the motor. For a few minutes we skim over the canal, light as water bugs. Stephen sits in front, and at this speed, his face becomes a windshield. As we cut through the water, bugs splatter against his forehead, get tangled in his beard.

"I should have brought goggles," he shouts, then swings around to squint out over the bow, the wind blowing his hair, brindled and freshly cut, back from his face.

Jay, meanwhile, is stationed by the Pro Drive, an air-cooled outboard motor that proves perfect for cutting through grasses and water hyacinths. He looks like a Cyclops in his lime green helmet with the big spotlight mounted on the front. As he glances from side to side the beam arcs over the water, illuminating the droplets splashing beside us and bathing the trees on either bank in warm yellow light.

"Smell that?" Jay says.

"Willow," Stephen answers before I smell anything. I didn't even know willows *had* a smell. *Who are these guys?* I wonder again, and remind myself that boys here grow up hunting, fishing, and wandering the woods in a way city boys never do. When my dad was a boy, he loved to hunt in the patch of dense woods behind his house. He carried the rabbits and raccoons, possums and squirrels that he shot home to his mother, who cooked them in stews. Once he shot and ate a crow.

"I used to spend hours out here when I was a kid," Stephen says, as if he's read my thoughts. "Once, before we had boats with motors, I paddled out here from the bayou behind my house. Took me all night."

I close my eyes and inhale the willow's vaguely flowery fragrance, the warm night air like a chamois against my skin.

*   *   *

There's dark and then there's bayou-dark—which is more like the darkness of deep space, I discover, when Jay switches off his headlamp. The banks and even the water vanish and we're floating in black, echoey nothingness. I can't see Stephen though he's right in front of me. I can't see Jay who's somewhere back there. *Please God, don't let us hit a log and flip this boat,* I think. *I'd have no clue which direction to swim.*

We glide like this for a while. The world out here is infinitely still, but not at all quiet. Crickets and cicadas compete to see who can chirp the loudest, water sloshes against the batteau, and all around us tree frogs croak and groan. Jay steers the boat like a master captain. How he knows where to go is a mystery, but as we cruise along, I feel the space around us open up, and as the moon shifts lower along the horizon, I can tell we're someplace different. The air feels less dense. Sure enough, when Jay flips on his headlamp, we're in a watery intersection as wide as a football field.

Franklin Canal is part of an intricate system of byways originally built to transport logs to the sawmill. Ultimately, the canal leads to the Intracoastal Waterway. Jay takes a hard left and we swing around in a wide semicircle, out of the intersection and into a narrower canal no wider than a two-lane country road. The air is thick and heavy with mildew and the trees are draped in so much pale gray moss I can barely see the branches.

We come upon someone's fish camp, a small cypress shack built on a dock. That's the third thing I've noticed: these Louisiana men love their camps. They spend hours, sometimes days, in their rustic waterfront man caves, cooking, lounging, telling stories. This one looks ghostly, floating there all creaky and weather-beaten, the two front windows like hooded eyes, the little porch a lazy mouth where it tilts down to meet the water.

Oh my God, I think, *this is exactly like the Pirates of the Caribbean ride at Disneyland*. But I keep the thought to myself, not wanting to sound like a tourist. Or a five-year-old.

Jay swings the light around, and out of nowhere, a mullet hurls itself from the water and into the batteau. It hits the deck with a dull thud, then lies there wide-eyed, silvery, and gasping through pink lips until Stephen tosses it over the side.

The foliage back at the boat ramp was anemic compared to what surrounds us out here. Spanish moss hangs low, like velvety drapes, and the canal is choked with tupelo, cypress, native grasses, and water hyacinths. The water hyacinths were first introduced to Louisiana at the 1888 Cotton Expo in New Orleans, on display at the Japanese Pavilion. Enchanted by the blossoms, people took cuttings home as souvenirs, but then discarded them in the waterways when the novelty wore off. Now the hyacinths choke out native species and clog every waterway in the state. A field of them blocks our passage. Jay glides over as best he can, then cuts through the rest by lifting and lowering the Pro Drive so the blades slice through the leaves. A lot of good *that* does. The moment we pass, the hyacinths close up behind us, our presence erased from history.

"I haven't been out in Quintana in over ten years," Stephen says. "We practically lived back here when we were in high school."

"Let's hope we catch something," Jay says. Like any gracious host, he wants to make sure I have a good time, and I can tell from his voice he's getting nervous. But just like that, as if it's been waiting for its cue, a tiny frog no bigger than Jay's thumb lands on his pant leg. "This is exactly what we're looking for," Jay says, sounding hopeful. "Only ten times bigger."

Frogging isn't a sport; it's an addiction. As we cruise through Quintana, Jay and Stephen trade stories about how many hours they've spent frogging on a given night—four, five, six—and how many pounds of frog legs they've eaten in one sitting. Stephen tells the story of a friend who started frogging as soon as the sun went down and didn't quit till it came up the next morning. Jay says that out in rice country, where farmers flood the fields, he's caught as many as one hundred twenty frogs in one night. All the time he's been talking, Jay has also been turning his head from left to right, his third eye sweeping along one bank and then the other, but now he goes quiet.

"There's one," he says, suddenly serious. "You see it? Right behind that cypress." He trains his lamp on the bank.

"I see it," Stephen says.

I follow the beam of light, but see nothing. No matter—Jay and Stephen are on the case. While Jay steers the boat closer to the bank and trains the beam of light on the spot, Stephen crawls on his belly till he's leaning over the front of the batteau.

I don't see any frogs, but I *do* see a tangle of knobby tree branches, stumps, spikey roots, spider webs, and black mud that looks like it would swallow you whole if you gave it a chance. There's no way our batteau can get in there, but Jay keeps steering us forward, holding the light still, until we're right up on the bank and I hear myself cry, "No way! No way!" as the top half of Stephen's body disappears in the underbrush.

"You got it?"

Stephen doesn't answer for a long time. His body is still. His orange life jacket glows like a flare. Then he inchworms himself back till his knees hit the deck and holds up a fat, grinning bullfrog, as big and juicy as a Porterhouse steak. I scream. I can't help it. The little frog that jumped onto Jay's pant leg was cute in a cartoonish sort of way, but Stephen has dragged a monster into our batteau. Its bulbous black eyes look like chunks of onyx under their partially lowered inner eyelids and stare at me accusingly; its skin, emerald green and dappled with black spots, glistens like enamel; its mouth extends in a lipless line from one side of his head to the other; its legs are fat as a baby's. As long as the spotlight is on it, though, the frog is hypnotized and won't move. That's the secret, the guys tell me, and I want desperately to believe them.

I need time to digest what I've gotten myself into. I could be back at Stephen's, sipping a Pimm's Cup and flipping through an auction catalog as the bayou drifts by, but *noooo*, I had to be bold, try something new. I remember what my dad used to say: you go looking for adventure, sometimes all you find is disaster.

Jay opens the purple crawfish sack that will serve as our cage, and after Stephen drops the frog in, he knots the opening and loops it through the cooler's handle just as the frog realizes what's happened to him and leaps angrily, bumping against the side of the cooler, the side of the batteau, until he's exhausted. One frog down, who knows how many to go. Stephen uses a long pole with what looks like a duck's bill on the end to push us away from the bank. As soon as we're dislodged and floating free, Jay guns the motor and we're off. The hunt has begun.

The night deepens. The moon has turned the color of orange sherbet, and the air feels like a warm bath. Jay strips off his camouflage windbreaker, down to his t-shirt, while Stephen rolls up his sleeves. Farther down Quintana, a sweet gum tree has fallen across the canal. For a moment, it looks like we won't go any farther, but then Jay sees that someone has cut one of the branches. With some expert maneuvering, we're on the other side, only to discover that a banana spider has spun her web across the width of the canal. She hangs there, big and black, right in the center of her masterpiece, and we have to duck in order to miss it.

Stephen shivers. "That's the worst feeling, walking into a spider's web."

And the storytelling portion of the evening begins. For the next twenty minutes, Jay and Stephen trade tales of their most frightening nature encounters, their accents thickening the longer they speak. My mind drifts off, and I think back to a boy I once knew. His name was Jacques; he was white, from south Louisiana. We met on a Caribbean cruise when we were both fifteen and for a few evenings, snuck out to the ship's top deck after dinner, until my dad found out and forbade me to talk to him, declaring no Louisiana white boy was good enough for his daughter. I was upset, but I didn't fight him or even try to argue my position. Now, all these years later, I can't remember what Jacques looked like—only that he was tall, with brown hair. But I do remember how it felt to stand on the top deck, his arms around me as we looked out at the ocean, the tropical summer evening against my skin.

Jay's headlamp sweeps over a raccoon scrounging for dinner on the far bank. An alligator, his nose as long as a shotgun barrel, drifts toward us, curious to see what all the fuss is about. Stephen and Jay tempt it by leaning over the side and splashing their hands in the water, but I don't think it's funny. The other day at Stephen's, his boys teased an alligator by casting their bobber into the water and reeling it in as fast as they could, the alligator in hot pursuit. I've never seen an animal move so fast.

"I've seen gators swim fast enough to keep up with a boat," Jay says, then recounts the recent news story about a swamp guide whose hand was bitten off when he tried to demonstrate, by dangling a piece of chicken, how high an alligator could jump out of the water. We all laugh nervously, imagining a boatload of horrified tourists, but I grab Stephen's collar and pull him back just in case.

"There's another one," Jay says, shining his light, and it's back to work.

This time, the frog is floating on a sea of duckweed—green, clover-shaped algae that blankets the water's surface. Jay trains his spotlight and suddenly I see what he sees: another fat frog, his eyes glowing silvery-white as aluminum foil in the light, his underbelly the color of a marshmallow. Stephen assumes his position, Jay drives us forward, and Bingo! Another frog drops into the sack.

It's illegal to catch frogs with anything but your hands, a net, or something called a "gig," a small pitchfork attached to a long pole. So when we spot a frog way back in a forest of cypress knees, Stephen grabs the gig and stands on the bow like Neptune as Jay pushes the boat as far forward as it will go. I can just see the frog. He's crouched and frozen, dazzled by glare, soothed by the spotlight's sudden warmth. Stephen leans forward, raises the gig like a spear, and takes aim. *What a way to go*, I think. *One minute you're minding your own business, enjoying a late night mosquito cocktail with a dragonfly chaser, next thing you're dangling from the end of a pitchfork.*

Jay is apologetic. "It's gory, but we try to be humane," he says. "We only use the gig when we have to."

I guess he thinks that since I'm from peace-loving San Francisco, I'll object. But I'm not squeamish, and besides, all this excitement has my blood running. "Don't worry," I say. "I've seen worse. We went to a bullfight in Spain on our honeymoon." Maybe an appreciation for life's cycles is what I inherited from my dad. Maybe this is one reason Louisiana has always felt like home.

Six or seven more frogs, then the guys say it's my turn. Jay finds the perfect specimen—not too big and not too small—lounging in an open space on the bank. It's mesmerized by the spotlight, and as Jay steers closer, I trade places with Stephen and assume the position. Closer, then closer still, till I'm a few inches away and that frog and I are looking each other in the eye.

"Grab it!" Stephen yells.

"Grab it!" Jay echoes. "Quick!"

Until this moment, I've been one of the boys, hurtling through the night, tooling up and down the murky canal, not caring how my hair looks or whether I have big sweat rings under my arms, laughing at tales of swamp guides dumb enough to taunt alligators with chicken breasts. In some ways, I've gone further in two hours than my dad was able to in a lifetime. But suddenly, I'm queasy. I can't make my arms move. All I can think about is the feel of that slimy, clammy frog skin in my hand. My head throbs with imaginary croaking.

"Grab it!" Stephen yells again.

It feels like forever that I'm hanging over the front of this batteau. Jay's spotlight illuminates a wide circle of ground around me, and for a second I think the sun has come up. I feel its warmth on my back, on my neck, on my arms, which are supposed to be reaching, but are instead plastered against my sides, rigid as a bayonettes.

"Grab it!" The batteau rocks gently as Stephen stands up to see what's happening, why I'm not moving. And then, something shifts. The trance is broken. The frog leaps away.

"Ah man, she girled out on us," Stephen says.

It's true.

I inch backward and take my seat on the bench, my tail between my legs. "I couldn't do it," I say. "I couldn't make my arms move."

"That's O.K.," Stephen says, and squeezes my shoulder. "At least you tried." If I were a dude, they'd never let me hear the end of it, but since I'm not, they go easy on me. As if he were my big brother, Jay offers to let me wear the headlamp again while he and Stephen catch half a dozen more, and by the time we turn toward home an hour later, fifteen bullfrogs are stepping over each other trying to climb out of the sack.

* * *

Three hours of frogging. It's almost midnight. We cut back up Quintana and out into the bigger canal, Jay's headlamp sweeping over the far banks where alligator eyes flash like brake lights. We re-hitch the boat and head home. Back at the Dog House, I shake Jay's hand and hug him.

"I'll never forget this," I say. "Thank you so much."

"Anytime," he says, yawning. It's Tuesday night. He has to get up for work in the morning. Luckily, he only has to walk next door.

Stephen is still amped up when he drops me off at my cottage. "So, what did you really think?"

"I loved it," I say, and I don't just mean the frogging—I mean all of it.

My dad had a change of heart in the last year of his life. He wanted to make one last trip home, to say goodbye to the parts of Louisiana he loved and wanted to remember—the land, the sky, the water, the food. He died before he could make the trip. But I'm here now, and I realize that my Louisiana is different; equally complicated, but easier to love.

ꝓ ꝓ ꝓ

Natalie Baszile's debut novel is Queen Sugar. *She earned an MFA from Warren Wilson's MFA Program for Writers, where she received the Holden Minority Scholarship. Natalie has had residencies at the Ragdale Foundation, the Virginia Center for the Creative Arts, and Hedgebrook. When she's not thinking about her next novel, she's scheming about how to spend more time in Louisiana. For more of her southern adventures, visit her at www.nataliebaszile.wordpress.com.*

♫ ♫ ♫

Remember this Night

The neighbors might talk—but it will be worth it.

The teenage girl you live with, the younger one with the jutting chin who rarely smiles, is laughing at *America's Funniest Home Videos*. She giggles as a kitten falls off a window ledge onto the back of a large dog, as a small dog runs so fast it trips and flips over itself, and as a parakeet recites words that have to be bleeped out for the viewing audience. Your legs are so sweaty that it's painful to pull them from the stuffed chairs you have swung them over. With your hands you try to separate your skin, swollen with heat and sun, from the vinyl, but after a few inches you wince, fall back in the chair, and decide there's really no need to move again tonight.

Just as you are settling into the home videos marathon with its echoing canned laughter, the TV begins to flip through channels. A denture commercial with lush bubbles surfacing over pearly teeth . . . a group of young, happy people wearing McDonald's t-shirts and dancing in line . . . an old episode of *Sanford and Son*. The changing continues, as if a higher power is trying to decide what's best for you to watch this evening. Finally, the pixels coalesce into a staticky image of two uncommonly attractive young people—male and female—and after one glance at the nonchalant grins of those faraway actors you've already divined the ending.

You and the girl are unmoving. Since neither of you comment on the fact that the television has changed its own channels, it's as if nothing has happened at all. Though you have only been in Guyana a little over a month, you've become accustomed to the shortage of options represented by just two television stations, one public, one private, both of which play mainly pirated shows from the United States. One evening you may be apprised of the weather in Tampa, and another you could see a live gospel concert from Dallas. The only things you can count on, really, are the local news broadcasts and a 4:00 P.M. daily showing of *Days of Our Lives,* the nation's favorite soap opera, which has spawned a generation of Guyanese children named Ashley and Alison. What you will watch tonight, however, is largely beyond your control, and this is a fact that you find strangely pleasing.

Sweat stipples your arms and legs, and for a moment you mourn the lack of air conditioning. You remember summer nights in Maryland and the whirring, icy breath on your forehead when you rested your face against the rumbling machine. The little plastic edge of the vent you bit against, causing the cold air to rush directly down your throat. Looking out the window at the dark, quiet streets as you sucked in the chill; these are some of your first memories of being alone as a child.

You allow yourself only a few minutes of self-pity tonight. It is true that you have never been hotter. That the relentless heat has inhabited and possessed your body in a way you could not have imagined before you arrived in this country. That your brain is fatigued by the heat, and your thoughts have frayed and gone soggy in the equally unmerciful humidity. But this is not the point. You look at the girl guiltily. She has probably never felt air-conditioning. There is no life for her without this heat.

Your legs and ankles are festooned with little pink-red dots, marks of fresh mosquito penetration. Languidly you imagine an *America's Funniest Home Videos* about mosquitoes. Guyanese lore has it that if you pinch the skin around the mosquito stinger as it is biting you, it will be forced to keep sucking your blood and explode. That might make for a good episode. The mosquitoes are staying away tonight because the girl has lit several "coils," flat, dark green solid chemicals that create a force field of noxious smoke around which the mosquitoes dance. Ash dropping from the smoldering ember slowly recreates the spiral shapes on the ground in gray, druidic markings. The odor permeates your skin and clothes. Tonight, in bed, you will smell it in your hair.

There's a knock on the door. No one is home except you and the girl, the appointed guards of the house. You pause and listen. Shirley, the girl's stepmother and your host for the next few months, has warned you about opening the door for anyone. "Teefmen come anytime," she has said. Another knock on the door and you emerge from the protective smoke into a swarm of eager black specks that, despite your swatting hands, fill with your blood and fly away. Your blood, flying all over the room, perching on the doilies and crawling back into the dark places under the sofa.

Between the metal bar and frilly curtains, you catch a glimpse of white skin. Todd. Flushed cheeks, slightly upturned, freckled nose, a pink Oxford shirt, khaki pants. Your neighbor, another young volunteer who has, like you, just graduated from college. Every day you walk together through the pitted roads of Georgetown to the training center to sit with the twelve other volunteers and listen to lectures on sustainable development, cultural sensitivity, and all the diseases you might contract while living in the tropics. You undo the many locks.

Todd looks wild-eyed, agitated. "Enid's Christian music is driving me crazy. What are you doing?"

You slap your leg, flick off a carcass, rub the red spot. "Nothing. You know, watching TV."

He comes into the house, and you lock the door immediately behind him. The girl had twisted in her chair briefly when Todd first appeared, but now she is chuckling again at the movie.

"Hey, Regina."

"Hello, Todd," from the back of her head.

He is rubbing his hands together nervously as he enters the house, which is crowded with furniture, rugs, stacks of telephone books, and piles of letters. He pushes the sweaty hair away from his head, surveying the room as if he's surveying the whole country, uncertain how he ended up here. Enid is an elderly widow, a born-again, Pentecostal Christian who really wants Todd to become one too.

Regina is laughing out loud now, and her laugh is thin and high-pitched. She has a voice that sounds like it's going to complain even when it isn't. Shirley told me from the beginning that she's "Uncle Reggie's daughter," born to another lighter-skinned, Portuguese woman during their marriage. Regina sometimes visits her birth mother on weekends, and returns saying nothing. While Shirley and Reggie have darker skin and call themselves "Afro-Guyanese," Regina has a long face more reminiscent of Madeira than Nigeria, and a tangle of wild eyebrows.

You feel the tension coming off Todd in waves. You see him assessing the mold that creeps from the windows down the baby blue walls, the cracked figurines in the alcoves, the crush of furniture and heat and smoke in the room. You can almost feel his loneliness too, with its pungent whiff of despair. "It's not the loneliness," he'll tell you later, "it's the aloneness."

Though you don't quite get the distinction, you begin to get the sense that he wants you to help him solve this problem.

"Are y'all hungry?" he asks us after a few minutes of watching the gorgeous, grainy movie characters flirt. A few hours ago, Shirley had served you rice and curried chicken from a dented pot. You and the girl both nod.

"O.K., I'm going to call for a pizza," he announces, as if this were a fine and honorable accomplishment. And, as if performing some kind of amazing circus trick, he adds, "and I think we should rent a movie, too. Anything."

You begin to protest. You are volunteers here; you are guests. You are supposed to be "living at the level of the people," you are supposed to be respectful of the resources of the country, you are supposed to be a model for sustainable development. You are supposed to take what you get, and be happy with less.

But Regina has already turned her head around. Her face, below her unkempt eyebrows, has changed. Her eyes are bright, and there is something like a faint smile on her face. Shirley is at a church meeting. Reggie is down the road playing dominoes. Nikki, the eighteen-year-old, is on a date with her forty-year old boyfriend, and Frankie, the older brother who comes and goes getting thinner and thinner, is out. The Americans are desperate, and now she's going to be the only one around to eat their pizza.

Todd is moving toward the phone. Curried rice and chicken, *America's Funniest Home Videos*. No options. To live with no options makes you feel noble, humbled to the situation. But Todd is not so settled with this arrangement. He's tired of pretending that he has no money, that his parents back in rural Virginia aren't well off, that he doesn't own a Jeep Cherokee across an ocean and won't be a lawyer in a few years anyway. This whole thing you're doing depends on your ability to feign you don't have access to luxuries—like air-conditioning—that Regina will never know. To endure the heat and mosquitoes when you know that not so very far away your college friends are sipping cosmos and gyrating under strobe lights in Manhattan nightspots.

Regina watches you.

"O.K.," you say, "go ahead."

Todd picks up the little plastic phone and dials the five digits he's memorized. Five numbers, you have realized, are much easier to remember than seven. The pizza place is new and brightly lit, located on the same circle where the city's most famous church, the tallest wooden building in the world, stands. But it's a tough market here on the tip of South America because the Guyanese do not eat pizza. This restaurant, like another Italian place where you will eat Thanksgiving dinner a few months later, is for people like you, people who are trickling in from Europe and the U.S. as the country opens up after decades of colonialism and dictatorship. But there are not enough of you, or you go home too quickly. Both places will be closed within the year.

"Yes, with pepperoni," Todd is saying. "Yes, and extra tomatoes. Thirty minutes, O.K. Directions? Let me put someone else on."

Regina comes to the phone and begins speaking with the most excitement you've ever heard in her voice. Her Creolese is so thick you only catch "up de back road," "Cuffy monument," "front house with cracked window." They hang up. You are officially waiting for your pizza to be delivered.

Todd is on a roll now. "I'll head down to the rum shop for sodas—why don't you two get the movie?"

You have no desire to peel yourself from your sticky chair again, but he is insistent. Todd's eyes are glistening with a kind of wild desperation you've never seen before. Then again you've only known him a month. Time has telescoped since you arrived here, and you often forget that your new friends—Todd—and your family—Regina—are essentially strangers.

You know Todd to be sheepish, reserved, making everyone laugh with his deadpan humor. He's polite, Southern, and he often looks down when he speaks. But tonight, tonight he is staring at you with manic hazel eyes, his thin hair plastered to his forehead like one possessed. *This night is going to be different,* he seems to be saying. *We are going to remember this night.*

Regina is happily along for the ride. She slides her feet into her plastic sandals and goes to wait by the door. Todd has already departed on his quest for sodas, thrusting a 500 Guyana dollar bill into your hand as he rushes out. As you leave, you will lock the door tightly and pray that the "teef-men" don't decide to show up in your absence. Shirley has had this house for fifty years and it's crammed with possessions from brightly painted cement wall to cement wall. To your jaundiced eye, much of it looks old and broken, but still you would feel terrible if any of it disappeared forever into the Guyana night. You leave the television on as a precaution, as if intruders might be kept at bay by scripted American wise-cracks and meaningful sidelong glances.

It's a short walk around the corner to the small video store. The night is starry and loud, men slamming dominoes down at the rum shop, babies crying, packs of dogs roaming the street, barking at nothing and each other. You can see Regina's face silhouetted in the moonlight, placid, unspeaking. You talk to fill the silence, asking her about her school, about Nikki's boyfriend George, about Shirley's church. She nods, or answers in a few words. You don't know if she's just shy or if she dislikes you, or if she is so excited by the pizza and movie she can't speak. You worry that you are too talkative and too foreign, and that you will never be accepted by this girl and, by association, her country where you are to live for the next two years. Then, suddenly, she slips her small warm hand into yours. You walk the rest of the way to the movie store afraid to breathe too hard because maybe the hand will fly back. But she does not move it.

There are a few hundred videos packed into the tiny store lit by a dangling bare bulb. The girl behind the counter is twirling her hair extensions and watching the same romantic comedy playing on your TV back at Shirley's. Dub music superstars are plastered on the walls: Petra, with bati-rider jeans perched on the top of her thighs, leers at you over her shoulder, while Beenie Man seems to thrust his pelvis right out of the poster. You think how unlike the characters in the American movie these Caribbean stars are, how bland and goofily uncertain the Americans seem compared with these brazen performers. You hope that by the time you leave this country, you will have absorbed some of this confidence and sheen.

It turns out Regina loves horror movies. She picks up several boxes showing people with axes jammed in their skulls, but you shake your head. Your suggestions of dramas and romances, even adventures, are greeted with solemn, silent disapproval. Finally, you compromise on *The Shining*, which both you and certainly Todd have seen before. You pay the equivalent of a two-week average Guyanese salary to become a member of the store, the girl writing your name in careful script on a little hand-printed cardboard card.

At home, Todd is prostrate on the stoop with the cold sodas pressed against his head and neck, an open one tipped precariously against his stomach. Back inside, you light more mosquito coils and turn up the fan so that smoke billows and gusts through the room. It has been half an hour, maybe more, since the call and you realize that you did not leave your number with the man who took the order. Georgetown is a city with few street signs, lit only by occasional guttering bulbs, and it's easy to imagine your driver—and your pizza—lost on the winding, unpaved roads.

Even though you were not that interested in the pizza to begin with, even though pizza sounded like a foreign and unwelcome intrusion to your night, the thought of it never arriving strikes panic in your heart. Not for you, you tell yourself—you'll be fine. But Todd. You look at him, swatting obsessively at his ankles, trying to focus on the television Americans. He is not all right. He's on the edge, talking more and more about going home to the States and to his dog Faulkner, a black lab puppy who just broke his leg. Talking about not knowing why he's here, not knowing how he'll make it. He is depressed and he is confused. He needs pizza.

Finally, you hear a car on the dirt road. It rumbles past the bonfires of trash wafting sweet smoke, past the cemetery with its gravestones sinking into the waterlogged ground, past where the neighbors' many roosters wander in the road all day. Halting in front of the house in front of yours, its lights shine brighter than anything else on the street. Walking over the planks to the road, you appreciate the fact that the delivery car is unmarked, that it looks like hundreds of other white Toyota Camrys that cruise the streets of Georgetown, white being the color used cars are painted when they are imported, refurbished, and resold. It could be a taxi, or a friend coming to visit. When the telltale flat white box is delivered through the window, however, you know the neighbors will begin talking.

But you forget: it is telltale only to you. The neighbors have never seen pizza delivered before; they have never tasted it. This delivery may as well be from another solar system, an alien handing over its mouthwatering intergalactic offering. When you give the driver the exorbitant amount of cash owed for the transaction, you cup it in your palm, concealing the colors of the high bills: the green-orange thousand, the pink-blue five hundred. This the neighbors will understand, and they would talk, though never to your face: *Look how de white gyal does trow money about*! They would think you wasteful, show-offish.

In the house, rejoicing has already begun. Regina and Todd have prepared the enamel plates. The box does not disappoint, its rich smell cutting right through the mosquito coil air. Pizza, the all-in-one food that requires no utensils, that completes itself in a perfect cycle of sauce, cheese, and bread. You and Todd are enraptured by the convenient, extravagant food of your country, and you dive into its comforting textures and tastes.

But you've forgotten Regina. She puts her fingers in the box gingerly, lifts a slice to her mouth. She has seen the commercials and so she knows how it should be eaten, tip first, raised up as if the entire piece could be descended to the gut in one gooey, delicious mess. Like all Guyanese, she does not waste food, crunching chicken bones between her teeth to suck out the marrow. She is a girl who knows how to eat. But this is a new delicacy, and you watch her face as she struggles to discern the strange spices on her tongue. It's as if you have taken her back home to feast in the kitchens, camps, and dorm rooms of your past. She is feeding on the food of your memories.

The box is empty soon enough, the soda bottles drained of their brilliant sugar water, and you feel satiated and guilty at the same time. The box holds only grease stains now, and little strands of cheese which Regina pries off with her fingernails. When she goes to throw it away it's far bigger than the barrel will allow, and it sits, balanced over the top, sharp angles jutting up to the ceiling. Shirley will wonder when she sees it, unaccustomed to finding trash like this in her house. She has already dug your strange rubbish out of the bin several times and transformed it into entirely new implements: empty metal tubes of toothpaste have become soap dishes, glass bottles now hold candlesticks, a wire hanger is used to clear the drain.

It's movie time. Even with the bright lights of the house, even in the thick nighttime heat, the scenes of mental breakdown and perilous snowstorms seem terrifying. The VCR clicks loudly and makes buzzing noises, and a message at the bottom of the screen "Bubba's Video Store—Not for resale" flashes at random, but still you find yourself quaking and jumping. The spectral twins appear and you release a small scream. Regina and Todd stare at you.

"Haven't you seen this before?" Todd asks.

Regina says nothing but seems to be communicating that the slasher films would have been much better.

Hours pass and the thrill of the evening begins to wear on you. Nothing has happened and everything has happened. By the time Jack appears with his long knife, Todd has fallen into a stupor of nostalgia, lethargy, and grease from which you wake him on the sofa. As his eyes flutter open, you meet them and see desire for many things, near and far, including you. You have also craved the long length of his body next to yours, but the raw need in his eyes still takes you by surprise. For now, you have no privacy, nowhere to go without Regina coming along. Looking back at the characters fighting their way through the blizzard in the labyrinth, you regain yourselves. Pizza will have to be enough, tonight.

"You need to go back to Enid's," you remind him, and he nods, shaking it off.

Calling goodnight to Regina, he shuffles toward the door. You hug him, and his rumpled shirt releases a familiar detergent smell because it is one of the ones that hasn't yet been washed here.

"I'll see you tomorrow," you say, and he nods silently.

He walks toward the dirt road, glancing back at you once. His expression is lost in the darkness.

The next morning you will wake up with a slight hangover from the chemical smoke. Nikki will be pulling dead frogs out of the shower. The TV will be blasting *The Price Is Right*. Shirley will have used your pizza box to patch a hole in the roof. And Regina will be quiet and sullen again. But as you pass by her on your way to the kitchen, where you'll reach for a glass of passion fruit juice, she will flash you a quick and startling smile.

Katherine Jamieson is a graduate of the Iowa Nonfiction Writer's Program, where she was an Iowa Arts Fellow. Her essays and articles have been published in the New York Times, Narrative, Meridian, Alimentum, Brevity, and The Best Women's Travel Writing 2011. Based in the woods of western Massachusetts, Katherine leads a dual life as a reclusive writer and road manager of an internationally touring musician (her husband). You can read more of her writing at www.katherinejamieson.com.

❧ ❧ ❧

Eight Million Miles

A friendship and a fever carry across the years.

RIO DE JANEIRO 2012
I spot Allyah at the base of the slum where she lives. Shacks the pale green of sea foam and the pink of flamingos cast midday shadows on the hill that rises behind her. Crumbling remnants of tin and brick form the jagged edges of each home. She sits like a small butterfly, perched on a ledge, clutching the strawberry colored wallet I sent her for Christmas. She is eleven and tiny, and full of confidence. My Portuguese feels thick and clumsy today, and as I walk I mutter the questions I want to ask her. Rio de Janeiro is a humid, sticky ninety-eight degrees farenheit and I've spent the last five days conducting interviews for the documentary I'm making. My brain needs a cold shower.

Allyah notices me and crosses the street to join me at the bus stop. I greet her with a kiss on the cheek and pass my hand over her thick, dark curls, but she remains silent. It's been two years since I was last here and it always takes her a while to start talking to me again. In the Western, middle class part of the world where I live, things happen at a fairly swift and easy pace. Calls are made, emails sent, meetings arranged. When I'm hungry I drive five minutes to the nearest grocery store and am back in my kitchen with my dinner cooked before the hour is up. This is a part of the world Allyah knows nothing about, and it makes the expanse between us feel like eight million miles. And sometimes it makes me shy around her. I become nervous as we board the bus and sit quietly as it rumbles down the green hills toward the city center. What can I say to remind us of each other? Allyah used to sleep next to me on a concrete floor with her face pressed into my arm. I'd wake up in the morning with a string of her drool around my elbow.

I start chattering in Portuguese. "So I thought I'd take you to the Folkloric Museum because it's got these really cool wooden statues from Northern Brazil and a garden out back and on the way we can swing in the park and then get some food after if you're hungry . . ."

Allyah was my translator in 2005 when I could only speak basic Portuguese. Our grammar then was at the same level, a foreigner and a four-year-old. Ever since, she's had a knack for understanding me when I stumble over words or when my accent skids on the slushy road of a Portuguese *r* or *h*. When I'm done with my suggestions she nods lightly and I recognize the hollow look in her eyes. She's hungry.

RIO 2007

I'm burning up with fever. Of the tropical variety. I've been on this couch for five days straight. They call dengue fever "bone break fever," and yes, my bones feel a crushing pressure like they might spontaneously shatter. Allyah's mother, aunt, and grandmother have been watching me around the clock to make sure I don't die. I've been living with them for over a year and they treat me like their cub. Jacque and Jessica are both at work and so Allyah's grandmother, Val, has dashed out with my wallet to buy water bottles and ramen noodles. The faucet is dry and the cupboard is empty.

Allyah sits cross-legged in her underwear on the floor with her little brothers Uri and Jon Pedro. They form a sloppy circle at my feet. There is only a little water in Allyah's pale yellow glass, and today it is wildly hot. She passes the cup to each boy and urges him to take the tiniest sip possible. The type of sip a ladybug might take out of the husk of a pumpkin seed. She then passes the glass to me and makes me take a similarly ladybug-sized sip. Finally she takes a sip for herself. This routine is repeated for the next thirty minutes until the glass is empty. As I lay there dazed by the sensation of an invisible weight pressing into my skeleton, I think: *holy shit . . . when you have few resources, you learn how to take care of people at a pretty damn early age*. And then I drift into a delirious sleep.

RIO 2012

As soon as we get off the bus I take us to an all-you-can-eat buffet.

"I'm so hungry!" I exclaim, piling my plate with black beans and rice, fresh fish and french fries, hoping Allyah will mimic my portions. I slide most of my fries onto her plate when she's finished and she eats every salty bite. We polish off two glasses of passion fruit juice. The hollow look has faded, and as we leave, I notice Allyah's steps are livelier. On our way to the museum my cell starts to buzz in my backpack, but I ignore it.

"Jô, your phone's ringing. Hey, crazy lady, you deaf?" Allyah arches her eyebrow and smacks the middle of my bag where the phone is vibrating. That's the confident, demanding edge I'm used to. I arch my eyebrow back at her and reach for my phone. The voice on the other end is speaking in Portuguese. "Can you meet me in ten minutes? There's a photo shoot and you should be there to film it. It's going to be a really good chance to get an interview."

I strain to understand him as the phone cuts in and out. Despite some years of fluency, Portuguese over the phone remains a challenge. I usually compensate by filling in the gaps with a shaky combo of intuition and logic. I remember that my friend André has a performance today in Copacabana, a beach neighborhood on the other side of town. This must be what he's talking about. I hang up and look at Allyah.

"You want to be a film assistant today?" Her eyes glow and she jumps in place, her frenzied nod making her curls bounce like rubber balls. I like seeing Allyah act like a child again. Over the past seven years she has become studious and serious as she's taken on more and more responsibilities to handle the extremes of her poverty and the needs of her family.

When I tell her we have to hightail it to the other side of town to film the photo shoot, she becomes all business. "Jô— let's catch the van at the corner of Catete—there's no stop, but they go right by there and they'll pull over if you yell real loud. It's fifty cents cheaper than the subway."

It dawns on me then that she must be her mother's personal organizer. She knows this dynamic—the no-time-for-bullshit attitude, the making something happen when there appears to be no easy way. She's in her element.

RIO 2007

Val returns and her eyes darken when she sees me.

"Jô, you don't look right, *amore*." She sits next to me on the couch and starts twisting the cap off of a water bottle. Allyah crawls into Val's lap and offers up her empty yellow cup.

"You've been taking care of the family while I was gone?" Val's tone is warm and honeyed. Allyah nods. "Good girl. You're so responsible." A smile, like a shadow, hovers behind Allyah's eyes. Val places her hand on my forehead and clucks her tongue. She holds the cup to my lips, but I choke out the water. It's too cold. Val's face is strained as she looks at the kids. "I have to get Jô to the hospital," she says. "Now."

RIO 2012

As we hustle away from the museum, I explain to Allyah who it is we're meeting. She remembers him as one of the dancers I've been filming since the beginning. He's from her neighborhood, and he always asked Allyah questions when he came over, and never left without giving her a hug. I tell her, "He's really making it big as a dancer. He's going on tour soon to France!"

This seems to connect with her. It's the type of possibility that hits close to home. It isn't mythical, like my life back in the States. I explain to her that I'll be filming him after his show and trying to get footage of him talking to other reporters, to show examples of what his professional life looks like. Allyah is interested, but much more focused on her production duties, and she cuts me off with a sharp yell in the direction of a speeding white van. "*O moco, o combi vai para Copa?*" Her sharp Rio slang makes it through the open window of the van and a harried-looking man leaning out the passenger window signals for the driver to slam on the brakes. "*Vamos!*" he snaps as the door opens. "Let's go!"

RIO 2007

Val is trying to help me walk to the door, but my limbs don't work. I haven't stood up in hours and my body isn't right. This is bad. I sense it. There are one hundred and twenty steps to climb to get out of Val's slum into the neighborhood street where there are buses and taxis that can take us to the hospital. The only other option is going through the slum in someone else's car. No taxis or buses pass through here.

Val is not your average grandmother. She had Allyah's mother at sixteen, so she is only forty, but with the vibrancy and strength of most twenty-year-olds. She is, however, a mere five feet tall and it's simply not realistic to expect her to drag me up a flight of one hundred and twenty stairs. Val cups her hand around Allyah's cheek.

"Honey, go find your uncle's friend, Wellington. The one who lives on the corner. Ask if I can borrow his cousin's car and drive us to the hospital. Tell him it's serious. Jô's real sick."

Allyah runs out the door in her underwear with a fierce look that is the mirror image of her grandmother. Val helps me sit on the floor by the open door, and the sensation of sun on my back makes me yelp.

"It's so hot, it's too hot!" I've lost my composure. I'm sobbing now in Val's lap and Val is stroking my matted hair with her red fingernails.

"When you're feeling better we're gonna go dancing at that new samba club in Lapa," she coos.

I met Val in a dance class I was teaching to a group of kids at a community center near her home. She heard the music and just decided to join on in, shimmying her shoulders and stomping her feet along with all the eight-year-olds. We felt familiar to each other immediately and inexplicably. When my volunteer housing arrangement ended, she insisted I move in with her and her family. Since then I've always felt buoyed by her optimistic determination, but my body knows this fever has a time limit, and I need to bring it down before it does irreversible damage.

Allyah is back in five minutes and out of breath.

"He's gonna pick you guys up outside. He wants to drive." I raise my head to see Allyah's triumphant look. We lock eyes and for a moment I feel certain that she is my big sister. I think about how fluid age is when there is a crisis. How the most important aspects of who we are come forward and the rest disappears into irrelevance.

Allyah kisses my cheek and then starts packing her brothers up to take them downstairs to their aunt's house, where she knows they'll stay while Val and I are gone.

Val takes my face between her hands and speaks slowly, but there is no denying the urgency in her words. "You need to get up and walk with me outside. It's gonna feel hot, but we've gotta get you to the hospital. You can lie down in the car, okay?" Then she smiles and I can see her left dimple. "How did you get this gringa skin, sister? It's not cut out for the tropics."

RIO 2012

I pour my change into the driver's hand, and Allyah and I scramble over a woman with a baby and three grocery bags as we exit the van. When we step into the street I'm disoriented; I've spent most of my time here on the other side of town. I went to Copacabana seven years ago when I was twenty-two and living in international volunteer housing. Copacabana Beach was our first group outing to a touristy, well-known part of Rio de Janeiro. I've been back only once or twice, but it remains one of the must-see destinations for most foreign travelers. Allyah reaches out to grab the elbow of a passing woman and quickly asks for directions to the Copacabana Theater where we're supposed to meet André. We're fifteen minutes late.

"Jô—it's just five blocks away, come on!" She's excited as she tugs at my hand, and I follow her through the crowded city.

We arrive at the theater out of breath and sweating. A security guard stops us at the front door. "The show isn't for another three hours," he says. "Theater's closed."

I stand with my mouth open and Allyah turns to look at me. I pull out my phone with a shaky hand and see a text message from the same number that called me earlier. I have no contacts saved in this borrowed cell, and my stomach sinks as I realize my mistake. "I'm at the Banco Cultural do Brasil," the text reads. "Where are you?"

Allyah is tugging at my wrist. "Let me read it, Jô! What happened?"

"I thought the person calling was André, and it wasn't." I say. "It was a different dancer, and the theater he was talking about is downtown, not in Copacabana. Looks like I messed up. We're out of luck."

I'm silently berating myself, but I try to keep calm for Allyah. This kind of stuff happens and it's part of the filming process. I'm usually a one-woman team and coordination is never easy, but it's always hard to gracefully let go of a missed opportunity. Allyah's shoulders slump as she sits down on a bench by the theater.

"Do you like the Copacabana Beach?" she asks me, gazing toward the break between two buildings where a sheet of green ocean glints in the distance.

"I think it's nice, a little crowded, but pretty. You?"

"I've never been." The vulnerability in Allyah's voice is not disguised.

I pause while I absorb the fact that she's lived eleven years in Rio and never been to Copacabana. I look out over the eight million miles between us and find her eyes.

"Well . . . the shoot's not happening. I'd love a walk along the beach, you?"

Allyah relinquishes her production duties with a grin and threads her fingers in mine.

"Yeah, I'd love that, too."

We approach a stretch of beach lined with sandcastle homages to the 2016 Rio Olympics. Allyah pulls off her sandals and holds them out for me to take, like she might do if she were with her mom and similarly overcome with the sudden need to be barefoot and free. I take her shoes and follow her lead toward the surfers and sun-worshipers who line the shore, calling out to her as she walks ahead of me.

"You're a natural production assistant, you know that? You're gonna have a credit in my film that says, 'Production Assistant 2012: Allyah Neves.'"

She doesn't respond, but her chest expands just enough to show that she's sucked in her breath. I believe she's trying to imagine sitting in a theater as the credits roll and the music plays and her name appears on the big screen.

"I'm not kidding, Allyah!"

She picks up her pace and so do I, until I'm chasing her into a white frill of foam that laces the sand like scattered diamonds.

RIO 2007

I spend the rest of the day in the hospital hooked to an IV that is rehydrating me and also pumping liquid aspirin into my veins to bring down the fever. By the time Val and I return home it's late and I'm by no means recovered, but certainly relieved. Dengue fever takes at least a few weeks to get out of your system, but my body is satiated with water and the pressure in my bones has eased, and that voice inside tells me I'm no longer in a life-threatening situation. I spend the next week in bed while Val and her daughters alternate caretaking duties—getting me to eat small spoonfuls of soup and drink copious amounts of water. Allyah quietly comes and goes from my bedside, and I know she's keeping her own watch just in case she can help again. One morning when I'm certain my fever has broken, I sit propped up against a pillow talking to her as she plays with a yellow and blue crayon and a piece of scrap paper at the other end of the mattress.

"You didn't get to film your friends 'cause you were sick, huh?" Allyah knows that I'm making a movie about a group of dancers—she often sees me leave the house with a small video camera in my backpack.

"Nope, no filming." I feel a strange, pervasive peace in my belly as I answer her, and an intuition that it's all going to work out. "I'll get other chances, though. These things happen."

Allyah looks in the direction of my backpack and raises her eyebrow. "Can I see your camera?" I nod my head and her face lights up.

"I'll show you how to turn it on and use it."

We sit in bed with my handheld Sony camcorder. She pushes the red button and pans the camera around the room with a tiny but steady hand.

"Can I interview you?" I ask. She nods and places the camera in my lap and I direct her to sit on a stool by the windowsill. I zoom in on her dark copper eyes, find the focus, and then zoom out so the shot captures her small body cross-legged on the stool and the shaft of sunlight illuminating one stray ebony curl.

"O.K. Tell me your name, where you live, and how old you are."

She becomes very serious as she sits up straighter and brushes a piece of lint off the edge of her dress. Instead of looking at the camera, her gaze lands on me.

"I'm Allyah Neves. I live in Rio de Janeiro and I'm six years old."

∽ ∽ ∽

Jocelyn Edelstein is a writer, filmmaker, and dancer based in Portland, Oregon. She has spent a lot of time dancing in Brazil, visiting a cherished community of loved ones in Rio and directing "Believe The Beat," a feature length documentary that follows a group of Brazilian hip-hop dancers. Jocelyn's other travels have taken her to Argentina, Uruguay, Scotland, Italy, the Czech Republic, and Spain. Her previous stories have been published in The Best Women's Travel Writing 2011 *and* The Best Women's Travel Writing Volume 8. *To preview "Believe The Beat" visit www.urbanbodyproject.com.*

ॐ ॐ ॐ

The Rice Man Cometh

In Italy, she learns the meaning of mastering risotto—
and herself.

*E*very once in a while, a guru crosses your path, one who can reveal meaning and mystery. We have to be ready for these moments of grace that can stir the soul—or in my case, the risotto.

Gurus don't usually announce themselves. You wouldn't expect, for example, that the driver who picked you up at your hotel to take you to a winery in Piedmont, Italy, would be a guru. But life is short, and you never know just who is driving your car, so you might as well ask a few questions.

Angelo Fornara, a friendly and outgoing man, was surprised I spoke Italian, and for the first moments of our forty-five-minute drive, we exchanged pleasantries. Then I asked him where he was from.

"Vercelli."

Vercelli may mean nothing to you. If you are not a devotee, like me, on a quest, the most you may know about Vercelli is that it is a handsome city of about forty-five thousand people in the Piedmont's Po River Valley. But to one who is searching to understand the mysteries, "Vercelli" means much more. It means *carnaroli*. It means, to a lesser extent, *arborio*. It means, in short, *risotto*. The best rice and the best risotti in the world come from Vercelli. People there have been stirring risotto since medieval times, when the Arabs brought rice north and some enterprising Italian flooded the Po River Valley and planted a few hectares.

For over ten years, I have been trying to make the perfect risotto. It sounds easy, and a lot of Italians make it look easy: You sauté some onions in a little butter or olive oil, toss in some rice, glaze it, add a splash of wine, then broth, one ladle at a time, stirring all the while, until the rice absorbs or your arm gives out. When it's almost ready, you throw in a few condiments (mushrooms, shrimp, asparagus, fresh peas, pancetta, whatever), and grate a little cheese on top at the end. *Voilá*. Risotto.

But risotto can go terribly wrong. You could use brown rice, for instance, and end up with a dish that not even the hippies in your college communal house would eat when they were stoned. You could use bouillon cubes instead of real stock and produce gruel that tastes thin and metallic. You could cook it too long and make glop. You could forget to stir, wander off to check your e-mail, and ruin your pot along with the risotto. You could add the condiments at the wrong time, making them tough and overcooked, or raw and crunchy. You could use old wine that's turned bad and wind up with risotto that tastes like old wine that's turned bad. You could add too much cheese, or the wrong cheese, and it would come out stringy. You could undercook the risotto and crack your teeth. You could, as most restaurants do, cook it halfway, then fire it up before serving it, ruining its consistency.

Risotto is all about learning from failure.

Risotto is a practice, one that requires patience, letting go of regrets about past attempts and expectations of the future. To make risotto, you have to be in the moment. You have to be alive to the ingredients, honor and understand them, and wait while their true natures are revealed. Risotto is egoless. To the degree that you have mastered risotto—and there is no perfection, only striving—you have mastered yourself.

That's why I had long been searching for a risotto guru. I don't want to brag, but I already make the best risotto in San Francisco, at least among people with no Italian blood, so there was no one to take me to that next level of transcendence. Now that I'd met someone from Vercelli—my culinary Mecca—I could barely contain my excitement.

"So," I asked Angelo, nonchalantly. "I guess you must eat risotto if you are from Vercelli."

He took his hands off the wheel for a moment to give me one of those fond Italian gestures that means, *Of course, you idiot.* The car swerved and he righted our direction just in time to avoid an oncoming car.

"So I suppose you make a pretty good risotto yourself," I ventured.

Angelo shrugged, with a little beatific smile on his face. Then he couldn't resist. "There are very few things in this world that I can say I am competent at," he said. "Risotto is one of them."

He went on to add that his friends considered him perhaps the best risottoist of their acquaintance, but he could take no credit for it—that was all due to his grandmother, who learned to make risotto from his great-grandmother, and etc., back to whomever in the Po Valley first had the wits to stir the rice and let the broth absorb slowly, releasing the creamy starch, instead of just putting the pot lid on and letting it cook.

I told Angelo that I like to make risotto. I'm no expert, like someone from Vercelli, but I like a nice asparagus version in the spring, maybe a butternut squash in the winter.

"*Zucca e gorgonzola,*" he said. Winter squash and gorgonzola. This was getting interesting.

For the next half hour, I peppered him with questions about the whole process. Do you use butter or oil in the *soffrito* (the sauté with the onions)? Alas, he never had an easy answer to my questions; they were always more like a riddle. Butter is better for some *risotti*—the heartier ones—and olive oil for the lighter, summer ones; often, however, he uses a mix (the proportions of which depend on the type of risotto). You just have to know your risotto.

O.K.. Red onions, white onions, or leeks? Again, it depends—but he tends to use scallions. Scallions? I had never used scallions. Really? Then I wracked the Italian side of my brain and realized: *scalogni*. Not scallions. Shallots. My next risotto nearly destroyed by one of those linguistic *falsi amici*, or "false friends."

So after the *soffrito* is nice and golden and the shallots are transparent, you add the rice. Angelo uses only *carnaroli* rice, which is a short-grained rice that is more absorptive even than arborio, which is acceptable, and more commonly used. (*Carnaroli* rice is not cheap. You will think you are buying the truffles for your risotto, not the rice.) Using any other kind of rice, Angelo said, is barbaric. Call it Chinese or Indian food if you want to use some other kind of rice, but don't call it risotto.

Then comes the wine, to *sfumare* the rice. This is the first time I have heard this term, a verb particular to risotto, and I am delighted. There is a whole verb that means infusing the rice with wine. I would run around for weeks afterward singing (to the tune of "Volare") "*Sfumare*, oh-oh-oh-oh."

But which wine? Angelo, it turns out, works at Batasiolo, a Piedmont winery famous for its Barolos, Spumantes, and Barberas, so he has quite a choice. There is no using up old bad wine for Angelo. He conceded to me that perhaps you could use a flat Spumante, but nothing that had truly gone off. Wine is an essential ingredient in risotto, like anything else, and all the ingredients have to be excellent. It's all about the "*material prima*," the prime materials. That's what makes risotto good.

So . . . red or white?

He shakes his head. Have I learned nothing? It *depends*. If you are making a delicate risotto with zucchini flowers, would you use red? Of course not. A nice frog's leg risotto? White! If it's winter and you have some meaty mushrooms? Maybe. Quail risotto? Barbera. White beans and sausage? Red.

O.K., now we have *sfumated* the rice. It is time to add broth. The broth, of course, must be hot. If you have cold broth, it will shock the rice or something. It will not absorb properly. It will make glue.

"*Che schifo*," I said. How disgusting. He nodded. I was catching on.

But, I wondered, what kind of broth? Chicken? Beef? "I suppose it depends," I said.

He nodded. In general, he said, he uses veal broth. They have very good veal in Piedmont, so naturally, the veal broth is very good.

"*Pollo?*"

With a lighter risotto, yes, he might use chicken—but actually no. He would only capons for his broth.

Capons.

Yes. Capons, he explained, are roosters with no *palle*, so they develop without sex hormones, which give the meat a vaguely nasty taste. Capons are more flavorful than hens, also because the flesh is a little more fatty, which makes it more tender.

I do not know where to get capons. It was becoming clear that my risotto broth was going to cost as much as a flight to Italy. I asked if I could get away with putting a chicken carcass in water with some celery, carrot, and a bay leaf, boil it up, call it stock, and use that for risotto. When I tell people in the

States that I make my own stock, instead of pouring it from the cardboard box, they are impressed. Angelo gave me a look that said, *You poor Americans.*

I asked him about *contorni*, the stuff you put into risotto. "There are so many *risotti* that this discussion could go on for the rest of our lives," he said. He pointed to a hill in the distance. "We're almost there."

I had only a few more minutes to get answers to some essential questions.

Al dente or creamy? Definitely *al dente*, chewy in the center of the rice. Texture is everything.

Cheese? A good Parmigiano-Reggiano, or even better, a salty sheep's cheese, a Sardinian pecorino.

Do you add a little cream at the end? Angelo gave a look of disgust. "Anyone who adds cream to risotto doesn't know how to make risotto. Risotto is creamy if you make it right."

We came in view of the hotel, a gorgeous, modern, five-star luxury hotel called Il Boscareto. I only wished that I could actually watch my guru make risotto, and taste his risotto, but I knew that was unlikely. I did actually hint about it, in case he wanted to invite me over for dinner. Then I thanked him and said, "*ciao, ciao.*"

The next day I was invited to eat with the owner of the winery and hotel and some friends at Batasiolo's Bofani vineyard. A table for twenty was set outside a villa, underneath some trellises overlooking hillsides covered with the best Barolo grapes anywhere. I suspected we were going to have *plin* for lunch, the little raviolis that Piedmont is famous for. The owner, Fiorenzo Dogliani, invited me into the kitchen to meet the chef.

To my surprise, there was Angelo, *sfumanding* the risotto. He had braised some pancetta with the shallots, reserving other pancetta to add at the end, for some difference in texture. He showed me his big pan, then shooed me out of the kitchen.

I wanted to stay, but he insisted I go drink some Spumante instead. I begged. But he was not about to give up all his secrets to any American who walked into his kitchen—or for that matter, to anyone.

In about twenty minutes, Angelo appeared with a beautiful ceramic platter filled with golden risotto. This risotto was his nod to spaghetti *carbonara*—a *risotto carbonara,* with egg yolks, parmesan, pancetta, and pepper. It was perfectly creamy and *al dente* at the same time, with both crunchy and soft pieces of pancetta, and amazing paired with a Batasiolo Sovrana Barbera d'Alba 2007.

"*Non é male*," I told Angelo. It's not bad. His face fell a bit. "It's the best," I said.

"There is one secret ingredient," Angelo told me.

I raised my eyebrows. I knew better than to ask outright.

"Passion," he said.

For everything I had learned from Angelo, what remained, after the last grains of the second plate of risotto were gone, was that all I knew about risotto was how little I really knew.

I could give you Angelo's recipe, but it wouldn't matter. It would never turn out like his. Besides, I'm sworn to secrecy.

♫♫   ♫♫   ♫♫

Laura Fraser's most recent book is All Over the Map, *a sequel to the best-selling travel memoir* An Italian Affair. *She also wrote* Losing It: America's Obsession with Weight and the Industry that Feeds on It, *an expose of the diet industry. An award-winning journalist, she has written features for many national magazines, including* Gourmet, More, O the Oprah Magazine, Vogue, Glamour, Self, The New York Times Magazine, Mother Jones, Good Housekeeping, Salon.com, Bon Appetit, Town and Country Travel, Islands, Yoga Journal, *and others. Her work has been frequently anthologized, including in* Best Food Writing of 2001 *and* 2002, *and* The Best Women's

Travel Writing 2005. *She has taught magazine writing at U.C. Berkeley's Graduate School of Journalism, Aspen Summer Words, U.C. Extension, and other venues. She recently traveled to Patagonia, the Atacama desert, Kangaroo Island, and to her house in San Miguele de Allende. A frequent traveler, last year she visited Sydney, Tasmania, Baja, Buenos Aires, Rome, and her favorite island in the Mediterranean, which she refuses to name.*

❧ ❧ ❧

A Day in Phnom Penh

No one ends up stuck in Cambodia on an expired visa
at the end of a winning streak.

*W*e called him Eat Pray Paul, because there were two
Pauls and they were more or less indistinguishable—
both red-faced old dudes who'd been kicking around Cambodia for years, smoking ice, shagging prostitutes and losing
teeth until there wasn't a whole lot left.

Both Pauls would wash up at George's Phnom Penh
house from time to time, when shit got bad enough and
they'd have to hop on the wagon for a bit. More than anything they'd be looking for a quiet place to hide out from
whatever mess they'd gotten themselves into, and George's
big fat villa was perfect for that: a place to smoke cigarettes, use a Western toilet, drink the Nescafe the house
staff provided, and maybe bum a meal or two from the
rest of us sober folks hanging around. Sometimes the Pauls
would piece a little time together—thirty, sixty, even ninety
days—before disappearing back behind the other side of
that razor-wired gate.

Eat Pray Paul's main problem was that he didn't have a
visa. It had expired and he hadn't gotten around to renewing
it. That was seven years ago. They charge you five dollars a

day for overstaying your visa, so you do the math. Or don't. Basically, Eat Pray Paul was fucked.

Without a valid visa, he could only get jobs teaching at the shadiest schools, the kind run by thugs and goons with ties to the government. Even then, after a few months immigration would come around and Eat Pray Paul would have to pay them off. The longer it went, the more expensive the bribes got. Eventually he was reduced to hiding out in the bathroom.

We knew this because he'd talk about it, ad nauseum, in that droning voice of his. He wouldn't talk about the obvious stuff—how he'd gotten into this situation or what was keeping him there—you know, questions that might occur to you, should you find yourself living in a third-world country in such a predicament.

Sammy wasn't as much of a cold-hearted hard-ass as me; he'd been in Cambodia longer but had less time clean. So one day he offered to take Paul out for lunch. Thought he was going to carry the message. They went to a roadside restaurant, nothing fancy—plastic chairs and chicken bones—and Sammy thought, you know, they'd talk about sobriety, recovery. Maybe Paul was finally ready to hear it.

No. Paul pulled a book out of the breast pocket of his dingy old blazer: *Eat, Pray, Love*. He held it in his battered old hands. Had Sammy read it? Paul asked. Sammy thought it was some kind of joke—he wasn't a middle-aged American housewife, so no, he hadn't read it.

Paul shook his head long and slow and began to enlighten Sammy on the great spiritual lessons inherent to the text. Elizabeth Gilbert, he said, had it figured out. This book had the answer; nay, it *was* the answer.

Sammy didn't know what to say. *Eat, Pray, Love* seemed about the last thing to solve Paul's addiction and visa woes, but you know, far be it from him. So he listened along, paid for the soup, and drove Paul back to his guesthouse.

Paul was staying at one of the few guesthouses still standing by the old lakeside. Not that there was even a lake for them to be on the side of anymore; after a Chinese company bought and drained the lake, and all the residents were evicted and their tin-roof shanties bulldozed, the former backpacker haunt became a bombed-out ghost town. The lake itself was just a vast stretch of sand, a sudden desert in the heart of the city.

But there were still a few spots left, three-dollar-a-night digs with cement beds and squat toilets, lobbies filled with dead-eyed souls who sat rocking themselves, murmuring and picking at scabs. Paul had been there for months now, though he was a few weeks late on the rent. Sammy saw him up to his room; Paul unlocked the door and there was jack shit in there—just a battered old suitcase and a pack of smokes. He set down his copy of *Eat, Pray, Love*.

Sammy told me about it all the next day while we were drinking lattes at one of those gleaming air-conditioned Western cafes I hated myself for loving. The nickname stuck.

A typical day in Phnom Penh:

Wake up at 6:30 A.M. The sound of horns honking. The fan is whirring and I've kicked the sheet off.

Do ten minutes of half-assed yoga poses. Muesli and coffee in front of the computer. Sweep terrace, water plants, wash face, wash dishes. Read the day's passage out of *Courage to Change*. Set timer and sit cross-legged for ten minutes of half-assed meditation.

All this takes an hour, over an hour actually, but I've found I can't skimp on it. Any of it. Remove one part of the equation—a downward dog, an unwashed bowl—and I feel wonky, unsettled, ungrounded, off-center. Like the city is glass about to shatter. Or, worse, like the glass between me and the city is about to shatter.

Leave the apartment by 7:45: crawl down the steep cement steps, squeeze past row of motorbikes parked in the hall, jiggle the key in the lock. Begin to sweat before I'm even on the street.

Eat Pray Paul had two things he loved to complain about. One was his visa situation and the other was getting robbed.

"I've been robbed seventeen times this year," he'd say, eyes trained down in a sallow fury. "They take my phone, my money, even my shoes."

I didn't go out much at night but seventeen seemed like an excessive number.

"You know he doesn't actually get robbed," Sammy whispered one day.

"What do you mean?"

"George told me," he said. "He was coming home one night and saw Paul, out of his mind on ice and God knows what else. Hollering and screaming and carrying on. And get this." Sammy pressed his fingertip into the plastic tabletop and leaned in. "He was pulling shit out of his pockets. And just throwing it"—Sammy flicked his thick hands open— "everywhere. The security guards were all laughing. And then he took off his shoes and chucked those too."

Sammy threw his hands up then let them flop back down in his lap.

But Eat Pray Paul started complaining less and less about the "robberies" and more and more about The Nephew. Kin to the owners of the shitty school where Eat Pray Paul worked, The Nephew was insisting on being paid to keep quiet about the visa. "He's threatening to go to the police." What The Nephew seemed to be failing to grasp was that no one winds up stuck in Cambodia on an expired visa at the end of a winning streak.

It got to be like a soap opera, with daily installments: Paul hiding out, Paul trying to go back to work, Paul getting stiffed for shifts he worked. "The Nephew says he could have me arrested," he droned. "They could deport me."

I sat on George's lush landscaped patio and watched the thin line of fire eating at my cigarette. I tried not to roll my eyes. It was all a bit world's-tiniest-violin for me, a little too boy-who-cried-wolf. I knew I should be more tolerant, but that dark-cloud Eeyore shit starts to wear on you. Starts to eat at you, long and slow and deep.

8 A.M.: Arrive at preschool. Put on tattoo-covering leggings and long-sleeve shirt, then the synthetic frock uniform that makes me sweat even more.

Sit cross-legged before a circle of three year olds, sing nursery rhymes, feel my anklebones digging into the linoleum. Make alphabet crafts, color worksheets, teach vocabulary. Snack time and playground. Give a series of high-fives as they file out the door.

Hide out in the "teachers' lounge," which is really just a closet crammed with three old Dells, and Internet so slow that only one person can use it at a time. But the AC is strong so that's where I usually while away my last half hour.

Since it's a preschool all the foreign teachers are women, which is nice because it negates the typical staff room discussions of girly bars and amphetamines. But honestly, sometimes I think I'd rather work with the sexpats and junkies; at least you know what their deal is. Mary is Sri Lankan, raised by missionaries; they'd promote her to head teacher, the owner had told her, if she weren't so dark skinned. Heather is an icy bleach blond with ashen skin and bulimic breath. Daria would be gorgeous if it weren't for the deep rings beneath her eyes. She came to Cambodia with her husband, some kind of businessman she's finally divorcing. One day she leaves a tab open on the computer; it's a Google search for "signs of domestic violence."

But the strangest is Shelly. She's young and American, so I try to chat with her. Her hands are jumpy and her eyes always rimmed with red. She's vampire-pale, damn near translucent, and fat in a weird way. Not like she eats too much—more like someone puffed her up with air. She talks a lot about how she can't sleep. "I was up till four last night," she'll gasp at 8 A.M.

One day she's crying in the principal's office; her dad had a heart attack and she needs to fly back to the States immediately, that night. She's a wreck—blubbering about what a great school it is, how sad she is to leave, begging them to still pay her even though she has to break her contract. It's hard to watch; I have to look away.

Three weeks later, I see her smoking outside a bar. I don't bother saying hi.

Walking home one night through the garbage and plastic bags lining the street, I got a text. I could hear the trash collectors coming, hanging off the sides of a big rattly dumpster—thin boys with hunger-sharp faces, in flip-flops and skinny jeans leaping off the dumpster to pick through the trash with bare hands.

I was sweaty in my exercise clothes, balancing an ice-cream cone, when I felt my phone vibrate. I tried with one hand to fish it out of the space where I'd wedged it between my hip and the spandex. It was a precarious operation: weaving through the trash and motorbikes while trying not to lose the scoop of hand-churned French-style tart yogurt with mango chunks. The little Nokia screen lit up and the text glowed green: "EP Paul arrested. Prolly getting deported. Don't know the deets."

I stopped in the middle of the trash pile and motorbike blaze. "Holy shit," I said aloud. I stood there for several seconds, blinking at my phone. After all that crying wolf, Eat Pray Paul's visa problems had finally caught up with him.

The dumpster heaved closer, boys scurrying like shadows around it.

12–4 p.m.: The hottest part of the day. It's all about survival during these hours. Avoiding dehydration and direct sunlight, keeping covered and lying low.

It's funny how it sneaks up on you—you won't *feel* thirsty and won't *feel* overheated but suddenly it hits: nausea, dizziness, the little black dots that swoon in your periphery, beckoning you to swim off into the corners with them.

So I go to an air-conditioned Western café, spend half my hourly wage on a beverage, and pretend to write but really just stream episodes of *The Colbert Report*. Or more often I stay home in my underpants in front of the fan with the lights off and pretend to write but really just stream episodes of *The Colbert Report*.

Sometimes I get stuck running errands. That's the worst. Riding a moto cuts a breeze, but the sun burns on my skin and my blue eyes squint fiercely into the glare. Buy spring rolls at Central Market, imported cans of V8 at Lucky Mart, six-dollar tampons at U-Care.

I have to go to the pharmacy occasionally to buy my thyroid medication. It's cheaper in Cambodia, which is nice, and I don't need a prescription. I wait for the pharmacist to get the box and try to avoid looking at the rows of other drugs— Valium, Ambien, Dexedrine, Xanax, Dramamine, all sealed, I imagine, with a thin layer of foil that sighs when you punch it open.

Next to the breath mints by the register, singles of Viagra are for sale. I avoid making eye contact with the customers who have come to buy these pills. They usually look surprisingly normal—sun-bleached and wiry and tired, but what Westerner doesn't after awhile?

*   *   *

Eat Pray Paul was being held at the Immigration Office, a peeling-paint building on a dusty lot directly across from the airport. We went out there the following Sunday, after our weekly visit to the "rehab," where we talked about sobriety to the inmates. It was more of a detention facility than a rehab or detox center; they just kind of held people there in cage-like cells, old fans shaking from precarious wires strung from the tin roof. The whole idea of addiction as a disease was new in Cambodia, and we could never tell what any of them made of us—a bunch of foreigners who came out each Sunday afternoon to sweat their asses off and talk about being sober.

"If anything," George shrugged, "we're the best show in town."

We rode out there in George's big Lexus. Being in a car at all made me feel fancy, so you can imagine. George had been in Cambodia a decade, married a Cambodian woman, sired a couple of kids. He had a way of laughing it all off, taking it all in stride that I hadn't yet mastered. Sometimes I thought I didn't want to master it.

But when he announced that on the way back from the rehab we were stopping by Immigration to drop off some stuff for Eat Pray Paul, there was nothing I could really say. Paul had been there a week by that point, just sitting there. No one knew what to do with him—there were massive fines and deportation fees the British Embassy wasn't keen to pay. It went without saying that Eat Pray Paul didn't have the money. And Cambodia sure as hell wasn't about to let him out without having paid something to someone.

"So there you have it," George said as we pulled onto the grounds.

A guard in a faded old uniform was napping in the shade. He roused himself from his plastic chair, smoothed his hair down as he walked belly-first over to the window. George talked to him in a jerky Khmer. The guard grumbled and disappeared.

"What'd you bring him?" I asked.

George grinned in the rearview at me. "A couple recovery books."

I laughed. "Oh, he's gonna love that."

We heard his voice then, coming from the second story of a back building. He called out and the sound ricocheted through the brown lot.

"Did you bring any eye drops?" he shouted.

"No," George leaned his head out of the window and yelled back. "We got a couple books for you." He waved them in the air.

"*Eat, Pray, Love?*"

"Oh for fuck's sake," I muttered.

"No, man," George shouted back, "just these here recovery books."

"I don't need those!" Paul's voice was gruff and strained, like it was choking from the dust and heat. I could see his arm flailing through the bars of the cell, battered old skin flashing in the light. "I need eye drops!"

George gave a good-natured laugh. "All right then, buddy." He handed the confused guard a plastic bag containing two sobriety-related texts. "I'll try to get those for next time. Now you take care." He gave a couple little toots of the horn as he maneuvered the car out of the brown lot.

"Eye drops!" Eat Pray Paul shouted after us, his voice disappearing as the automatic window zipped shut.

We pulled back on to the street, through motorbikes and SUVs and vendors pushing carts with checkered krama scarves wrapped around their faces. Across the road, a line of tuk-tuks waited for passengers. A plane angled up into the sky, away from all the chaos and dust, taking its passengers somewhere far, I imagined—far from Cambodia.

*   *   *

5:30 P.M.: Evening. The Golden Hour, when the sky is pink and the heat has broken and on the best of days, there's a breeze. If it's not raining or about to rain—branches whipping in the howling black—I go to Olympic Stadium. Dusty track and stair sprints, a ring of women doing aerobic dancing to an electric version of "Hotel California." Run for thirty minutes before the dehydration makes me queasy. Sit at the top of the stadium, drink sugar cane juice, watch bats swoop in the neon sky.

Go to writing group; meet a friend for dinner; stroll down the Riverside.

But kickboxing nights are the best. Sour gloves and slick sweat, splinters and bits of glass jammed into my bare feet. It's Khmer style, more rugged than Muay Thai, and in each class comes a moment when I feel the thwack of my body's weight against the pads and then an anger rise up, through and out of me. An anger I hadn't known was there.

I walk home, flip-flops splashing little bits of rubble and dirt against the backs of my legs. Feel warm and tired and good. Pass all the girls, skinny with hot pants and malnutrition limbs; pass the Western men with their glassy eyes and crispy skin, the teenagers huffing out of plastic bags, the tourists with their feet in tanks while swarms of starved fish eat off the dead skin. Pass the two attendants in front of Tin Tin Hotel who smile and wave and say, "I love you!" Buy a coconut from a vendor in rubber boots who hacks the top off with a machete, hands it to me, and grins.

I climb those concrete steps back up, yank open the little wire gate, plastic tarp flapping, and duck my head through the frame. Shower. Cut up a bowl of jackfruit. I rarely go out after 9 P.M.

Weeks went by. I kept getting little updates—Eat Pray Paul was still in detention, George and Sammy were still bringing things to him. He'd gotten in touch with his family and they had actually wired money over, enough for the flight and fees. But only a third of the money arrived, and by that time the fees had almost doubled.

Every week it was "only one more week." By the seventh week I decided to go out there with Sammy and George. I'd like to say it was a flash of Christian compassion—though I'm not Christian—but it was something else. Perhaps some need to see the other side, see what I'd been insulating myself against, pushing away or judging or blocking out. A long ride in an air-conditioned car sounded nice, too.

We got there and the heat was dense, thick. By that time the guards all knew Sammy and George; they barely looked up from their card game, smoke curling around their faces and the TV behind them blaring. We sat on plastic chairs and waited.

Eventually a guard went to get Eat Pray Paul but when he walked in, it was him but not him. He wore a clean shirt and his skin was less red. He'd put on weight—not a lot, but enough. He no longer looked skeletal. And there was a lightness in the way he moved, and a difference in how the air moved around him.

I watched him sit down and fold his hands calmly on the table.

Sammy handed him a brown bag. "We got everything but the eye drops."

Paul reached in his pocket, pulled out a modest fold of bills. Sammy waved his thick hand. Paul nodded and put his money back.

I studied him. "You look good," I said cautiously.

He nodded.

"They're feeding you out here, eh?" I asked with a smile.

He looked at his clasped hands. "Just the usual rice and soup. But a lot of the guys don't eat, so they give me extra."

"Paul here's a downright favorite!" George exclaimed, slapping his oven-mitt hand on Paul's shoulder. "These guys love him!" he pointed his thumb at the guards, who nodded at us and smiled.

"Yeah?" I asked, raising an eyebrow.

"Well sure. They've got some real firecrackers in here. Who was that guy?" George leaned toward Paul. "The South African fellow? Would fly into rages and holler all damn day?"

Paul nodded.

"Well, compared to that, Paul here's a saint. A regular model citizen!" George chuckled and something happened then: Paul smiled. I didn't realize till then that I'd never seen him smile. It was a timid and unaccustomed smile, full of moldy teeth and thin lips, but an honest-to-God smile.

"How long has it been now?" Sammy asked. "Since you drank?"

Paul looked sheepishly at his hands. "Six weeks, I suppose."

"Six weeks!" George exclaimed and slapped the table.

"It'd be easy to," Paul began to explain. "I mean, the guards bring beer for any of us who'll pay. But after the first week, I just decided, you know. . . ." He trailed off and looked up at me for a moment. Our eyes met, and I realized it was also the first time we'd met eyes in the months I'd known him.

We sat around talking for a while. It was ungodly hot, even beside the fan. The guards had been telling him he'd get to leave in a few days, a week at most. "I'll believe it when I'm on the plane," he said, but without rancor or self-pity, or even resignation. Something like acceptance.

I gave him a hug when we got up to leave.

"Well, hey," I said, "if I don't see you again, good luck back in the UK."

He nodded. "Thank you, Lauren." He paused then looked back up at me. "Good luck to you, too."

We walked through the heat back toward George's car. Sammy sucked on a cigarette.

"I've never seen Paul that good," I said.

Sammy nodded. "Blessing in disguise, this arrest. Probably end up saving his life."

George looked back at the detention building, his face suddenly serious. "He had to get out, man." He said it without his usual joking gusto. It was a voice I hadn't heard him use before. He stared at the cement structure, squinted into the sun. "It was killing him."

He didn't say what "it" was, but I knew. "It" wasn't Cambodia and "it" wasn't Paul. "It" was Paul *in* Cambodia. We got in the car and headed back toward the center. Planes arched into the sky behind us.

11 P.M.: Cigarette on the terrace before bed. I don't smoke much in Cambodia, less than I have in a year or so, but I always have one at night, when the day is done and the heat has usually passed. There'll be a breeze; the traffic will have died down, and the neighbor's dog yaps from the next balcony over. The lights down on the median will cast orange halos on the tile and the city will seem like a still, gentle place.

The cigarettes are cheap and burn fast, but they allow me a few minutes to just sit and watch the leaves sigh. To watch the stray motorbikes whiz and weave, dangling limbs of teenagers. To see the glow of the bank tower, the domed roof of the silly mall a few blocks away. To hear the clack-clack-clack of the late-night noodle vendor. To look down on it all from a distance.

Do you ever sit on balconies and think about that scene from *Forrest Gump*? The one where Jenny stands on the railing in platform heels and closes her eyes in the wind and almost lets herself fall? Do you ever understand that impulse? Like there's a certain kind of person who, when standing safely at a great height, will always feel the urge to jump. Even when they don't really want to—like their bodies are beckoning, like there's some kind of gravity that only certain bodies feel.

Not that I ever actually want to jump. But the thought will come, and sometimes that's enough to scare you.

Then the cigarette will be done. I'll stub it out and stand up. Lock the chain link fence, click the light out, and yank the metal doors shut, bits of Phnom Penh still blowing in through the cracks.

❧ ❧ ❧

Lauren Quinn is a writer and kindergarten teacher currently living in Hanoi. She is a contributing editor for Vela, *an online magazine of travel-inspired creative nonfiction, written by women. She will always be an Oakland girl at heart.*

❦ ❦ ❦

Rangefinder Girl

She wanted so badly not to be afraid of it.

Maybe this is about rhinoceros. But it is just as much about the smell of myrrh, or the warm grit of water from a desert spring—how it coats the mouth with salt, as if even the land were sweating. It is about the men who were our guides, and the ways I misunderstood them—the ways I misunderstood all of it. Mostly it's about how the desert looks when viewed through a rangefinder—shrunken and precise, with neat crosshairs through the center and a digital number showing just how far away it all is, the whole world so small and clean you could serve it in a teacup. And then you lower the rangefinder, let it swing from your neck, and everything rushes up around you, from the hot sand in your shoes to the red-black hills and the white of a dusty sky, closer than you could imagine.

I had come to Namibia with six other American students to do research on desert-adapted black rhinoceros. We would be tracking them for the next two weeks through the Ugab desert, a stretch of wilderness so barren that its name, according to the Damara people, means *place of silence*. At home in Maine, I often fantasized about the outdoors, about adventure, and I had been looking forward to the trip for months. Deserts could be tough, sure, but I had done fieldwork before, high in the Rocky Mountains and on glaciers in Alaska. I was prepared.

It took twenty hours to drive to the Ugab from Windhoek, the capital, and we left pavement behind after the first thirty minutes. The dirt road passed over flatland scattered with cement sheds and stick huts, brown goats and skinny dogs. In one village, a few kids played soccer in a field, barefoot, kicking a cool-green melon that spat dust as it rolled. Donkeys and cattle leaned against tree trunks, pressed into fragments of shade. After a while there were no more houses, and then there were no more trees. Cracked dirt spread in every direction, as if it had been poured from a great height.

Finally we came to a spring—a round pool in the center of a plain, almost perfectly ringed with hills—where we had arranged to meet our guides, who worked for the organization Save the Rhino Trust (SRT). Fresh ostrich and zebra tracks crisscrossed the sand, circling and spreading from the pool like threads from the center of a spider web. Meeting times in the bush are flexible—even the day is uncertain—and so we took time to explore, shuffling over rocks to find crinkled layers of basalt and chunks of deep purple amethyst. It was drizzling, each drop a pinprick of cold on my hot skin, and the ground shone.

Another student, Erin, and I found a darkling beetle meandering on legs like stilts, and we bent close, listening to the gentle scraping of its belly against the ground. Its body was black and perfectly round, its back striated and glistening such that the grooves caught light and appeared, at certain angles, to be stripes of clean white, which flickered on and off with the beetle's every step. The beetle was struggling to cross the humps and divots in the sand. It would come to a crest, totter, and careen down the other side, landing on its back with legs and long antennae swiveling. After rocking back and forth it would right itself, hesitate—as if pausing for breath—and start up the next mountain. Finally, after several minutes, the beetle came to the top of a ridge and stopped. Very slowly, it bent its front legs, raising its rear until it was nearly balanced on its head. I leaned closer. The beetle was quite still.

A raindrop splattered onto its domed back. Then the water pulled into itself, pearling into a ball that rolled down the center groove like a steel bead along a track, landing finally on its head. Something moved in the little face; the antennae twitched. Erin and I looked at each other, astonished: the beetle was catching rainwater to drink! It stood frozen for several more minutes; then, as the rain slowed, it continued on its laborious path across the sand.

Erin and I were still glowing from the joy of entomological discovery when we heard the first mutterings of a vehicle. Bernd, a Namibian-born German with skinny legs and a white beard, pulled up in a Land Rover as filthy as our own, its dirt-splattered sides dented and scarred. There was an open gash in the driver's-side door; I could see movement through the hole.

We had been told that our guide would be a military man— Bernd had fought in the Namibian War of Independence— and I sensed this in the way his eyes ticked over us from the cab, his head inclined with a soldier's stiffness. A dog perched on the front seat beside him; we would later learn that she was a Rhodesian ridgeback named Shamira, and that he brought her with him everywhere. Two men rode cross-legged on the roof, as dark and sun-creased as Bernd was pale, bundled in heavy canvas parkas with hoods pulled over their foreheads to block the raindrops. Here in the rain, it was probably eighty degrees—cold by Namibian standards. When I reached up to introduce myself they glanced at each other before taking my hand. Their names, they said, were Johannes and Fulai—pronounced *fly*. "Like the bug," Bernd noted from the front seat.

The trackers were Damara, a minority tribe in Namibia that once lived primarily as cattle herders. They understood some Afrikaans but spoke to each other in a dialect of Khoekhoe, a click language, rarely raising their voices above a murmur. The words and clicks happened at once: two strings of sound, layered on top of each other. But when Bernd spoke to them, they nodded without responding.

Now nine in number, we left the watering hole and drove onward, whether on a road or not it was difficult to tell. Bernd led the way. We bucked over rocks and spun in deep sand, heaved left and right with such force I was thrown into the laps of the students beside me, and at times tipped so precariously that the vehicle froze for an instant, as if deciding whether or not to topple; each time this happened, we would fling ourselves sideways in an attempt to sway the outcome. The driving reminded me of something else I had seen that day, but it took me over an hour to identify what it was. I felt an understanding for the beetle.

Hills rose about us, first grassy and later sharp with rocks, and we rode the channels between them, curving through serpentine gullies. As the day cooled, the Brandberg Mountains appeared silhouetted to the south, as smooth and flat as if torn from paper. After five hours of driving we came to our camping place in a dry basin. The Ugab River ran underground here, coming up only in occasional springs: a sure draw for rhinos and other wildlife. The sand was flattened with elephant tracks—"Big Guys," Bernd called them, as in, "Did you hear about the tourists who got stomped by the Big Guys?"—and we set up our tents under a canopy of tall acacias, which were heavy with pink-orange seedpods. When it was quiet, I could hear the pods snap and fall, rustling through layers of branches.

For dinner we cooked potatoes and springbok meat in cauldrons over a fire, and though Johannes and Fulai came to our circle to fill their bowls, they retreated into the shadows to eat alone. I stood to invite them over, but Bernd stopped me. "Stay here," he said. "They'll be eating on their own."

"They're welcome to join us," said Amber, one of the students, who sat hunched beside Bernd with her bowl on her knees.

Bernd shook his head. "Don't you get it?" he said, tapping pointedly at the skin on her arm. "They see themselves as different."

The next morning we built our breakfast fire in the dark and left camp before sunrise to get a head start on the heat. I rode on the roof of Bernd's truck, between the trackers. I learned that Johannes focused intently while he worked—he glared at the ground, as if daring it to reveal its secrets—but was quick to smile, and would answer a question in Afrikaans if I asked him directly. Fulai was tall and very thin, with delicate spectacles and a bit of white in his hair. He didn't speak, but his eyes flicked constantly across the horizon, as if he were reading, with mild interest, the world as it presented itself to him. Both men had red in the whites of their eyes, and they wore fitted green cargo pants, khaki shirts, and caps with SRT logos. Fulai wore his cap forwards, and Johannes rotated his hat to match the direction of the sun.

We started out driving along the broad sand of the riverbed, between rocky hills. In an aerial photograph, the long, curving hills of the Ugab look like the ridges on a fingertip; from the ground, every narrow valley looked alike. Bernd navigated without hesitating.

Our goal was to pass a rhino spoor, a trail we could follow on foot to the creature itself. We had been trained on how to act during a sighting—silent, with little movement—and how to gather data, marking down GPS points and the animals' physical features so that Save the Rhino Trust could analyze the health and number of rhinos in the region. We each had a job, and I was Rangefinder Girl. I carried it around my neck, a heavy black cube that punished my every movement, and I peered through it occasionally to practice: 12 meters to the nearest hill; 2 to the ground; 170 to the base of the Brandberg.

It was hard to range-find from the vehicles, though, which bounced constantly, powering over boulders and through dry brush. "These Land Rovers can drive sideways across a 45-degree angle," Bernd said, but when he tried to demonstrate, the truck leaned so horribly that he accelerated off the slope. "Maybe not with people on top," he amended.

There were low guardrails fencing the top of the truck, and I clung to them the whole time, squeezing the hot metal, struggling to stay on as the Land Rover bucked beneath me. Meanwhile the trackers rested their hands in their laps and hardly blinked when the vehicle threatened to fling them off. At one point the wheels on one side lifted entirely into the air; I tensed my legs and tried to guess the distance to the ground, preparing to jump off if the lean should worsen. I was embarrassed about my response, and mentioned it to Bernd later, feeling that I should be honest. I thought he should know of the limitations of his team members.

But Bernd only nodded. "Ach, good for you. Fear is a way of being careful—it is the ultimate respect. If something feels unsafe, get out. I did that in the war once, and it saved my life." He paused and fluffed his white beard with his fingertips. "Some of the others weren't so lucky."

By the end of the day, we had spent a lot of time scrambling and driving but hadn't seen anything like a rhino—only a few dozen zebras and ostriches, and two giraffes. There was so much poaching in the area that the animals were constantly on edge. On the drive from Windhoek, the wildlife had looked at us like we were in their way, but here they were galloping off by the time we entered the far side of a valley, a speck of dust in the distance.

I noticed also that Bernd and Fulai carried walking sticks everywhere; when I asked why, Bernd said they were for killing snakes and "whacking rhino." Why would you want to whack a rhino? "If the rhino is already on top of you," Bernd said, "then you can reach up with your stick and whack it in the face."

"Couldn't you, I don't know, throw rocks? If you needed to scare it away?"

"Oh, no," said Bernd. "That would only make it angry, and the last thing you want is an angry rhino. They can stab you, trample you—just like that."

I considered this. Then, feeling I was being duped, I approached Johannes. "Why does Fulai carry a stick?"

"For snakes and rhinos," said Johannes, swinging an invisible bat through the air. "Whack whack!"

Early the next day, we came to a spoor. Rhino tracks are distinctive, about the size of my open hand, with three rounded toes like the leaves of a clover. Johannes and Fulai started ahead, scanning the landscape beneath their feet, whacking sticks held loosely. Bernd pointed out bent grass, chewed twigs, even a puddle of rhino drool—not yet dried—and we grabbed our packs and water and started off, pacing in single file. Even Shamira fell into line beside Bernd, her head down, sniffing the ground as she walked.

We followed the trail over hills, sidestepping sliding blocks of shale, then down to a grassland and through a swamp, up again, over, around, until it seemed we could be back where we started or else a hundred miles away. We walked without speaking, sweat dripping from our shirt hems. The heat felt like warm palms pressing against my skin; it filled my mouth

when I breathed. Then we came to a valley and Bernd raised
an arm.

There was a rhino, lying in the shade of a Salvadora bush,
ears and horns poking from the grass like periscopes. I measured: 120 meters. We crouched behind a tree to fill out data
forms—my hand shook so much I had trouble recording the
digits—then edged closer. For ten minutes nothing moved;
the scene solidified around us, the great boulder of a creature
lying sharp and sleepy in the sun. Then those ears swiveled
like satellite dishes and the bull was up, running off with its
tail straight in the air, at once tremendously heavy and agile as
a dancer. Its shovel-shaped head was lifted, as if in pride, and
the skin on its legs fell in heavy folds, slapping together with
each step. I felt like I was watching a dinosaur.

That evening I took the fly off my tent so I could see the
stars, and sometime in the night it started to rain, just enough
to wake me up. Though most nights in the Ugab were cold,
the clouds had contained the day's heat like a blanket. I lay on
my sleeping bag with raindrops falling on my arms and legs,
marveling at the world.

That was the beginning. I felt, at every moment, like a child
pressing her face to window glass, watching scenery flow by
in a bright and jubilant stream. And though I didn't realize
it, I had a child's faith that the glass was impermeable—that
it displayed a world wholly separate from my own, and if the
car shook a little, it only bettered the illusion.

The following day I rode inside the truck with Bernd and
took advantage of the enclosed space to ask some of the questions I had been collecting. Why rhinos? What was it like to
grow up in Namibia during apartheid? Why do you choose
to live in the bush, and to take students with you? Are you
lonely, so far from other people? His eyes never left the terrain, but he was accommodating in his answers, telling stories

of people he had encountered and dangers he had seen. Once, he told me, he awoke from his cot in a sandy clearing to find that a herd of elephants had surrounded him while he slept. I tried to imagine it—their vast bodies in the early morning darkness like pieces of night broken apart from the rest. A young bull came toward Bernd and gripped the foot of his sleeping bag with its trunk, tugging at it lightly, then harder, so that the bag strained under Bernd's body.

As Bernd lay there, certain he was about to die, the matriarch of the herd appeared at his head, so close that her skin brushed his hair. She lifted her face and let a rumble roll through her chest, and instantly, the bull released the sleeping bag and drew away: she had reprimanded him.

"And here is the part of the story you'll like," said Bernd, "but first I must tell you something else. One morning, during the war, a soldier in my division refused to rise from his cot. 'There's a snake in my bed,' he said. 'I can't get up.'

"'Yes,' we answered, 'then none of us can get up, we all have snakes in our beds.' But it soon became clear that this man was telling the truth. There was more sweat on his face than is on ours right now, though the air was cool."

"What did you do?" I said.

"We poured diesel over his body, to make the snake sleepy. Then we unzipped his sleeping bag one centimeter at a time. Curled between his legs was a black mamba. The mamba was dazed from the fumes, and the soldier managed to get out. But I tell you, he was quiet a long time after that.

"Now, you must keep this in mind while I return to my first story. The ellies had scared a mouse, and it climbed into my sleeping bag to hide. I felt that mouse moving and—*woop*—I was out of the cot so fast, dancing like I stood on scorpions! So there you go. A herd of elephants I can tolerate, but a little mouse was too much for big, brave Bernd."

We didn't pass a spoor that day, and after returning to camp, I joined Fulai and Johannes where they were looking at camera trap photos with Bernd. The photos had been loaded onto an old laptop, which plugged into a solar panel. There were more than seven hundred images, grainy and green-black on the small screen. Most showed rock doves and springbok, but there was one oryx, her horns curling back halfway across her body, and a few low, tense jackals dipping their heads to the mirror surface of the pool. Then several blurry night shots, and finally, what we were waiting for—a rhino right there, square-on, nose so close to the camera that you could see the wrinkles and craters in her skin, a whole topography in itself.

Johannes and Fulai filled out forms for the rhino, under Bernd's supervision. I noticed that around the trackers, Bernd lost his lightheartedness—he didn't smile at all.

I asked Johannes how long he had been working with rhinos. "I be assistant to an SRT tracker two years," he said, careful with the words. "After two years"—here his mouth twitched and split into a grin, which he pulled in after glancing at Bernd—"I become permanent staff. And Fulai, he been permanent much longer. Thirteen, fourteen years longer than me."

"That's wrong, Johannes," Bernd said. "The longest-running trackers at SRT only came on a decade ago."

Johannes nodded. "Yes, *meneer*." And he was silent the rest of the night.

I read in my field guide that you can tell how poisonous a scorpion is, roughly, by the ratio of pincer to tail. Big pincers, and the scorp is making up for a feeble sting. But the bigger the stinger—and the more lethal the sting—the less it needs pincers for defense.

During the day, yellow-legged ticks the size of pumpkin seeds patrolled the sandy ground in the riverbed, and after dusk the scorpions came out. They were black, and two or three inches long; looking at them, I couldn't see pincers at all.

In the morning we found a trail early, just a kilometer out of camp. We were heading to the spring to fill our water cans and saw that the spoor had overlapped the previous day's tire tracks. By watching the trackers, I was learning what to look for in a spoor: wrinkled footprints, dampness in the sand, whether fallen leaves along the trail had fresh edges where they had been torn from bushes. And then there were the signs I could never hope to see: the faintest of smudges on solid rock; the places where a rhino had touched its nose to the ground and breathed.

All of these things told us that the spoor had been made since sunrise, less than two hours ago. We followed the tracks for an hour, two, three, as the sun rose higher and shadows shrank away. We turned, backtracked, backtracked again. And then, at the edge of a small valley, Johannes pointed ahead and we all dropped to the ground. There stood a bull, sixty meters away—I was surprised to find that after the past days' practice, I had gained an intuition for distances, and used the rangefinder only to double-check my estimates. This rhino had his head lifted, and his ears swiveled in our direction. His eyes were small holes in the side of his face. We were closer than we wanted to be—for rhinos, a safe viewing distance is around a hundred meters—and so we crept backwards, crouched low; we didn't speak until we had made it up the nearest hill, safe above a cliff, and the rhino was just a bulge in the grass below us.

Later, as I peeled squash for dinner, Fulai came over and stood beside me. "*Was dit naby?*" I said quietly. Was that close?

Fulai squinted at me, then looked down at his hands, which clutched the end of his whacking stick. He was missing a thumbnail, had only a swollen scar in its place. "*Ja*," he said. "*Dit was baie naby.*" Too close.

* * *

The next afternoon I went for a walk by myself; I was eager to explore on my own. I hiked up to a nearby ridge, enjoying the solitude and the late-afternoon wind. The hills were black, and ribboned with parallel ridges of stone; dry grasses pushed between rocks, and here and there grew tangles of myrrh, its fragrant sap bleeding from bare twisted branches. The air seemed to soften around them, to take on a slight blush as it filled with a scent like pine and roses. When we had come up here the other day, Amber called these "the hills of the dead." The description didn't seem far off.

The sun was low in the sky and I had promised to return by dusk, when the leopards came out. As I walked I was aware of, though not concerned by, the homogeneity of the terrain— the way each naked hill melted into the next, the way stones rose up and blocked the view behind me. I noted landmarks as I passed them—a faint game trail, a stack of broken rocks, a zebra wallowing hole—and played with them in my head, twisting things around, trying to figure out how to navigate back. *After the deepest wallow, walk perpendicular to the veins of shale,* or *Just past the dead myrrh, turn away from the sun.* It was a game, a way to entertain myself. I walked for forty minutes or so, then stood for a while admiring the Brandberg. The mountain was dark red, its rock edges serrated, and there was a stillness in the air around it, as if not even the wind wanted to be there. I decided to turn around.

Every direction looked the same.

As I began to retrace my steps, the sun slid down the sky as if greased; suddenly the landmarks meant everything. It would be so easy, I realized, to miss one sign and lose my whole system, to wander off a hidden cliff or into the wrong valley. Even if I wasn't eaten, I wore only a t-shirt, and the night would be cold; then morning would come and with it the heat, and how could I hope to find a spring?

It was already growing cool; the day's sweat had long since dried from my arms, and now goose bumps rose in its place. As I walked, I became keenly aware of sensations around me. I noticed the movement of rocks under my feet, the crunching sound as they rolled against each other. When I passed a myrrh tree that stood alone in the center of the ridge, its branches gnarled and contorted, I reached out to touch it, seeking, I suppose, some comfort in its solidity; I withdrew my fingertips glossy with sap. I tried to wipe the sap off on the ground, but grains and pebbles only stuck to my skin, as dark as the hills themselves. I looked down at my hand and started to cry.

I thought of the darkling beetle, its struggle against a land too big to negotiate, and I saw now that I had been wrong to identify with it. The beetle was clumsy, yes, but he was designed for this world, was designed to pull water from the air itself. I could no sooner pull water from the air than a springbok from my back pocket. I was pink and soft, blunt-nailed and flat-toothed, inflexible in my constant dependence on so many physical resources: food, water, warmth, shade.

Finally, as the first stars appeared in the sky, I caught sight of bright colors below me: the tents back at camp. Most of the others were gathered around the fire, and did not notice my return. To get to my tent I had to pass Johannes and Fulai, who were sitting on the hood of the Land Rover, eating dinner. Johannes watched me as I passed—looked hard at my eyes, which, although I had rubbed them dry, still stung. "A good walk, miss?" he asked quietly. But when I looked at him, he dropped his gaze.

I was determined that the following day would be better— that I would be responsible, and focused, and diligent in my recording of data. There would be no recklessness, and certainly no getting lost. The desert was a remarkable place, and I was lucky to be there.

Sure enough, the morning started well: we came across a herd of elephants just outside of camp. They passed through the Salvadora bushes like boats through water, all moving forward at the same slow pace, ears waving in the damp air. Beside the largest was a baby, gray and wrinkled with baggy skin; although its back barely reached its mother's stomach, it was still the size of a Volkswagen Beetle. Bernd told us that this was one of the largest herds in the Kunene region, led by a matriarch named Mama Africa—and that based on their tracks, they must have passed through camp last night while we slept. Remembering Bernd's story, I sent a silent thank-you to Mama Africa for leading the herd safely past us. Then I twisted backwards on the Land Rover, watching until the elephants were long out of sight, unable to stop smiling.

Not ten minutes later, we came to a plain that opened from the riverbed. A cheetah ran on the yellow slope before us, stretching and compacting its long limbs. It passed the way a shooting star might—a streak through my vision, gone before I blinked.

When we found the rhino tracks, it was still early, the sun just over the horizon. A breeze blew the grasses against our ankles. The spoor curled around itself in elaborate loops; we entered dead-end valleys only to find that the rhino had climbed a steep slope, or passed through a narrow opening in the rocks. By afternoon we were thirsty and hurting. My feet had blistered and bled along the sides, where I had slipped against thorns or rocks. But there was something meditative about the tracking, something I liked, the heat and the sips of warm water and the quiet patience of it all, the way we chased a goal but not a destination. We decided that if we found nothing by three o'clock, we would turn back.

At five to three, we came around a boulder and Fulai froze; I had never seen someone stand so still so quickly. We dropped, pressing ourselves to the dirt, still unsure of what had happened. The air smelled of dust, and something rotting. Then I saw it: a gray head emerging from the grass, a sleeping rhino so close that in a few strides I could have touched its horns. Four meters, I thought, at most.

Two ears perked, then rose, as the bull heaved itself to its feet. It took a step toward us. Shamira pressed herself against Bernd's legs, and he grabbed a wad of skin from her neck in his fist, twisting it to pull her closer. His nails dug sharply into her fur.

Still low, we crawled as one, backwards up the slope behind us; scree fell beneath our hands and knees and rocks clattered against each other. The bull followed, head raised. It stood where we had been a moment before.

How to describe it, facing a rhino head-on? I could hear its breathing quicken. I could see the black hairs tufting from its ears and bursting from the point of its upper lip. The rhino came to the base of the slope and stood. Five, six minutes it stood, staring at us. I tried to make myself small and silent. I tried to make myself into air.

Something in the rhino's expression reminded me of an old man lowering his glasses to squint across a table. And then I understood: it couldn't see us. It knew we were there, but it didn't know *what* we were. Rhinos are nearly blind. They sense only motion, and bright colors, and we wore faded, dirty clothing; we blended into the rock. The wind swept our scent away from it. It was confused.

There was a movement. To my left, Bernd had pulled a camera from his backpack and was moving forward. It must have been a new rhino, one that SRT didn't yet have a photo of in their database. The animal tensed. It watched Bernd come closer, and then it snorted.

Fulai lifted a hand in signal to Johannes; both trackers shook their heads. They nodded to each other in wordless, delicate communication, and Johannes motioned for Bernd to move away, to back up. *Nie doen*, Johannes mouthed. Don't do it. Bernd looked at Johannes for a long moment. Then he lifted his chin slightly and turned away, toward the rhino. He raised his camera and snapped the shutter.

The rhino charged. It lowered its head, horns splitting the air, the skin on its sides bouncing as it came. Pebbles flew up and fell against the rocks around us; I closed my eyes as they hit my shoulders, my arms, my face. The rhino skidded to a stop when it reached Bernd, sending up a spray of dust that engulfed him completely. For several moments there was silence, a sudden calm as the red cloud hung opaque before us, and then, as it began to settle, a figure stepped backwards, camera still in hand.

The rhino stood watching. Then it kicked at the ground, turned, and trotted away in a zigzag, peering over alternate shoulders every few steps. As I watched it leave, I exhaled fully for the first time since rounding the bend.

But the rhino wheeled and ran toward us again, stopping at the base of the hill, then retreated. It repeated this eight or nine times, running away and coming back, and each time I was sure we were done for. My legs were long asleep from squatting, and when I glanced at my watch I saw that we had been trapped there for close to forty minutes. Finally, when it seemed the rhino wasn't coming any closer, Fulai gestured instructions and we crept sideways around the hill; the trackers led, and Bernd fell into step behind them, among the students. The rhino stood with horns high, watching us go.

By the time we got back to camp it was evening, and according to our GPS we had walked twenty-one miles. I helped Bernd refill our water cans at a spring, and I asked him why the rhino had charged—what it had been thinking. And why had it stopped?

Bernd tapped the ground with his stick. "It didn't know whether to be afraid of us," he said. "It was saying: 'I don't know what you are, but *I* am *very big*.'"

Later, as we ate dinner by the fire, there came a rustling in the darkness. First Johannes and then Fulai entered the circle of students, the firelight casting sharp, flickering shadows across their faces, and sat down on a log beside us. They did not look at Bernd, nor did he look at them; nobody spoke. Bernd stirred his food methodically, lifting his spoon from the bowl of stew and dipping it in again. He looked up as if to say something, clearing his throat, but he only stared at the fire for a moment, then resumed eating.

Everyone overslept the next morning. We didn't start the breakfast fire until 6:30, and didn't leave camp until 7:15. After five hours of fruitless searching we headed back. That was fine with me; I was still shaken from the day before, and from my hike the day before that. I couldn't admit it to the others, but I suspected, in truth, that I didn't want to see another rhino. Not up close, at least.

The whole landscape felt too big; it was too far out of my control, beyond my understanding. I had lived in wilderness before, had loved how real it felt, how important and forgotten, but the Ugab frightened me. It was the most beautiful, dangerous place I had ever been.

I watched the trackers, the way the land spoke to them in words I couldn't begin to follow, and it made me miss the places whose languages I *did* speak. I felt foolish to have come to a place where I didn't fully know how to protect myself. I didn't want to get hurt. I thought of this when I checked for scorpions in my shoes and when I took my anti-malaria pills, swallowed with water I had scooped up between clumps of slime in an open pool. I thought of it when I climbed out of my tent at night to pee, and checked with the beam of my headlamp for the glowing eyes of leopards and lions. Or when I saw the thin, curving trails of spitting cobras in the sand. Or when I learned that thirty percent of the people in Namibia have AIDS.

I stood in the grasses under an open sky and felt the warmth of the sun, and watched the looping flight of a Cape glossy starling, and listened to the grating of cicadas in the soil around me, and thought: Why have I come here? This is not my place.

I wanted so badly not to be afraid of it.

We spent our last full day cleaning up camp, organizing rhino forms, and entering data into the laptop. In the hottest part of the afternoon, Erin began to vomit. She was sick for over an hour, then fell asleep. The rest of us boiled water for coffee in a kettle over the fire. After we had drunk a cup or two, another student looked into her mug and yelped—there were insects' wings floating at the bottom. She opened the coffee press and found half a dozen bees wedged under the screen. Then she peered into the kettle and screamed.

The bottom of the kettle was covered with several inches of dead, crispy bees; when we shook it, they made a brittle, grating sound. All we could guess was that the swarm must have crawled in through the spout one by one, desperate for what little moisture remained inside. In the fifteen minutes or so that it took the water to boil, we had essentially been making bee tea, steeping their bodies into a hot broth. The water that remained at the bottom was thick and brown.

No one was sure if the bees would make us sick. We sat there, feeling for something unpleasant in our guts, and finally decided we were fine. Probably. And then someone remembered Erin, who was sleeping off her illness in the shade of her tent. If she hadn't been sick, she too would have drunk the coffee.

But Erin is allergic to bees.

In the evening, after we had recovered from the afternoon's scare, Bernd made fresh *vetkoek*, jelly donuts, to celebrate our last night. As we ate I found a scorpion on my leg, crawling up the back of my calf; I swallowed once, then twice, and managed to flick it off with a jelly knife. Fulai caught it in a jar so we could see it up close—firelight shone on its dark shell, and its stinger straightened and curled like a beckoning finger.

We leaned in, raising the jar above our heads to see the scorpion's ridged belly, its sharp feet. Despite the glass, I felt a shiver of adrenaline in my chest. I thought about what Bernd had said on the first day about fear—carefulness—as the ultimate respect.

When we were finished examining it, Johannes released the scorpion on the far side of the riverbed. "We just be putting you here," he told the scorpion. "Thank you for sharing your home."

On the drive back to Windhoek, a low haze spread across the horizon, what I took at first for fog. It obscured the hills so that even the closest were little more than brown outlines against a gray sky. I sat in the front seat with my window halfway up, and it wasn't until I felt grains hitting my face that I realized the fog was a sandstorm.

It was funny, I thought, brushing the grit from my cheeks, how a thing could surprise you up close—fog into sand, and the sting of it through a window; a rhinoceros at a hundred meters, and a rhinoceros suddenly before you; the desert itself. I had returned the rangefinder to Bernd that morning. My shoulders felt light, unfamiliar without the weight of it hanging before me, and when I touched the back of my neck I felt a crease where the leather cord had bitten my skin.

I was glad to be done with the rangefinder; I had begun to doubt its usefulness. Numbers, it seemed, were a poor measure of distance. After all, what separated a night alone in the desert and a mere close call, a closed throat and a cup of coffee, a white man and his black assistants? What of the distance between me *then*, and me now?

Proximity blurs perception; we are more frightened of the mouse in our sleeping bag than we are of the elephant in the darkness. The trick is to know this, to recognize the real meaning of *too close*. The trick is to see clearly through the glass.

We left the desert and passed through a field of dunes, where the wind was stronger. The landscape crumpled and folded around us. As the sun fell in the sky, the horizon melted purple, then blue, and the dunes shimmered with colors, a sea of opals. Lines of sand rose from the ground and swam in the air.

It was one of those moments when the world lifts up and beneath it you glimpse something else, a place so big and different that when you breathe it fills you. I held each breath as long as I could.

ॐ ॐ ॐ

Blair Braverman is an Arts Fellow at the University of Iowa's Nonfiction Writing Program. She has worked as a naturalist and dogsled guide in Norway, Alaska, and Colorado.

❧ ❧ ❧

The Codeine of Jordan

One woman's quest for adventure, romance,
and antibiotics.

*W*hen you're a Jewish woman in a Muslim country,
having a fling with a nineteen-year-old Mexican
whom your boyfriend knows nothing about, and you've got a
raging urinary tract infection—your thighs sore from squatting over the hole in the floor that passes for a hotel toilet—
and you can't find an open pharmacy, never mind a female
pharmacist who speaks English, you can be expected to get a
little cranky.

"*Aie*," Mateo says, wounded. "You don't have to snap," after
I grab from his hands the guidebook that supposedly reveals
the location of English-speaking drugstores. I thumb through
it again, as if I hadn't just studied it a half-hour before, scour-
ing the pages of this glib book written by college students half
a world away. Twenty-four hours, it said about the last pharmacy we checked. Open all the time, it promised.

We're back at the hotel now, waiting until 8:30 A.M., when
I'm guessing the pharmacies might open. I have this dream
right now, as I run to the toilet for the fifth time in as many
minutes, unable to eke out the stream that is both razor sharp
and oddly relieving at the same time. A dream that I will walk

into a pharmacy and say, "Bactrim, please," and a kind female pharmacist with understanding eyes and a hijab over her hair will smile knowingly and hand over a bottle. True, at home in Seattle, Bactrim requires a doctor's visit and a prescription, but this is Wadi Musa, Jordan, so maybe it's different here. After all, you can get Tylenol with codeine without a prescription in Canada. Maybe Bactrim is the codeine of Jordan.

Mateo gently tries to rub my shoulders, but I shrug him off. "*Huevos*," he says, *eggs* being the hip swear word of the month. His tone is mock tough, but I can hear his worry. He—a Mexican-born Jew of Syrian parents—is as misplaced as I. His dark skin and Semitic nose allow him to blend in here in a way that I, even when I'm wearing a long skirt and modest shirt, cannot. "What can I do?" he asks, nuzzling his stubbled chin against my neck. His accent is fierce. Mateo speaks four languages, none of them well.

An hour later at the drugstore, a sour-looking man of no more than forty stares at me after my brief, quiet utterance of my ailment. He's wearing a button-down white shirt and black pants, and his face is so smooth, so absent of wrinkles that it looks as if he hasn't cracked the merest of smiles in ages. As his silence continues, my panic mounts. If he doesn't know what a urinary tract infection is, I'm certainly not going to explain it, although perhaps I could somehow draw a picture?

I'm sweating through my LOVE YOUR MOTHER EARTH t-shirt, having given up all semblance of modesty in my agony, even though there's a chill in the morning desert air. I need to use the toilet again, and I'm fighting back tears, because I just don't know how I got into this. Which is, of course, a lie. I know exactly how I got into this, how I didn't want to marry the guy back home so I took a short trip abroad to find myself and found myself taking up with a gorgeous, thin-as-a-reed, dark-toned boy nine years my junior, whom I met on the kibbutz and who was willing to travel with me to Jordan and who didn't remind me—as the boyfriend always did—to go the bathroom after having sex. Jordan was as far away from Seattle as I could fathom, which days ago had seemed a superb idea, but now, with the misery between my legs, loomed large in my list of travel regrets.

The pharmacist's eyes are a deep brown, and his eyebrows meet dangerously close in the center of his forehead. He hasn't blinked. "You need to see a doctor," he says.

I am in a country I never imagined I would visit, far on the other side of the earth, and I am supposed to be having a phenomenal adventure. Instead I'm back in the shared hotel bathroom, squatting and noticing little more than the pink tile. I have no idea what I ate an hour ago (I think I ate; I must have eaten). I'm unsure how we returned to the hotel from the pharmacy. We must have walked—we *had* to have walked—but I couldn't tell you what I saw on the street or if I talked to anyone besides the pharmacist. I'm focused like I've never been able to focus on anything before, focused on this shooting pain, which is not the kind of adventure I signed up for.

Actually, I *could* tell stories about the bathroom, I've been here so long. The showerhead is in the middle of the wall with no separation from the toilet, so water can spray everywhere. Not that it sprays; it trickles slowly when off and in a steady stream when on. A stream like I wish I could produce right now. There are indents in the tile where my feet fit nicely, and so I have to watch where I pee so as not to wet my feet. That is, if I could pee. The smell of rancid urine mixes with pine-scented deodorizer, giving the room a decayed odor, like that of a roadside gas station restroom. The door doesn't seem to lock all the way, and I lean precariously, a delicate balancing act, squatting here with one hand reaching toward the door so no unsuspecting tourist can wander in to see me perpetually posed for leap frog.

*   *   *

At the Green Crescent Medical Society, the doctor seems surprised to see me. "How can I help you?" he asks clearly, although with a distinct accent. He is a thin man with a caterpillar-like mustache, wearing a crisply ironed white shirt and tie, which appears to be the uniform of Jordanian professional men. His face is pockmarked, dotted with acne scars. The office is cluttered with a living-room sofa, complete with tears on the side of the dark red fabric and a pile of papers fluttering beneath a rocklike paperweight on an ornately carved wooden desk. It looks more like the study of a professor in an underfunded college than a medical doctor's office.

"I, uh, have a urinary tract infection."

His surprised expression quickly turns into a look of skepticism.

"I've had them before," I add. "At home I take Bactrim."

His gaze is sharp, scrutinizing. "That is a diagnosis."

I just nod.

"Are you married or single?"

Ah, the all-important medical question about my marital situation. The question that will determine all that is right with the world and all that is wrong with me. A question that gets to the root of who I am and what my worth is in life. But I didn't reach the age of twenty-eight without becoming used to this question, and it makes me instantly wary. A good five beats pass as I debate how to answer. If I say I'm married, he'll never know the difference. I wear a ring to discourage the men who need to be discouraged. But if there's one thing I've learned in life it's that you never, ever lie to doctors. Doctors are your friends. Doctors help you.

I respond, finally. "Single."

He continues with his questions, which are more in line with those I would be asked at home. Discoloration? Blood? Discharge? He's not getting the answers he wants. When

I confess to a kidney infection about seven years back, he becomes concerned.

"We need to do an ultrasound!"

"An ultrasound?" An emotion finally surfaces through the pain: dismay. I know about ultrasounds. Rather, I know about the cost of ultrasounds, and there's no room for one in a traveler's budget.

"When you've had a childhood kidney infection, you must be careful."

"But I wasn't a child! I was twenty-one!"

"How old are you now?"

"Twenty-eight."

Is that a slight smile? A bit of relief I see in his gaze? No, I finally realize—it's actually a bug on his forehead that he's trying to swat away by furrowing his brow and dodging his head slightly. "I would have thought you were sixteen."

For fifteen minutes the doctor grills me on my medical history, before an idea hits him. "Do you engage in non-marital intercourse?"

Again the pause, but there's no point in lying. I think of Mateo waiting nervously in the lobby, the darling thing who whispers to me in Spanish as we lie in bed, who tells me his father always said difficult women are worth the challenge, which, I suppose given the circumstance, is lucky for me. "Yeah," I mutter.

A piercing look. A deafening moment of silence. Finally, *finally*, he says, in a reprimanding tone, "Do you think this could have something to do with that?"

Why hadn't it occurred to me that "single" immediately translated into "virgin" in his mind? Perhaps the contortions I have twisted my body into, trying to lessen the pain, have put a kink in my brain. "Single." "Not married." Ergo "virgin."

"Yes." I simply respond. Contrition is what I am going for. I'm not sure it is working.

"Are you here with a friend?"

A friend, a friend! Yes, I'm here with a friend. Oh joy, oh happiness, I finally have the correct answer, the thing he wants to hear. "Yes!" I practically shout.

"Tell her to come in and then hop up on the table."

Foiled.

"Actually, my friend is male."

He nods, at this point not surprised by anything. He calls into the waiting room, and a woman with a chubby face and a dark blue chador covering her heavy body comes in and sits on the couch in the corner. The flow of the fabric obscures her, erasing any feature that could make her distinct, and I can't even determine if she's a teenager or middle-aged. I try to look at her face, but she turns her head downward. She doesn't read; she doesn't pick at her fingernails; she just sits.

"O.K., get on the table," says the doctor. And for a moment I panic. This man is *not* going to give me an internal! But I feel like a junkie, so desperate for the prescription, for the pretty oval green pill that's going to make my life all better, that I lie on the beige medical table, surprised when he covers me with a gray wool blanket. How hygienic can that be? He lifts my shirt not even high enough to expose my belly ring, and presses on my stomach.

"Does it hurt here?" I shake my head, and he moves his hand around until he reaches my bladder and I say yes.

Ten minutes and one ultrasound later ("Look, here's your kidney," he says, his tone implying the obvious, when all I see are wavy lines), he declares, "You have a urinary tract infection."

Isn't that where we began? Isn't that what started this conversation? I nod.

"Are you in much pain?" he asks, his voice stoic, simply trying to gather the facts.

"Yes," I say. What I'm thinking is, *Oh God yes I'm in dying pain, isn't that obvious, why else would I be here? Please save me.*

"O.K., I'll give you a shot and a prescription. Lie down."

Briefly I think of autoclaves and disposable needles, but those thoughts fade when I think of the Bactrim. I turn on my stomach, knowing what's coming next but not quite believing it. He ever so slightly pulls down my black leggings. No comment is made about the tiny daisy tattooed on my ass.

I turn toward the woman on the couch, who hasn't moved but seems to be peering at me from the corner of her eye, and comment, "I can't remember the last time I got a shot down there," but she says nothing, and I can only assume she doesn't speak English. I flinch slightly as he gives me the injection.

He and the woman leave the room so I can leap off the table and pull my leggings up the inch he has drawn them. He returns to hand me a bill, written in both Arabic and English, the words and numbers in big block letters as if a grade-schooler had written them. Sixteen dinars. Ten dollars. I try not to grin as I hand him the cash.

Afterward, Mateo walks me to the pharmacy, where I triumphantly hand my prescription to the man with one eyebrow. Now that the shot has taken effect and the pain is subsiding, I can browse the shelves as he prepares my drug, eying the unfamiliar boxes with the unfamiliar writing, noticing these details that escaped me before.

Pills in pocket, we head for the street, where Mateo buys me *esh al-bulbul*, the tiny treat that means "bird's nest," a pocket of dough filled with pistachios. As we walk, I notice for the first time the empty beauty of the desert town, the store windows that look like a Midwestern town caught in the 1950s, and the smell of *mansaf*, lamb in fragrant yogurt sauce, being cooked for dinner in the small restaurants lining the road. I finally see the women draped in rich blue, pure white, pale peach head scarves walking in the streets; my mouth waters at the flaky squares of nut-filled baklava that are being laid out in delicate rows in the bakery shop window; I watch the boxy, pale yellow cabs already lining up to ferry tourists to Petra.

Mateo distracts me with talk of what we'll see in Petra as I clutch my beloved prescription of Bactrim—O, how I love thee!—and swear to myself that I won't have sex until I get back home, safe and sound in Seattle, no matter how long that takes. And I mean it. For another eight hours, anyway.

ॐ ॐ ॐ

J. S. Brown lives in the suburbs of Boston, almost within walking distance of her HMO'd doctor. Her travels have taken her across the U.S., Europe, and the Middle East. Now traveling with two children, her explorations are different, yet still adventurous, and her family thrills at the journey as much as she does. Her writing has been published in The Bellevue Literary Review, Natural Bridge, Under the Sun, Sojourn, *and* The Southeast Review. *She has an MFA from the University of Washington and is currently at work on her first novel.*

ॐ ॐ ॐ

The Risky Path

How do you keep your fears from shrinking your world?

The dirt lane that passes through Porabari, a village on the Dhaleswari River, in Bangladesh, is lined with dozens of nondescript wooden crates stacked on top of one another. A waft of hot cooking oil from a nearby food stand makes its way through the sweltering air. A dozen men, women, and children offer curious, placid stares as I walk past the crates. Sweat streams down my face and body, but it's not the 98-degree heat and punishing humidity that leave me sopping. It's raw panic. Some of the crates appear to move, ever so slightly. One jiggles. A devilish forked tongue flickers out of a slit.

Snakes, I think to myself with Indiana Jones dread. *It had to be snakes.*

All my life, I've had nightmares about snakes; in these dreams, serpents wrap around my head in a twisted tiara and across my neck in mocking threat. Awake, my fear has diminished me, limited my experience. I've walked miles to avoid crossing giant rock fields (likely snake habitats) and passed up the opportunity to fish alpine lakes teeming with cutthroat trout but reputed to have rattlers, because I know an encounter will leave me an irrational mess. This fear, stuck in my craw for decades now, may not be just about snakes. I have a hunch it's somehow related to my Big Fear: a life of stagnation, of narrowed options, of arriving at the pearly gates with a rucksack of regret. More than a decade ago, when desk life felt stultifying, I looked at fear and renamed it potential. I quit my steady job to travel the globe in search of women who live by their inner compass and make change in the world. I found a professional outlet for that ethos by making these women the focus of a travel series, Adventure Divas, and sold it to PBS. Then I hit the road to produce the program.

The crazy lady in my attic had been released, and she had a passport. I've since learned that I'm my best self in motion, courting the unexpected and running not away from what I fear but toward it. Still, the snake nightmares persist.

Here in Porabari, the Bede people revere snakes. They catch hundreds of them a year to sell, trade and charm, including deadly species such as krait, viper, and cobra. They milk snakes for their venom, which is used in antivenin. Charmers from all over the region shop here, where a six-foot cobra costs the equivalent of $10, and snakes for pets or culinary delicacy abound. In a town where every house has a pet snake, the love for the species is palpable. Indeed, fear of snakes is mostly a Western phenomenon. For the Hindus, the serpenty Kundalini life force that winds up and down our spines is a source of enlightenment. If you were born in the Year of the Snake, as I was, the Chinese say you will be wise, romantic, and calm.

Calm? Hardly. Part of my job for Adventure Divas, and nowadays as a host of Globe Trekker, is to hurl myself into dodgy situations, sometimes physical, sometimes political. I've become a student of fear, and everywhere I go, I ask people what they fear most, trying to learn from their answers. In India, I met Kiran Bedi, a police chief then in charge of training all of Delhi's forces. In her career, she's gone toe to toe with rioters and endured death threats from corrupt colleagues while at the same time fighting to introduce vipassana meditation to inmates and guards at the infamously brutal Tihar prison (where under her watch violence and corruption plummeted). After seeing her put hundreds of cadets through a 5 A.M. silent meditation and later supervise their target practice at the range, I asked her, "What do you fear?" She tipped back her military hat, all the tough drained from her face, and said, "Nothing since my mother died. After that, there was nothing left to lose. I lost what I loved most. It made me realize the transience of life, and now I fear nothing."

I tell myself that missing out on an experience because of fear is not an option (snakes notwithstanding). Once, while trekking through Niger's Sahara, I entered a camel race. Sitting atop my leggy nine-foot mount, I feared being trampled, as a seasoned rider had been minutes before. But as we thundered off in a hail of hooves and Arabic hollers, I reached for that sweet spot where fear gets transformed, through action, into vitality—and possibility. As I held on for dear life, mine expanded.

Of course, testing myself against fear and trying to learn from it is a luxury. Many people don't choose to tangle with danger; they're forced to. I remember a caste-oppression activist I met in Rajasthan who, after her unjust arrest and persecution and the torture of her colleague, said, "I don't have any fear since this attack. It has made us stronger." And I'll never forget the village woman turned elite mountain climber who was buried alive in a massive night avalanche on Everest. She and her team were dug out within hours, and most of the climbers descended the mountain. She chose to continue her ascent the next morning, becoming the first Indian woman to summit Everest. "The experience of the night drained all the fear out of me," she said. Then there was the filmmaker who was threatened by a knife-wielding john in a brothel. The prostitutes protected her by surrounding the man, changing her fear to power: "Their strength gave me strength. They trusted me, and my strength came from their trust, and so I had no fear."

The dance with fear (be it of snakes, failure, loneliness, bad guys, death) is a process. And here in Bangladesh, I've been processing my heinie off.

Three days ago, I joined a group of honey hunters in the fetid Sundarbans forests, where Bengal tiger attacks are common; a man had been mauled and killed only hours before we arrived. But all I could think of was snakes. My translator, Bachchu, who grew up in these forests and now worked as a guide with the Tiger Conservation Project, told me his father once sat down on a log to take a break and chew betel nut. When he nicked the log with his knife (a bit of wood is part of the betel-nut-chewing pastiche), it moved. "It was not a log," said Bachchu. "It was a giant python."

But Bachchu wasn't afraid of snakes. He and all the honey hunters were afraid only of tigers. Of the approximately three hundred foragers who will enter the forests this season, driven by economic need, about twenty will be killed by Bengal tigers. Of course they are afraid, the leader told me, but they have to support their families. Then he wrapped a multicolored woven scarf around my jugular. "Tigers like necks," he warned.

We proceeded through the soppy mangrove forests in a loose line, a dozen bare feet (and two in boots—mine) stepping around spiky roots. The hunters scanned the treetops for hives and the tangled green foliage at ground level for tigers. I was the only one who trained her eyes on the forest floor, looking for suspiciously moving logs. The men hollered in lilting Bengali, calling on God, making noise to keep track of one another, to make sure no one had been taken. It can happen silently.

The hive was about twenty feet off the ground. The hunters gathered a bundle of giant mangrove leaves, like floppy elephant ears, bound them together with bark twine and set them afire. A young man took the smoking torch, wrapped a cloth around his face and shinnied up the trunk. Amid a billow of smoke and angry bees, he hacked off a third of the dripping hive with his machete, leaving the remainder for the bees to rebuild, and for the hunters, someday, to return to. We huddled below, cloths wrapped around our heads, tense, waiting for the stings. A cloud of thousands of very angry bees blotted out the sunlight and created a viscous surround-sound buzz. But I was not scared of the bees: I had a calm, deep knowledge that all would be fine.

The thin, buttery, delicate honey was otherworldly. We were huddled together tasting it, distracted and happy, but then I scanned the forest. Tigers will stalk the hunters for hours before pouncing on one of them, often during the relaxed moment of joy after the hive has come down. "Bach-chu," I asked, "are you afraid?"

"Yes," he said. "Every time I return from the forest safely, I feel as if I've been born again." After we talked for a while, I realized that his "rebirth" was not about the relief of surviving danger but about coming very close to the thing he both fears and cares about deeply—tigers—and finding a way for those opposing feelings to coexist. When we parted, I understood better the taut, vital balance that comes from facing fear in pursuit of your passion.

Only yesterday I made a certain peace with Bangladesh's most ferocious and cold-blooded reptile. In the town of Bagerhat, several hours south of the snake village of Porabari, crocodiles troll the ponds surrounding the mausoleum of Sufi mystic

Khan Jahan Ali. Pilgrims gather there to honor Khan Jahan and receive the powerful blessing that comes from touching a crocodile; I was slightly befuddled by, and envious of, their faith, which had a template, a history, a clear path.

As I stepped forward to share in the ritual, the mazar, the keeper of the tomb, called out "Kalapar, dalapar!" (Come!), and a crocodile emerged. The mazar guided my hand toward the behemoth, now dead-still except for the two eyes fluttering on top of its head, the monstrous jaw jagged with prehistoric incisors. I thought of an acquaintance of mine who was snatched, lickety-split, off his canoe in Zambia and dragged under, never seen again. Crocodiles move fast when they want to. The mazar offered me encouragement in Bengali, then English. "Blessing. Blessing," he said, pushing my arm farther down toward the croc.

I was anxious but not white-knuckle scared. The crocodiles were used to brown Bengali arms; nobody knew how they'd react to my pale one. But surely no sensible host would want his foreign guest to lose an arm? I gently grazed my fingers across the clammy, rough snout, wishing only that my bare white arm remain attached. Suddenly another bite of meat—a live chicken—was thrown from behind me toward the crocodile, and the beast exploded forward, crushing the bird in its gargantuan jaws. Feathers flew and the chicken screeched, until both creatures were submerged, silent. The reptile's eyes went under last. I'll never know if that sacrifice was made to honor Khan Jahan Ali or to ensure that the croc chose the right white meat.

But here in Porabari, as the snake crates jiggle, it's not mere trepidation that I feel. Can I, without sedatives or psycho-analysis, transform stifling, panicking fear into something else? Some say faith can be a powerful tool in facing hardship or fear, but I don't believe in God/Allah, destiny, or a cosmic order. Instead, I can only trust the path I've chosen, where the willingness to step outside what's safe and known has become an article of faith. "Salvation is being on the right road," said Martin Luther King Jr., "not having reached a destination."

I approach a vendor who nods and slides back the wooden slats. Out they slither. A pile of small bright-green snakes wind together frenetically; a four-foot-long, lithe grayish snake strikes the vendor and draws blood from the back of his hand. The man is unfazed by the bite and after a few minutes pushes the serpent back into its crate. He carefully opens the next box, and a pair of king cobras spring out of the top, necks flared. He twists his fist in front of their lidless gaze. Arched and ready, the snakes sway and follow the movements. What looks like lilting compliance is actually their attempt to get a fix on the prey. Although the villagers are said to have magical powers that protect them from cobras, the truth is many snake charmers eventually die from bites. Thousands die of snakebites in rural Bangladesh every year.

There is one more crate. Through a slit, I see a thick shadow move. The man slides back the top and lifts the three-foot-long snake. "Around your neck, around your neck," he says in Bengali, which I understand all too well as he gestures for the fat red sand boa to become my garland. The creature's tail looks like a head, so it's referred to as the two-headed snake; both heads twist my way.

I am sickened but determined. I try to channel the brave women I've met. The snake is not poisonous, but the real risk is that if I don't engage this fear—if I walk around it, as I have for decades—I will remain its hostage. When I see a wet paddy field (as I did yesterday), I will again fail to revel in the jubilant green, or in the sturdiness of villages built on stilts at its center, and will instead focus on unseen creatures, on bad things that might lie in wait. I will narrow my life.

I take a deep breath. He puts the snake around my neck. It wraps, one head cuddling my jugular, the other tentatively exploring my cleavage. My eyes are shut and my heart races. I can't open my eyes.

I just can't.

Suddenly in my head I hear the words spat at me by my grandfatherly guide on a particularly sheer edge of the Matterhorn, when I was frozen in fear and exhaustion:

"You are a tough girl! Action! Action!"

I open my eyes.

And the world gets bigger.

ॐ   ॐ   ॐ

Holly Morris is the author of Adventure Divas: Searching the Globe for a New Kind of Heroine, *a* New York Times *"Editor's Choice," and writer/director and executive producer of the companion PBS documentary series, "Adventure Divas." A former* National Geographic Adventure *columnist and widely anthologized essayist, Morris is also a regular contributor to* The New York Times Book Review *among other national publications. Morris presents the PBS television series "Globe Trekker," "Treks in a Wild World," and "Outdoor Investigations." Her recent feature story, "A Country of Women," about a group of survivors living in the shadow of Chernobyl, won the Meredith Editorial Excellence Award, and was reprinted in London's* Daily Telegraph, The Week, *and in the book* The Best Travel Writing Volume 9. *Currently, the story is being made into a documentary film and is the subject of Morris's popular TED Talk. She's based in Brooklyn, New York.*

ॐ ॐ ॐ

Chasing Tornadoes

"The Suck Zone . . . it's the point, basically, at
which the twister sucks you up."
— *Dusty from* *Twister*

"Go, go, go! Towards it!" Ron bellowed. He must have
sensed my hesitation.

Was I supposed to pull a one-eighty and drive away from
the tornado or actually haul ass through a Nebraskan cornfield toward it? Then the twister flickered and was gone.

"It's coming back," Ron yelled. "It's going to come down on
the track right in front of us!" And then it did. A full vortex.
"GO!"

I stomped on the accelerator pedal of the intercept vehicle,
a hail-dented little Pontiac Vibe. We were doing eighty in a
cornfield. Getting stuck was not an option.

The Star Trek-sounding computer voice on Ron's laptop
said, "Warning. You are approaching severe weather."

We were approaching my first tornado, now just five hundred feet in front of me. The dark, jagged cord of wind looked
like it could loop and lasso me from my seat. Now two hundred feet. I thought about the tornado in the *Wizard of Oz*—
it was made by spinning a black sock. It was ingenious and

inexpensive. I was living a movie, a nightmare, and a dream come true. My heart pounded in my temples. This was *real*.

"Gone." Ron slammed his laptop shut. "There was another one there on the hill as well. So what did you think?"

I whooped my reply cowgirl-style. It was time for a bar, drinks, dancing, screaming, bloody steaks, mashed potatoes, do the twist.

It was the last day of the storm chase, and I'd driven 12,365.3 miles through the summer while Ron Gravelle, storm predictor, forecaster, and certified chaser, navigated us to the best storms across the United States. The weather had been a storm chaser's worst nightmare, sunny and dry. Yet Ron overlaid hundreds of weather maps and found a variety of extreme conditions: killer fork lightning in Louisiana, an isolated cell in New Mexico with a cactus and canyon backdrop, a Kansas storm that looked like it could plough a house across a field, a front in Colorado that resembled an alien ship from *Independence Day*. I'd finally seen my first tornado. But not my last.

"So, you heard what happened with Ben and the thirty thousand dollars at the border?" Len, the South African stock car racer, asked me when we picked up the Chevy Suburbans at Will Rogers Airport in Oklahoma City.

It was four years since my first chase, when I had—upon whim—begged Ron to take me on as a driver to pursue extreme weather, one of the things that both frightened and fascinated me most on the planet. Now I was back in Tornado Alley, the expansive swath of the United States between the Rockies and Appalachians, stretching from North Dakota all the way south through Texas. I was here with Ron again— he'd been hired by a television network from Hong Kong for a ten-day storm chase and had asked me to drive for him. Ron was sporting a t-shirt that showcased a spectacular Colorado tornado, an image of his that had been published in *National Geographic*. I desperately wanted to take a picture like Ron's. That was the only problem with being an intercept driver— less opportunity to shoot photos. But it was also the only way I could afford to keep doing this.

Ron handed me a set of keys to a brand-new silver Suburban, extra-long. I'd already heard the story from Ron about his brother-in-law Ben and the thirty thousand dollars. "He had loose change in his pocket," I said, "which put you guys over your limit of ten thousand each in cash that you could bring in from Canada. But I can't believe the border officials seized the entire thirty-grand because of a couple coins? Freaking disaster."

Stock-Car-Len grappled me in a bumper-grinding hug. There was nothing sexual about it. "The entire trip budget, gone," he said, shaking his head, "and all Ron has is a little slip of paper so maybe he can get it back from someplace in Canada. Those machines at the airport can see what you're carrying."

Later that morning we made our introductions with the Chinese celebrities and film crew in the lobby of the airport Ramada.

Keiky, the scriptwriter, shook my hand. "Nice to meet you. This is He."

"Who?"

"He."

He shook my hand. He was China's George Clooney.

"And this is Lawlaw Law." Law had evidence of a former harelip. His job was to report on his colleagues, back to China.

It was our turn to introduce a few members of the storm-chase team. "This is Ben, Len, and Jen." Nine Asian faces stared at us in disbelief.

Soon our trio of storm-chase SUVs was on the highway and heading away from Oklahoma, where the weather was going to remain sunny and dry for a week. Stock-Car Len overtook us slowly so that Ron's cameraman, Ben, could film us. As they passed, I waved to Justin, a student from Singapore who'd signed on at the last minute and was hoping his mother would never know he spent his summer vacation chasing tornadoes instead of girls. It would be a difficult secret to keep, though, since it was a major television production and his parents were fans of Wong He. Then Stock-Car Len sped ahead to get a shot of the lead vehicle.

I had the two Hong Kong celebrities in the backseats of the cavernous Suburban. I inhaled the glorious toxic scent of new car. Keiky, the researcher and scriptwriter, sat beside me in the passenger seat. Lawlaw Law was already sawing logs from the back row.

"Nice leather," Wong He said, admiring the Suburban. He was a Buddhist. Leather seemed an odd thing for a Buddhist to admire.

Yen, the female star, put on a coat even though it was almost a hundred degrees outside. I examined her prettiness in my rearview mirror. According to Justin, she wasn't just a TV presenter but also a famous singer.

"Where are we going?" Keiky asked me excitedly.

"To The Big Texan, in Amarillo, Texas, to eat rattlesnake, bull testicles, and a free seventy-two-ounce steak—free, that is, if you can eat the whole thing in an hour," I drawled, and then felt like an idiot for drawling. "Have you been doing a lot of research about storms?" I asked her. I wasn't sure what I should explain. As the scriptwriter, she really should have been riding in the lead vehicle with Ron.

"Have you seen a tornado before?" she asked.

"Yes, with Ron, in Nebraska. I drove right toward it."

"Was it an F4 or F5?" Keiky was schoolgirl cute, adorned in kittens and bows, but I had the sneaking suspicion she could be as deadly as a crouching tiger.

"A tornado only gets an F-rating if it hits something like a barn, bridge, outhouse, or Walmart, and then the damage is assessed," I explained. "The tornado I saw didn't hit anything, so it wouldn't even be counted. Even if we drive toward a tornado that's a whopping F5 in power and size, it's a zero if it doesn't hit something. Practically every year you hear it's a record-breaking year for tornadoes, right . . . yes?"

Keiky nodded—but she might have been nodding off to sleep.

"It isn't that there are more tornadoes. There are just more housing developments and shopping centers being built in their paths," I continued, trying to make my voice more animated, like a teacher during story time. "More twisters are being counted with F-ratings because there are simply more objects for them to hit."

"Uh-huh," Keiky said, rooting through her enormous purse—probably looking for a pair of earplugs.

"Anyway, we're not going to get any severe weather for a few days—it's been really hot and dry. And we're going to have to head far north for the weather coming over the Rocky Mountains. There's been a drought in the U.S. all summer. For a big storm you need a few main ingredients—moisture for starts, and there hasn't been any, instability, and lifting agents . . . ." I saw Keiky's eyes glaze.

Ron explained it so well. He used ice fishing as an analogy. I decided to channel him. "Hunting for tornadoes is like going on an ice-fishing trip," I said. "You aren't going to try and drill a hole through ice that's one thousand feet thick—you're going to look for where it's thin. If the ice is thin, it's easier to break, and then you get a hole. It's when the weather conditions such as updrafts, lift, moisture, and instability can penetrate the CAP, where the hole is, that you can get a tornado. Ron will be looking for where the ice is thin." I loved this so much. It turned my crank, but something about my explanation wasn't working. Did they even go ice fishing in China?

"Have you seen the movie *Twister*?" I asked.

"Oh, yes," Keiky applauded. "We watched this for research."

"It's just like *Twister*," I said. "But I've never seen flying cows."

"How long until we will be in Texas?" Keiky asked.

"Just a couple hours."

She sat back and closed her eyes. Lawlaw was snoring, and Wong He and Yen were hunched over their phones.

A few hours later, while the Hong Kong film crew ran around the leaning water tower of Texas, the storm chasers watched a single cell storm, in the middle of a horizon-to-horizon blue sky, making its way across the plains.

Ron nudged me. "I told you." He pointed north. "We're heading to Colorado and Nebraska, then over to the Dakotas. We should get something big in the Dakotas."

Wong He saw me taking pictures of the little storm. "What?" He asked.

"It's exactly what we need. It's a great sign. It means there's now moisture." I was thrilled.

"It's just some rain. Pffft," he said, dismissing it with his hand. "It's not a tornado."

It hit me: No wonder Ron's brilliant ice-fishing analogy failed to make an impression. The TV crew was here to see a tornado—they weren't interested in the process. And because of that, unless they saw a tornado, the trip would be a write-off. The work that went into finding a tornado was part of the journey. But the Chinese group was snacking and snoozing and gaming, Facebooking and tweeting and texting. They were more involved in their virtual lives than with what was happening in the here and now. They'd seen *Twister*.

Day two: Texas, New Mexico, Colorado, all in one day's drive, and now on our third day we were back in Nebraska and the weather was severe. I kept my eyes on Jen's taillights while also watching for deer or livestock that might fly across the road. Wind rocked the Suburban, and my passengers sounded like spectators at a fireworks show as they *oohed* and *ahhed* over the forks of lightning. Nobody was hunched over a hand-held device now; their faces were pressed to the windows. I angled my rearview mirror back at the road. Stock-Car was right behind me, but not too close. The man could kiss your license plate on a highway. I recognized this roller coaster of road—we were near Valentine.

When the lead vehicle pulled to the shoulder in front of me, I stopped and told everyone they could get out. I left the engine running, as you always do during a chase. Then I grabbed my cameras and ran up the sandy, grassy slope. I knew this exact field. It even smelled the same, almost like ocean. I'd photographed a funnel cloud here the day before I saw my first tornado.

Lightning eviscerated the sky.

"There's rotation!" Ron yelled over the thunder from behind.

I stood under the power lines between Wong He and Justin. Sand fleas attacked my shins, but I didn't move. The Chinese cameraman, soundman, and tech all struggled with their wires and equipment while I took photos. Bright yellow grass angled in the wind against an ash blue sky. Then, out of the revolving super cell above us, a funnel descended. I was transfixed. It was right over us. Hell from the heavens was reaching for me. In order to be a proper tornado, it would have to come in contact with the ground. I prayed it would.

My first tornado had looked like barbed wire, but this funnel was smooth—almost sexual. I looked behind me and clocked where the Suburban was, to calculate when I'd need to run. Maybe now was the time to run. Was now the time to run? Ron, Ben, and Jen, whose long blonde hair whipped up over her head like a science experiment, were on the road beside the vehicles. Why was I standing on a hill under the power lines with a tornado trying to materialize above me? In *Twister,* the character Dusty warned that one should stay out of the suck zone. And if this cone reached the ground, we'd be right in it.

"We're going east!" Ron yelled.

We bolted to the vehicles and headed down the road alongside the storm. Then the rain hit. We had been ahead of the front. Now we were behind it, and it was like driving through a waterfall. I masked my slight state of panic with my "business as usual" face. Storm chasing becomes dangerous when you can't see. This was now officially death defying, and just like the time I was on an airplane with malfunctioning landing gear, my son Rigel, now thirteen, popped into my head.

I didn't want to die and be Rigel's big disappointment and life-long baggage. Regardless, I was still annoyed by my mother's gym acquaintances. They thought it was so cool that I was tornado chasing until they found out from my mother that I was also a mother, and then they disapproved. I white-knuckled the steering wheel as we hydroplaned. You don't have to stop living life to the fullest just because you've given birth. Rigel was proud of my quests.

We turned onto a gravel road.

"You're going to get to try out your helmets," I shouted. "We might get hail." I grinned at Wong He and Yen. They'd brought helmets from China.

Wong He smacked the top of his helmet to prove its strength, and then before I knew it he was out of the Suburban and leaping across the grasslands, talking to his video camera in the torrential downpour and deadly lightning while the crew set up.

Lawlaw Law made a sarcastic comment in Chinese. Tone of voice can be universal.

I videoed He as he jogged to the lead vehicle to stand under the shelter of the rear door with the crew. Suddenly Woody, whose job was a mystery to me, pushed Wong He and grabbed his camera, then tossed it into the back of the SUV. There was rapid-fire shouting in Cantonese. When Woody turned his head—maybe he felt me watching—Wong He lunged for his camera and marched back to our Suburban with it.

I wanted to ask what had happened, but Lawlaw Law was sitting in the back with folded arms and an expression of extreme distaste on his face. What I saw in the rearview mirror frightened me more than an unseen tornado. I saw primal loathing, maybe even utter hatred. I fiddled with the skipping rope that Ben had bought me in Colorado so I'd have something to jump over at rest breaks. (For the first few days I'd been air-skipping in parking lots across five states—you had to do something to counteract the fast food diet, arguably the most dangerous part of tornado chasing.) I looked back in the rearview mirror. Wong He was peeling off his sopping clothes. He was gorgeous. He was living on apple slices and water.

I, on the other hand, was living on Quarter Pounders. I was hooked. It happened every time I did this. Maybe I was partly doing this as an excuse to eat salty, greasy, splendid junk? I angled the mirror at myself. *Yuck*, I thought. *You really are what you eat.* I turned the mirror back to He. It was perfectly fine to admire the guy—even if I was married. Surely it was acceptable to admire the George Clooneys on our planet. I grabbed my pulled pork sandwich out of the center console and took a huge bite. Fat ran down my chin as rain pounded the roof of the Suburban. *Oh, God,* I thought, *I love this job.*

Nebraska, and then just one day later, Iowa and Missouri, and the following morning Minneapolis, Minnesota—where Stock-Car was rear-ended during morning rush hour traffic. The SUV was fine, but the car that hit Len, Ben, and Justin was totaled. Len figured the young driver must have been texting to miss the large SUV right in front of him.

Day six, South Dakota—the Chinese group were still texting and tweeting and Facebooking; in restaurants and on the road, they never stopped looking at their handheld devices. Day seven, North Dakota—Ron filed official weather reports over his radio. A road sign for Winnipeg, a sign for Fargo, and many wood chipper jokes amongst the westerners later, we were now parked on a dirt road as dust sandblasted anyone who dared to stand outside. A super cell worth risking my camera lenses for was fast approaching. I could barely see due to the flying dirt, but I recorded Yen being blown right off her feet. The sound-man's plastic raincoat flapped loudly as it was shredded by the wind. The ingredients were almost perfect for a tornado.

"If a tornado is going to come down, it's coming down right there!" Ron stood with his hands on his hips, apparently oblivious to the stones hitting his bald head. He did the same thing in hail. He was so intent on the weather I doubted he'd notice flying monkeys. I was terrified of the flying monkeys.

A whirlwind of grit scoured my eyeballs, and I ducked inside the Suburban to retrieve my sunglasses. Today I was driving for Ron in the lead vehicle. Wong He was sitting in the back of the 4x4 on his own. Now was my chance to ask.

"He, what's going on? Everyone seems mad at you. They're obviously ignoring you. It's practically a Mennonite-style shunning."

"You noticed?" He threw his hands up in exasperation. "They want me to lie and say I saw a tornado, when I haven't. They're all mad at me because I won't do it. I was hired for my integrity, for my reputation. I'm not going to ruin my reputation."

"The trip isn't over. You could still get a tornado. Maybe any minute. . . ." I hoped we would, but this storm was so spectacular, it didn't matter if we didn't.

"You know what Yen's line in the script was, just then, when she was blown over? Her line was, 'It's windy.' That's the type of lines they're giving us. That's like filming someone eating chicken and they say, 'It tastes like chicken.' They're giving me nothing. They don't care about the storms or how they're made. They just want to see a tornado." He picked up his camera. "Did you see them take my camera yesterday? They told me I wasn't to film anything myself because they're paying for me to be here. I took my camera back."

"I saw that. It was terrible."

"I feel sorry for them too, though," he said. "There's so much pressure. They have to film a tornado. They can't go back to China without one—it will be seen as their failure. That's why they want me to lie. I talked to the executive producer in China today. He said I should just say on camera that I saw one, and he won't use it in the show, but that way I can at least get along with the crew."

I had a bad feeling about that. But I said nothing. I was here to drive, not give advice. I put on my sunglasses and dusted off my lens before stepping back outside.

Ron was looking at his camera's viewer. Then he lowered it and squinted at the field, now just a wall of debris heading right at us.

"GO!!!" Ron ran full-speed toward the SUV with me right behind him.

I jumped into the driver's seat, heard doors slamming behind me, and floored it, spitting up stones. I looked in my mirror. Jen was screaming at the Chinese crew to get in the vehicle. You didn't have to be an expert lip reader to see she was tossing F-bombs at them through the dust.

"Jen isn't following yet," I said to Ron, who was looking at Baron Mobile Threat Net, his live weather software that showed our vehicle in relation to the storm. We crested a hill and were airborne, then sped down the far side.

"Take the next left," Ron ordered.

We were at the next left. I hit the brakes. "They're still not here!" They wouldn't know if we went straight or left. I didn't have my walkie-talkie. It was in the other truck. Where was Jen? I purposely held back and watched the top of the hill.

"GO!" Ron commanded.

I saw Jen crest the hill. I hit the gas and braked and attempted to drift around the corner on the loose gravel, but the vehicle's excellent traction control made it difficult.

"My camera picked up a tornado but we couldn't see it," Ron said. "It was behind the debris. It was right there. Exactly where I said it would be." Ron tilted his camera so I could see, but I didn't want to take my eyes off the road.

Ron liked my driving because he said it was "smooth." I could pass traffic on the shoulder of the fast lane doing one hundred miles an hour while he calmly worked the weather.

Just then, a blinding ball of light exploded behind me. Stock-Car's SUV had been hit by lightning. But they were still coming. Now *that* man could really drive. Hail pummeled the windscreen; I was driving sightless and knew it was wrong, but I didn't want Ron to see me fail. And I didn't want the TV crew to miss a tornado because of me. The barrage of ice stones on the roof was deafening. I kept driving. Ron told me to take the next right. I missed it. He gave me the "special" look, the "how especially stupid are you" look—the one he saved for dimwitted hotel receptionists and waitresses.

*   *   *

Day eight was the other kind of "suck zone." It had been a fruitless trek back and forth between the Dakotas. And now, on day nine, we had to drive nine hundred miles back to Oklahoma. The trip was over. For the Canadian crew, it was a success. We were chasing storms. For the Chinese crew it was a failure. They were chasing tornadoes.

There was a camera attached to my side-view mirror that was focused on me (or maybe my crop of fast-food pimples), and another on the front of my vehicle, plus one on the passenger mirror trained on Wong He. We both wore microphones. The cameraman and soundman were squished between us, capturing our road-trip banter. We talked about Facebook etiquette and the chiropractic back cracking He had given me the day before. But I desperately wanted to ask him whether he'd lied about seeing the tornado. Jen had told me as we loaded the trucks in the morning that both the director and Keiky had asked Ron if they could buy footage of past tornadoes he'd captured, but they didn't give him the reason. You couldn't just lie about a tornado. I knew Ron would never sell it to them if he thought they were going to lie. But I couldn't ask He about this while on camera.

I was relieved to see Wong He back in the passenger seat. He'd driven for a stretch earlier in the day—he wanted to drive, he said, to help me out, because I was exhausted. He'd said it was his gift to me. Then he overtook a truck on a blind hill, which was the closest any of us had come to dying on this trip.

"Stock-Car Len sure tore a strip off your hide for your driving earlier today," I said.

The cameraman leapt in for a close-up of my face. I hadn't known the man spoke English until that moment.

If I had a crystal ball, like the Wicked Witch of the West, I'd have learned that nine months later the Chinese crew's disappointment over not filming a tornado would be nothing compared to Ron's frustration over never reclaiming from U.S. customs the thirty thousand dollars he'd ponied up to fund the trip. And that the storm chasing episode had yet to air in Hong Kong due to a bureaucratic quagmire—so I still wouldn't know if Wong He had to lie or if he'd told the truth.

But for now, I ignored the cameraman. Keeping my hands on the wheel, my eyes on the road, and my mouth shut, I drove on. I was getting better at navigating a storm.

$$\mathcal{S} \quad \mathcal{S} \quad \mathcal{S}$$

Kirsten Koza is the author of Lost in Moscow: A Brat in the USSR. *Her travel writing and photographs have been published in newspapers and magazines around the world. She once even made the front page of Kyrgyzstan's national newspaper. Her essays have appeared in* The Best Women's Travel Writing Volume 8 *and* Leave the Lipstick, Take the Iguana. *Kirsten's areas of passion when traveling are kayaking and mountain biking (she's mountain biked across twenty countries), culture shock, almost anything with adventure in the title, unusual destinations (especially if there is a revolution or a Stan in the country name), men with guns, trip partnering with strangers, exotic food, and meeting locals. Photos and videos from this trip and others can be seen at www.kirstenkoza.com.*

༝ ༝ ༝

The Women's Sitting Room

And this is she
with whom I tried to speak, whose hurt, expressive head
turning aside from pain . . .
and soon I shall know I was talking to my own soul.
— *Adrienne Rich,*
"Twenty-One Love Poems"

We stood before the bright blue wooden door, a single spot of color in the long, white compound wall and the dun, rubble-strewn city. Fumes from the diesel engines and open sewers of Kabul swirled around us, mixing with the dust of the unpaved road.

"This is it," said Laila, my Afghan-American interpreter and travel companion.

On the other side of the wall, I would soon meet a woman I had been hearing about for three years. She was illiterate and had never attended school, but her sons in America were gruff, stoic, educated men who held university professorships and high-level government jobs, and spoke proudly of their Pashtun roots. In English, the men called her one thing and one thing only: Our Dear Mother. Laila simply called her Grandma.

*   *   *

It was May 2004. After September 11, I had begun reporting on the Shirzais, an Oregon-based Afghan immigrant family, for a major daily newspaper. Grandma's oldest son, Daoud, a university professor who returned to Afghanistan to serve in the new Karzai government, had invited me to visit them in Kabul.

I'd traveled more than thirty hours, arriving at the house after a bumpy, dusty car ride from the Kabul airport. Laila's grandmother was waiting for us in the women's sitting room. What would I say to her, I wondered? Even with Laila's help, could we ever understand each other?

Daoud had purchased this house before the Soviet War, soon after taking his first university teaching job in Portland. On the northwest outskirts of the city, it had been built amid wheat fields, which reminded him of Shinzmaray, his family's rural village in the Ghazni province. Those fields were long gone now, replaced by a sprawl of other homes crowding the unpaved roads. Daoud had originally intended to return one day and live there. But then his younger brother Mohammed was captured and executed by the communists. Guilty by association with his brother and with the United States, he knew he could not come back as the Soviet War, and the wars that followed, raged. Other family members, those who remained, had taken over the compound.

Behind the blue door was a courtyard dotted with rosebushes and fig trees—a rare spot of lushness in the arid, brown city. The neatly trimmed grass was still damp from its midday watering. Leaving our shoes with the others piled near the doorway, we stepped up into a small vestibule, the entrance to the women's side of the compound. Through the filmy white fabric draped across the doorway, I could see a squat, dark shape slowly rising from a cushion.

Entering an Afghan home, whether a modern compound in Kabul or a mud-brick house in a village, happens in stages.

Guests first enter through an outer wall that shields its inhabitants from outsiders. Male guests are then ushered into the most accessible room from the courtyard, usually the formal sitting room for men. As a woman, I was guided through a smaller side entrance that led to the innermost rooms, which weren't visible from the courtyard. This positioning allowed the females protection from prying eyes, and full-length curtains hung in the entryways for added privacy.

Purdah, the Islamic term for keeping women hidden from men through separation and veiling, comes from the Hindi word for "curtain." To westerners, these protected spaces tend to symbolize sexism and oppression. But during my weeks in Afghanistan I would come to understand that the women I met regarded this separation as a form of freedom. *Purdah* meant they could be themselves in half the home, sometimes without headscarves, knowing that men would rarely enter. Inside the inner sanctum, women developed a fierce closeness and formed their own society, where the elders would watch over and nurture the younger. Inside those rooms, girls became women, marriages were arranged, widows were comforted. Entering an Afghan women's room truly lifted a veil into another, hidden world.

As Laila parted the curtain, Grandma came toward us. I had practiced the traditional greeting with Laila's older female relatives in America: the embrace, the left-right-left cheek kisses, and a rapid-fire series of Pashto greetings. Still, I worried I might mess it up, as I sometimes did, going right instead of left and awkwardly almost kissing the other woman on the lips.

I practically stumbled into Grandma's outstretched arms, and she engulfed me in an iron embrace, hugging me with more force than any of Laila's American relatives ever had. Her grip was cushioned, though, by the black fabric of her large *chador* and a voluminous traditional Afghan dress. How did a woman who had appeared so frail standing up possess such strength? She placed a soft hand on each side of my face and regarded me at arm's length, her glittering black eyes attempting to focus on me. Her hands firmly guided my head from side to side, training wheels for the kissing, as she pressed her lips into my cheeks.

"*Salaam aleikum*! *Tsenga ye*? *Jora ye*? *Stere me se*!" she said. Peace be with you! How are you? How is your health? May you not be tired! I repeated the words as best I could, trying to roll my "r" on *Stere*, "tired," just right.

The octogenarian before me had lost five of her fourteen children to disease or accidents when they were small. Then Mohammed was taken. She endured the Soviet bombing of her village and stayed as her children and grandchildren left to start new lives all over the world. She had been there through the civil war, the Taliban, and now, the U.S.-led war. And then six years ago, she lost her husband to illness. Who was I to tell her not to be tired?

Grandma motioned for us to sit on the pomegranate-colored velour cushions flanking the room, then took a seat near the center, smoothing her full skirt over her crossed legs. I had expected to see Daoud when I arrived, but there was no sign of any of the men.

Laila's cousin whisked in a tray with a large teapot and glass cups. The warm cardamom-scented liquid washed over my dust-parched tongue and throat, and Grandma smiled and sipped hers as I downed mine in a couple of gulps. It was refilled immediately, and I resolved to drink more daintily.

When I set down my cup, Grandma began to talk. I instinctively sat at her side, and Laila settled opposite me so she could interpret from Pashto. She spoke first of Shinzmaray, and the family's traditional mud-brick compound where she spent most of her time. She was only in Kabul now because Daoud was here, she explained. She preferred the village to the city. "It's peaceful there," she said. But it hadn't always been that way.

"One day," she said, "from seven in the morning to seven at night, the planes kept circling and bombing." Her voice rose and fell, at times getting caught in a warbling spot in her throat. She gestured with her hands, sticking her thumb and pinky finger out like wings to demonstrate the swoops of the Soviet bombers. "I can't hear well because of the bombs."

Indeed, later, when I would finally gather the courage to try the rudimentary Pashto I had learned from diplomatic language tapes, Laila would instruct me to lean close to Grandma's good ear and shout.

"The bombs dropped on people's crops and tractors," she continued. "Their livelihoods were destroyed. Before the war started, people had so much land. Horses couldn't go from one end to the other. Now the land is destroyed. People hardly get by."

Grandma beckoned to me. She put on a pair of thick glasses that covered half her round face and pulled something out of the folds of her scarf, like a magician. It was a tiny black crayon, pointed at one end.

"She does this to everyone," Laila said. "She wants to put kohl on your eyes to beautify you."

Grandma firmly propped my face with one hand and trained the point of the crayon straight toward my left eye with the other. Laila instructed me to blink down on the tip as her grandmother drew it across my inner eyelids. Seeing the results, the matriarch threw up her hands and made a soft sound of delight. In this world of women, familiarity occurred through actions, not words. This instant intimacy was hospitality and, more subtly, a way of keeping me in line. Absorbed into the intricate social order of the household, I'd be far less likely to disrupt it.

Over the next few weeks, I would be alternately praised and reprimanded by Grandma and the other women of the household on the finer points of protocol: I could remove my headscarf in front of the younger women, but should keep it on for Grandma and the older women. I should not make eye contact with any of the men, particularly the younger, unmarried ones, in front of Grandma. Even though Daoud and I always shook hands to greet each other in Portland, I should absolutely refrain from doing so in Kabul. In fact, one evening in the sitting room, Laila would translate a message from Grandma: the women had decided that I tended to stand too close to Daoud when talking to him in the courtyard, the compound's only gender-neutral space.

Now with her glasses on, Grandma studied me again.

"Are you married? How old are you? Where is your family?"

Laila mumbled in English, "I'm going to tell her you're twenty-five, not thirty, because otherwise you'll get an earful about not being married yet." She then shouted into Grandma's ear in Pashto.

"Twenty-five?" Grandma said. "Why aren't you married yet? And Laila too. You should tell her to get married, too."

Laila, who actually *was* twenty-five, rolled her eyes.

As Grandma continued to espouse the virtues of marriage, Laila stopped translating and whispered, "Change the subject."

"O.K," I said. I turned to Grandma. "I'd like to show you what I do for a living."

Only twenty percent of Afghan women were literate, and nearly all of those who could read had grown up in urban areas. How many times in her life, if ever, had Grandma picked up a newspaper? Would she be able to comprehend what a journalist did, and that I had written about her family?

I pulled out a newspaper from the year 2000 with my first article about the Shirzais. The story had run with many photos, including an old family snapshot from the seventies.

Seeing the front page, Grandma exclaimed over a portrait of Daoud giving a university lecture. She picked up the paper and kissed her firstborn son's image. Then she honed in on the old black-and-white family shot of Mohammed and his three children. In the photo, Mohammed wore horn-rimmed glasses and an argyle sweater. His children, all under the age of six, piled on top of him as he reclined on a bed. Mohib, the oldest, had curly hair and a petulant look on his face. Sarasa had a pageboy haircut and a mischievous glint in her eye; Mina, the baby, was wearing feet pajamas, barely able to sit up. They were grown now, Laila's age, and also living in Portland. Though Afghans typically didn't smile for photos, Mohammed's lips were pressed together with the corners of his mouth turned up, as if he couldn't help himself.

Later that year he was kidnapped from his home by the KGB, imprisoned and eventually executed for helping to organize a coup against the communists. His body was never recovered, but was likely one of the fifty thousand believed to have been disposed of in mass graves in Kabul. Those found had broken bones and gunshot holes to the skulls. Grandma's smile fell. She extended a finger toward the newsprint, caressing her late son's slim face, and then each of the children's.

"Mohib, Sarasa, Mina, their father was taken. And now they are all the way in America," she said. Laila's voice grew quiet as she translated. "The war broke so many families."

I felt instant regret. "Should I not have shown her that photo?" I whispered.

"It's O.K.," Laila whispered back. "It's good, actually."

Grandma blinked hard behind her thick lenses. She folded back the sides of the newspaper and kissed Mohammed's image, then smoothed the paper down on her knee and let her son and grandchildren gaze up at her. She removed her glasses. The late afternoon sun through the sitting room window caught the wetness in her eyes and made her round face glow. She smiled and gripped my hand fiercely. I squeezed back and swallowed all that I had planned to tell her about the newspaper and my job. She had already shown me more about both than I could have possibly imagined.

Note: The Afghans and Afghan Americans' names have been changed for their protection. They were threatened for cooperating with an American journalist.

♫ ♫ ♫

Angie Chuang is a Washington, D.C.-based writer and educator. Her work has appeared in Creative Nonfiction, CALYX, Washingtonian Magazine, Asian American Literary Review, Consequence, *as well as the anthologies* The Best Women's Travel Writing Volume 8, The Best Women's Travel Writing 2011, The Best Travel Writing Volume 9, *and* Tales from Nowhere. *She is on the faculty of American University School of Communication. "The Women's Sitting Room" is an excerpt from her book manuscript*, The Four Words for Home, *which was the Santa Fe Writers Project Literary Awards 2011 second place winner.*

❧ ❧ ❧

The Mighty Big Love Test

Thunder, lightning: the way he loved her
was frightening.

We were camped at the deserted Highland Beach, one hundred miles into a one-hundred-fifty-mile kayaking trip in the Gulf of Mexico, paddling from Florida's Everglade City to the Flamingo visitor center and back.

I had a suspicion then, which has since been confirmed, that this was my relationship test. Don't pretend you have never been subjected to one or devised one yourself. My practical-to-the-extreme and water-savvy new boyfriend had been a kayaking instructor with Outward Bound, and he wanted to make sure his new girlfriend, me, could make such a trip.

Though admittedly not the most athletic person on the planet, nor the most fearless (not fearless at all for that matter), I had only one thing going for me: I don't get seasick, and we were encountering unseasonably rough seas.

But by the third twenty-mile kayaking day, my forearms squeaked like rusty door hinges when I tried to move my wrists or my hands. Later I would learn the medical term for this: *crepitus*, making it sound like the death of an arm, which in some ways it was.

And then on the fourth day, we ran over a shark in the shallow waters between mangroves, and I had a little tantrum. O.K., a big tantrum, which was quite a feat considering I was squeezed into my kayak compartment like a wrapped mummy.

"It's just a nurse shark," Practical Boyfriend said.

"So?" I screamed. "Shark! Shaaaarrrk!"

"Calm down. I don't even think they have teeth."

I grew up in the 1970s at the height of the *Jaws* paranoia. Most of my friends would not set one toe into the ocean. While never that extreme, the sight of a dorsal fin brought me right back to my five-year-old self and the trochaic meter of that Jaws music, the thrashing, and the blood blooming like a red begonia under the sea. One now has to wonder why parents ever let their small children see such a film.

And for the record, Nurse sharks do have teeth.

But so far—though I wouldn't know this until much later—I was passing the test. I paddled through my crepitus and didn't sink the boat during said shark tantrum. I even agreed to hit a fellow boater over the head with a paddle, if need be.

A school group was out at a rough point, not ironically called "Shark Point." Their canoes had tipped in the wind, and the waves were lashing at their boats and their now-submerged bodies. They were screaming. A lot.

"Listen," Practical Boyfriend said, "I have a towline. We've got to go out and get them."

"We do?" I asked.

My question was not rhetorical. Apparently this particular corner of ocean was popular with the hammerheads, who even Practical Boyfriend admitted had teeth. But he had been a boy scout and an outdoor trip leader—there was no way we were going to paddle past them in their time of need. They were all bobbing about the angry gray sea like eggs boiling in a pot. One of their canoes was upside down. The other was out of their reach.

"But if they try to grab at you," Practical Boyfriend warned, "hit them with your paddle, so they don't capsize the boat."

I was poised with my paddle, but still, as you might imagine, full of doubt. How could I crack the head of someone in need with my hard plastic paddle? Thankfully, Practical Boyfriend saved the day with his towline and quick wits, and no head smashing was called for. I certainly would have failed that test.

That night, we arrived to Highland Beach on our way back to Everglade City and set up our small blue tent between two palm trees. We watched bald eagles try to steal fish from osprey, and then the salty sky turned blue to pink. The sun streaked across the sea; its face tilted on the edge of the ocean, the neck, a pathway of light to the sand. Scattered conch shells shined white like bones. The wind rustled the palm fronds above and kept the black flies away. A hawk caught in a draft of wind, flashed a brown triangle tip of wing, a red tail.

At first I thought there must have been an explosion in the distant horizon because of the brewing electricity over the sea. The storm erupted like a volcano, a commotion of orange and yellow light flashing from the line between the black sky and gray sea. We listened to the transistor radio with its mechanical warnings to small craft about the electrical storms, the high seas, the winds. There on the horizon, it seemed so very far away.

But not for long.

We woke at dawn, and the radio issued new, more urgent warnings to the small craft that had been dumb enough not to heed initial warnings. Then the rain fell in pleats against the roof and walls of the tent. Then the rumble of thunder. But still an ocean away. Or so it seemed. Even Practical Boyfriend didn't appear worried, so we reached for each other.

That is, until the rain turned to hailstones and the small tent lit up with each new crack of lightning. And the distant rumble of thunder became detonations on our sandy beach, between our two lovely palms, around our little love tent.

"Listen," Practical Boyfriend said. "If anything happens, here's how you call out on the radio." He showed me.

"What do you mean anything? Why would I call? Who would I call?"

"If anything happens to me," he said. This was not a man who overreacted, so I tried to concentrate on what button to push and when.

"And we better get in lightning position," he said between cracks of thunder and flashes of lightning. The air smelled like burning things. My hair was standing on end. Until this moment, I had always thought of this as a cliché. But sometimes, I was learning, there's truth in cliché.

"O.K.," I said. "Lightning position. What's that?"

Practical Boyfriend demonstrated. He rolled up his thermarest and kneeled on it. I copied him. "You have to have your knees and feet together," he warned. "So even if we are hit by ground current, there's one entry and exit place. It's safer that way."

"Ground current?" I asked.

"Yes," he said. "Kneel like this."

I didn't find out what this meant until later, that if lightning struck close enough, it could reach us by traveling down one of our palm trees and through the sand. Practical Boyfriend knew a fellow outdoor leader who died exactly this way. One point of entry and exit meant less burning of the body.

So there we kneeled, naked and knees together on our thermarests. Not a terribly romantic position.

When it got to be too much, I started to cry.

"It'll be O.K.," he tried.

The blue tent lit up with each strike, followed by another crashing ka-boom and the smell of something like sulfur. I was scared, but it wasn't that. Well, at least it wasn't that *exactly*.

"I have to poo," I finally admitted.

And the fear, plus this knee-together position meant that I might not be able to hold it. It was one thing to be scared of sharks in front of a new boyfriend or even fail to smash a fellow boater in the head with your paddle should the need arise. This was another thing entirely.

But ever-Practical Boyfriend reached for his knit beanie, and then he said those six words every woman longs to hear: "You can poop in my hat."

Let me be clear: Practical Boyfriend had not yet told me he loved me, or even that he liked me. But this was something more even than that.

Of course I could not poop in his hat. Willpower is also something else. Because of my practiced yoga postures, a strong will, sheer embarrassment, and an offering of the hat that I interpreted as true love, I was able to hold off until the storm finally moved on, and I could sprint from the tent and squat in privacy behind a palm.

In the end, it was he who passed the test, one I never could have devised for him. Practical Boyfriend is now Practical Husband, and for the record, I have never, ever pooped in his hat. At least not yet.

♫   ♫   ♫

Suzanne Roberts is the author of the memoir Almost Somewhere: Twenty-Eight Days on the John Muir Trail *(winner of the 2012 National Outdoor Book Award), and four collections of poetry, including* Three Hours to Burn a Body: Poems on Travel. *She was named "The Next Great Travel Writer" by National Geographic Traveler, and her work has been published in many journals and anthologies, including* The Pacific Crest Trailside Reader. *She writes and teaches in South Lake Tahoe, California. More information may be found at www.suzanneroberts.net.*

MOLLY BEER

ॐ ॐ ॐ

Who Made this Grave?

A child's encounters in Mexico:
elegant skeletons and drug war soldiers.

One day in late October, my son Avery and I left his Mexican preschool and wandered up the Calzada toward
Morelia's pink stone aqueduct. He was collecting sticks
snarled with epiphytes, and I was walking backwards so I
could watch him—his red plaid uniform, his white-blonde
hair—while I lured him toward our home. Behind him,
through the ficus that lined the old cobblestone pedestrian
avenue, I could see the façade of San Nicolás, the university
where Mexico's revolutionary priest, Father Hidalgo, was
teacher to Morelia's namesake, José María Morelos. It was
2010. My son was two; the independent Mexico of Hidalgo
and Morelos, two hundred. I found the contrast alternately
fascinating and terrifying.

Since I was looking backwards, it was Avery who noticed
the crowd gathering up ahead.

"Look, Mama!" he cried out as he threw down his sticks
and began, at last, to walk with purpose.

In the months we had roamed our temporary city together,
me pregnant and waddling, my son barely done toddling, we
had happened upon the sorts of spectacles that made living in

Michoacán's capital just a little bit magical. With Michoacán stewing in the heat of Mexico's escalating drug war, this magic helped. A few weeks earlier, we'd watched a crew filming a telenovela, while off-camera cast members dressed as revolutionary soldiers hoisted passing children onto their half-sleeping horses and women in petticoats sat on the old stone benches sending texts. And once, for reasons we never quite discerned, we came upon the Calzada to find it carpeted end to end in a mural made entirely of flower petals, grains, dried leaves, and pine needles.

This day, we joined the milling crowd and found that the attraction was a group of girls from the Catholic high school standing still as statues in little sets they had made to represent an old family portrait, or a garden party, a wake or a wedding. The girls in their tableaux were dressed in gowns and veiled hats or cross-dressed in suits, but their faces were made up in black and white and ash gray, and their bare arms were painted with bones. They were "elegant skeletons"—*calaveras de la Catrina*, or simply "Catrinas"—like the delicate ceramic figurines of skeletons made in the campo outside Morelia. They were the lovely living, living dead of Mexico.

Just in time for the Day of the Dead festivities, Avery happened to be entering the incessant-question stage.

"Who made this?" he asked three hundred times a day.

"Who made this book?"

"Dr. Seuss."

"Who made this food?"

"Your daddy made your omelet from eggs that a chicken made and *calabacitas* that a farmer grew in a field from a seed."

But so far, in situations like the one in which I now found myself, I'd been lucky: 1) *who made this* was the extent of his interrogative repertoire, and 2) he had not yet learned to ask *why*.

My son had no idea what a skeleton was. He didn't even know the word "dead" could pertain to anything beyond the grasshoppers he'd left locked in the driver's seats of toy cars on the roof of our apartment or the desiccated scorpion we'd saved to show him. Death was not yet a bewilderment: it was an all but blank space in his conception of the world.

This isn't to say that I minced words when explaining to him the finite mortality of grasshoppers.

"He's dead, honey," I told him when he tried to goad his latest, legless victim back into action. Or when he was served roasted *chapulines* in lime and chile in a restaurant: "That's a grasshopper, like the grasshopper you play with on the roof." And, as he examined the scorpion carcass, "This *alacrán* is dead. Your daddy squashed it with a shoe so it cannot pinch you with those pincers or sting you with its tail. But remember what it looks like, and if you ever see another one, back away and call a grown-up."

I would not lie and say they were sleeping, I would not disappear a corpse, and I would not get metaphysical. But the pedagogy of bugs only went so far in Mexico.

As he hadn't done with the dead scorpion, despite my fear tactics, my son sensed there was something fearful about the Catrinas. He didn't even ask who made them—a good thing, since I had no answer planned.

"Uppy," whined Avery, who was ordinarily bold with strangers.

He pawed at my hip until I hoisted him and, by maternal reflex, told him everything was O.K.—although it occurred to me as I said it that I didn't really know. By "everything," in the case of Day of the Dead, didn't I mean mortality and death and grief? In Mexico, all of the above were exposed, stripped bare and apparent. But so, in contrast, was joy. Newlyweds posed in the park as security convoys rolled past. Quinceañera girls waved from their pink limousines while the headlines of *La Jornada Michoacán* tallied the newly dead.

Back home, in the shelter of familiar customs, I probably would have defaulted to the typical trajectory of an American child's education in death. He would be initiated with the passing of a pet or distant elderly relative, and then graduate to weeping by flashlight onto the pages of books like *Charlotte's Web* or *Bridge to Terabithia*. I would keep him away from deathbeds, funerals, and graveyards until he was "old enough to understand"—as if grieving were something we grow into knowing how to do. Somehow, intrinsically, he would come to his own understanding of mortality and contrive coping mechanisms for dealing with such knowledge. In a pinch, if death refused to keep to my schedule, I could always fall back on therapists to talk him through.

But we were in Mexico, and just as Mexico teaches its children to eat fiery food by feeding them chile candies, it coats its day of remembrance with sugar (candy skulls, sweet breads, and fruit *ates* set out on altars). And it is a simple inevitability—however much a mother chafes at the fact—that one raises a child in the context of culture.

Mexican culture, I knew and yet kept relearning, was very interested in the raising of children. Even these elegant skeletons, realizing they had scared Avery with their painted faces, were ready to guide me.

The girls already knew Avery from our afternoon walks down the Calzada where they loitered in the afternoons. At the start of the school year, they'd been fascinated by his hair—stuff so fine and pale that it had compelled more than one passerby in Mexico to cross a busy street just to touch it—but soon the novelty wore off. In the afternoons, when we strolled past, they had begun to tease him. "¡*Que ojos!*" they'd gush as they flocked around him, quickly drawing their cell phones to snap his picture (or just get his goat). Some afternoons, like a celebrity dodging paparazzi, he walked past them with his hands over his blue eyes, just in case they were looking at him—so they oohed and ahhed even louder.

Now, seeing that he was frightened, a girl in one tableau whispered his name through her frozen smile. Then, keeping the rest of her body still, she held out to him a plate of sugar-coated guava *ate*. Soon he was shaking hands with each of the Catrinas, his pink cheeks bulging with sweets.

In 2010, as Avery and I wandered around Morelia, the country was commemorating even more dead than usual. Twice in September, on the anniversary of Hidalgo's *Grito de Dolores* that, two hundred years earlier, had heralded the war for Mexico's independence, and then again on Morelos's birthday, the town had shut down its main thoroughfare for grand *desfiles*. There were marching columns of men and women in period dress, prancing horses sat by proud *charros*, and cruising low-rider classic cars upon whose sides ghost flames consumed skeleton beauties. There were jet fly-bys and marching troops and slow-rolling tanks and, if President Calderón (a native of Morelia) happened to be in the audience, metal detectors at the cross streets. And the festivities were to continue into November, at which point Pancho Villa would become the hero of the parade.

No events were scheduled to honor the current war—the drug war that was "Mexico's" or "Calderón's" or "the U.S.'s," depending on one's politics—but every so often a caravan of dark blue military trucks would roll down Avenida Francisco Madero, each with a masked soldier standing face to the wind in the back, clutching the mounted machine gun. There was no honoring of this war, but no ignoring it either. Two Septembers earlier a grenade had been tossed into the crowd during the governor's *vivas*, and turnout was accordingly low at this year's two hundredth *Grito* in Morelia's plaza. Or so I heard; on the advice of the one-legged man who shined shoes in the park near my house, I had skipped the celebration.

Throughout these displays of military might, nostalgic or otherwise, Avery kept up his questions.

Who made this cathedral? Who made this mango? Who made these streets?

I wasn't even tripped up by the slippery ones:

"Who made this elephant?"

"The elephant's mama and daddy made him."

"Who made the elephant's mama and daddy?"

"Their mamas and daddies made them."

I had a few rules for my answers. First and foremost, I always answered as fully and truthfully as I knew how to do within the range of a two-year-old's vocabulary. Second, I steered clear of my mother's rebuttal for when things crossed into the ridiculous: "That's a God question." As in, *how could I possibly know who made an elephant?* By extension, I never defaulted to God as the grand maker—as in, "God made the elephant." I knew the inevitable next question would trap me in tautological loops too tangled for a mind addled by pregnancy and sleep deprivation (and made worse by the all-night Mexican karaoke reverberating from every cobblestone and pink stonework wall). *Who made God?* I couldn't handle, not so close to so human a problem. God didn't make or consume Mexican meth. God didn't make or sell or run or fire American guns. And the cynical side of me couldn't help but think humans had made God so they could blame someone else. The way Mexico blamed the U.S.; the way the U.S. blamed Mexico.

I admit, however honest I pretended to be as a parent, I consciously withheld key vocabulary. Before Day of the Dead, my son hadn't known the word "skeleton," or the full meaning of the word "dead," and he still didn't know the words "gun" or "war." Without the words, I reasoned, there were questions he simply could not ask and I therefore would not have to answer. But he was learning quickly.

"Who made this?" he would ask about the dancing plastic skeleton bride in the café and the giant papier-mâché skeleton towering over the crowds in the plaza on Day of the Dead.

"Who made this?" he would ask about the sugar skulls and the shimmering funeral wreaths for sale in the market.

Even without God, *who made this* was downright easy next to *why*. I was terrified that *why* would come while we were living in Mexico.

Why were soldiers standing over there? Why was that altar covered with toys and teddy bears?

"It's the soldiers' job to keep everybody safe," I explained preemptively whenever trucks of masked *federales* sped past us. Of course, this was only a benign, arguably untrue half of the answer to the question he hadn't asked: I never attempted to explain why or from what we needed to be kept safe.

Because my son didn't know the questions or the words, he didn't know there was a war. Because he did not know there was a war, he did not ask who made it. But people in Morelia told me all the time: the U.S. made it. The U.S. and its wildly out-of-control drug addiction. Why, just that month Mexican authorities had torched 134 tons of U.S.-bound marijuana in Tijuana—about three ounces of pot per adult resident of my entire home state.

Drug addiction or no, if we still lived in the U.S., I might have avoided talking to Avery about guns for another year or two or three. He would have play-dated other kids raised on free-range, whole-grain organic innocence. I liked to think that if he lived in the U.S.—where it was easy to see no evil if you just turned off the TV—he would not already be pointing sticks at everything around him and shouting *ppppchu*! I liked to think that, given the good health of his dogs and grandparents, I might have avoided the subject of death for even longer. Especially if we followed our own precedent: when our dog killed his chicken, we got a new one pronto, so what if it was a different color. But here in Mexico, the chicken meat was sold with feet attached—there was less glossing over of life's messier facts.

In the four years leading up to this Day of the Dead, thirty thousand Mexicans had died as a result of the drug war, whomever's it was. This messy fact didn't put Mexico's murder rate above Washington D.C.'s, but as a mother of small children living in a city that was not beyond the fray, it certainly had my attention.

Like all parents, in the U.S. and in Mexico and everywhere else on this planet, my husband and I want to protect our children from any and all things that might hurt them physically or psychological. This does not mean we wall ourselves in, but it does mean we take reasonable precautions. But what constitutes "reasonable," I was learning that year in Mexico, is highly dependent upon where one lives.

In Mexico, when I was warned against going to the *Grito*, I skipped it. When we passed *policia* or *federales* patrolling the street, if we could not cross over, I positioned my own body between my son's and their downward-turned rifles or holstered handguns (both of whose muzzles were at the level of a child's head, but usually below a pregnant woman's belly). And I heeded the advice I'd been given to stay away from soldiers and police, particularly during public events: if anything went down, the logic went, law enforcement would be shooting, or being shot at, or both.

But then something happened that's hard for me to explain. It isn't that I got inured or numb to the guns, but rather that I began to feel compelled to shelter my son not from the guns, but from the fear that necessitated them.

"Let's go say *hola* to the *policia*," I suggested one day, out of the blue, as if it were the polite thing to do, like saying *gracias* to the waiters and cooks in restaurants, like telling his teachers *hasta mañana* after school or waving each morning to the elderly lady who lived around the corner and sometimes gave him old tortillas to feed to the pigeons. I hadn't thought it up beforehand, hadn't planned to send my son up to a group of men with guns. It just came out of my mouth.

Avery, a natural glad-hander anyway (albeit not with oohing, cell phone-wielding teenaged girls), promptly trotted over to the cluster of soldiers with the wrong little hand thrust out. Each soldier in turn leaned down to shake it.

In that act, and its subsequent repetition, I learned that in Mexico traffic cops, *federales*, state police, and pretty much everyone else would reciprocate my son's advances. They shook his hand. They spoke to him in whatever words of English they knew. Once a pair of soldiers hoisted him up on the tank they were guarding so he could pretend to drive it. And each time this strange scene happened, I watched an armed man's face change from the frozen expression of an officer on duty, of a man with a gun, into something soft and human.

It was a logic I was learning in and from Mexico, a logic that underpins the celebration of Day of the Dead.

Before moving to Morelia, I hadn't visited a graveyard—a place I connote with riderless horses, bagpipes played lowly on a hillside, the hollow thud of dirt falling on wood—for over a decade. Avery most certainly had never been to one. But when—beginning with the afternoon of the Catrinas and in the days that followed—our adopted city bedecked itself in a heady profusion of orange marigolds and purple cockscombs, I learned a less passive approach to the subject of death.

Morelia's Day of the Dead festivities began with altars set up around the city, in businesses and lining the Calzada. Most altars were built to commemorate Mexican historic figures—Pancho Villa, Hidalgo and Morelos, Frida Kahlo. Others were not so romantic: one altar commemorated women who had been the victims of domestic violence and, another, unborn babies.

"Who made this?" Avery asked incessantly. Usually, the creator of a particular altar was right there, ready to shake his hand and reward his interest with sweetbread or *dulces*.

Altars were one thing. But I didn't intend to visit any of the cemeteries in the hills around Morelia, though many tourists do. It seemed invasive, voyeuristic, disrespectful—at least to my more somber sensibilities. My conception of mourning is intimate and inexpressible, not public and celebratory. But this, of course, is cultural.

In spite of my reservations, driving through the countryside in the afternoon, we happened to pass under a pedestrian bridge crowded with people carrying armloads of calla lilies and cockscombs. I couldn't resist stopping. In the graveyard these people were walking to, the smell of marigolds mixed with that of freshly turned earth and incense. Rather than the hush I associate with holy grounds, there was a clamor of several hundred people chatting with one another, of children hollering and ice cream hawkers calling out their flavors: ¡de coco de coco de coco de coco! No one seemed surprised that foreigners would visit the bones of other people's dead. No one seemed upset about much at all as they shoveled fresh dirt on their loved ones' graves, set out teddy bears and photographs, placed wreaths, and sprinkled the ground with sunny, pungent petals. Avery perched on my shoulders, begging for a wedge of *sandia* or to be set free to play with the kids in the reeds around a pond below the cemetery.

Too soon, I knew, *why* would come. And when it did, my little boy would learn that soldiers fight wars, that he was born in a time of global war, that in Mexico he was cradled in the very middle of one. He would know what *pppppchu!* means and why his mother doesn't like it. He would come to know in the most concrete terms that the dead do not come back. And I know, as Mexico well knows, that however many sweets and flower petals are strewn about, there is no way to keep a child from knowing sadness.

But I hope that, in part due to his time in Mexico, he will always be able to reach past fear and shake hands with the human on its other side.

ஃ ஃ ஃ

A correspondent and international teacher, Molly Beer has published her subsequent writing on culture and culture clash widely. She is a graduate of the Bread Loaf School and the MFA program at the University of New Mexico, and has served as an Olive B. O'Connor Fellow in Creative Writing at Colgate University. After spending many of her "odyssey years" living in Latin America, Molly Beer returned to Mexico in 2010, this time with her husband, son, and baby-on-the-way, and found navigating family as well as place to be an entirely new sort of adventure. She is currently a contributing editor at Vela Magazine, *where this story originally appeared.*

න්‍ර න්‍ර න්‍ර

Fill in the Blanks

A latter-day Don Quixote makes windmill
fighting seem perfectly sane.

*M*ine, I admit, is an unorthodox quest—lacking, as
it is, in magical treasures, meddling deities, sinister
beasts, and epic loves. Yet it has nonetheless consumed me
since the fateful winter's day twelve years ago when I wandered into the deceptively unremarkable Barnes & Noble near
my Midtown Manhattan apartment.

With my first trip to South America looming—but only
loosely planned—I wanted to browse the store's most ency-
clopedic guide to the continent. And the fattest of them all
was . . . let's just call it F—r's (because honestly, I can't remember which of the two it was). No sooner had I grabbed the
book and turned to the map page than I noticed a grave error.
Four countries were missing. Yes, *four*: Paraguay, Guyana,
Suriname, and French Guiana. Literally left off the map—
blank gray spaces in place of actual name-bearing nations.
(O.K., technically French Guiana is an "Overseas Department" of France. But still.)

Willing to suspend disbelief and accept that maybe I'd
picked up an oddly defective specimen, I reached for the
other copy on the shelf. But again the four were conspicuously

absent—unidentified bits of irregular geometry alongside Argentina, Bolivia, Brazil, and Venezuela. Now I was truly stunned.

I understood that no guidebook editor was going to spring for entire chapters on virtually untouristed places. Still, to go so far as to make deletions from the map was something altogether different—the sort of behavior traditionally reserved for, say, terrorist organizations.

And somehow, I felt so personally offended (perhaps by the idea that a *guidebook*, of all things, would play into the stereotype that Americans are willfully ignorant—if not totally dismissive—of whatever's beyond our borders) that I vowed right then and there to avenge the omission. Precisely because these places were left off the map, I had to go see them and—though I lay no claim to sanity here—discover at least one spectacularly cool element of each that could be found nowhere else.

The quest was on.

And then just as quickly, it was on hold: Of the nearly nonexistent flight options I found, each seemed to be priced somewhere between mildly amusing and criminally insane, topping out in the $10,000 neighborhood. For economy. Periodically, I'd recheck the fares—the days turning into weeks, the weeks turning into months, and the months, alas, turning into years.

Meanwhile, as magazine assignments took me ever more frequently to South America, over the years I managed to see every country on the continent *but* the Forgotten Four—until the day I realized I had enough LAN-Pass miles to tack a quick Paraguay stop onto my next work trip to Peru.

Be still my quixotic heart.

The next morning at the Paraguayan consulate, I was met with total bewilderment: Why, the visa application ladies asked, would I want to visit their homeland if I didn't intend to conduct business there or volunteer for an NGO (as did the only other American applicants they'd ever dealt with)?

"Why not?" I countered.

The truth was, despite Paraguay's war-ravaged, dictator-intensive, narco-and-Nazi-harboring history, there was, I'd read, much to recommend the place: the faded glory of Itapúa's UNESCO World Heritage-ranked Jesuit ruins, the stark beauty of the Chaco, the biodiversity of the Pantanal, and—of course—the consumer electronics district of Ciudad del Este. (This last attraction was responsible for the majority of the country's tourists: Argentines and Brazilians whose appliance budgets went significantly further here than at home.) Though I would have loved to see all of the above, a forthcoming magazine-editing gig dictated a highly abridged intro to Paraguay. I'd have to satisfy my craving—and the terms of my quest—during the course of a few days in and around Asunción.

Finally, at 2 A.M. on the tenth day of the twelfth month of the year 2010—surely some sort of auspicious numerical alignment—I landed at Silvio Pettirossi International Airport, where I was again met with total bewilderment (the official Paraguayan response to American tourism, as I was quickly picking up). But neither the immigration officer's line of questioning—"What the hell brings you here?"—nor the ungodly hour could temper my euphoria. I had, after all, arrived. And as soon as I could take a real look around, I liked the place.

Despite being utterly unconcerned with appearances (because really, who was there to impress?), Asunción was full of beauty, starting with the intense greenness of the streets. Given the average daily temperature of a trillion degrees, shade trees were everywhere—heavily accessorized in seasonal reds, pinks, oranges, and purples. Equally gorgeous and abundant was the centuries-old architecture, all spires, columns, friezes, and domes. And though the twenty-first century occupants of these buildings consisted largely of bootleg CD vendors, the juxtaposition somehow worked. But the most distinctive local beauty was invisible. Rather, it was something I learned to listen for.

Guaraní, the country's indigenous language, is such a breathy, vowel-icious confection, I could have gorged on it nonstop. And I essentially did. It's spoken to varying degrees by more or less every local, which distinguishes it—considerably—from all other indigenous languages in the Americas. Not that Spanish doesn't get equal play, but Paraguayans constantly weave back and forth between the two—in a way that felt sweetly familiar to me. Much as my grandparents (shtetlniks who raised their family in Cuba) would switch from Spanish to Yiddish mid-sentence when the most tender and affectionate of terms were required, Paraguayans of all stripes slip into Guaraní when discussing, say, kids. Or pets. Or a particularly beloved dish.

Even the colonial Jesuits—who weren't exactly known for their staunch preservation of indigenous culture—were taken with this language. Father Antonio Ruiz de Montoya, the seventeenth-century author of an entire book on the subject, deemed Guaraní "so copious and elegant that it can compete with the most famous [of languages]." Ruiz de Montoya retained the title of Most Unlikely Guaraní Proponent until 1970, when a man named James Carson was appointed U.S. ambassador to Paraguay. The diplomat went on to not only become fluent in the language, but to record an entire album of folk songs in it.

Sadly, the only word I myself mastered was *aguyje*, or thank you—but it was good for some of the best taxi driver smiles I've ever gotten.

Mission A accomplished.

*   *   *

Apparently my success in Paraguay triggered the exact cosmic momentum I needed. Shortly after I returned, I received—as if from on high—a newsletter from a tour company called Adventure Life about a certain "Jungle Rivers and Tropical Islands" trip. This two-week expedition cruise, departing exactly one day after my editing stint was set to end, would include stops in the prize ports of Suriname and Guyana. French Guiana, unfortunately, didn't make the cut (too expensive a stop even for cruise operators, I later learned), but in the immortal words of Meat Loaf, two out of three ain't bad. And if I could simply manage to get assignments on Brazil and Curaçao—the ship's first and last stops—the trip would pay for itself. Or close enough, I told myself, factoring in the mammoth quest payoff. So, like Odysseus and Sir Galahad before me, I landed a couple of bridal magazine stories.

And thus did I tell Adventure Life to count me in.

Again, my introductions to each country would be brief—a day in Suriname and two in Guyana—but I'd learned in Paraguay to relish the extra layer of the challenge. Not only did I have to find something uniquely amazing, I had to find it fast.

Things took a turn for the discouraging, however, as soon as we pulled into the Guyanese capital of Georgetown. The country was so untouristed—to the tune of 500 annual foreign arrivals, max—that it rolled out a special brand of red carpet for us: Everywhere we went in our two little buses, motorcycle cops accompanied us, as if we were a UN envoy instead of the AARP quorum and travel writer we were. Not only were the sirens wailing the entire time; the lead officer would part multiple lanes of traffic—Moses-like—with a simple wave of his hand. And as we rolled through town unimpeded by such nuisances as traffic lights and other vehicles, the locals had to

swerve to the side of the road and wait. Death by mortifica-
tion seemed a distinct possibility.

Yes, the capital had a bit of a reputation for violence. Yes,
caution was advised. But a motorcade? Really?

To the extent possible when there's weaponry at the ready,
I did enjoy the natural history museum (best life-sized giant
sloth replica ever) and the weather-beaten British colonial
architecture that housed everything from churches to Chinese quickie-marts. Still, the police escorts made any genuine
experience of the place seem endlessly elusive—and quest ful-
fillment increasingly unlikely.

Mercifully, they didn't follow our convoy of fourteen-seat
Trans Guyana Airways planes into the jungle. Our destination was Kaieteur Falls, where none of the stats I'd read pre-
departure (five times higher than Niagara; two times higher
than Victoria; a total drop of 822 feet) meant anything in
the face of such ridiculous beauty. Cutting a ferocious path
through a vast and otherwise undisturbed tract of rainforest,
the Potaro River dumped what appeared to be Kahlúa and
cream at a rate of 23,400 cubic feet per second over the sheer-
est of cliffs into a mist-expelling cauldron below. Ignoring the
PLEASE STAY A MINIMUM OF 8FT FROM THE EDGE sign (with silent
apologies to my parents), I walked out as far as I could to look
for the rainbow that reportedly turned up on command in
the gorge. And when the vapors below and the clouds above
cleared all at once, there appeared, as if on cue, the mythic
prism. It was almost too much.

For all the gorgeous elements present, however, just as
notable were the absentees: the mega-falls souvenir vendors,
snack shops, commemorative photographers and, um . . .
guard rails. Indeed, there was no trace of humanity, save the
aforementioned—and abundantly disregarded—warning
sign. Just little old us—and *big* old wilderness.

Once the group had gotten its fill and decided to depart, I lingered at the edge for as long as I could without losing sight of the last diminishing body. I knew I was never going to get any closer to being one—quite literally, *one*—with nature.

Mission B accomplished.

Next came Suriname, where things were almost too easy: Despite being the continent's smallest sovereign state, it offers a sampler platter of humanity that exists nowhere else on earth. Among the country's 490,000 or so residents—most of whom live in and around the capital of Paramaribo—are Amerindians (Suriname's original inhabitants), Hindoestanen (descendants of contract laborers from India); Surinamese Creoles (descendants of West African slaves and mostly Dutch Europeans); Javanese (descendants of contract laborers from Indonesia); Surinamese Maroons (descendants of escaped West African slaves); Chinese (both descendants of contract laborers and new arrivals); Boeroes (descendants of Dutch farmers); and Sephardic Jews (descendants of the first Jewish community in the Americas).

And this crazy cultural stew is what I fell for at first sight (or sight, sound, and smell, if you count all the languages and foods that figure into the equation). In fact, despite the perfectly lovely rainforest that carpets much of Suriname's surface, I found the comparatively unstunning Keizerstraat—a long, mostly commercial street in the middle of Paramaribo—to house the nation's most beautiful sight: a mosque and a synagogue standing side by side, or minaret by mikvah as the case may be. The very picture of improbable coexistence, it turns out to be fairly emblematic of the country as a whole—the implications ranging from Caribbean-spiced Dutch Indonesian food to state-sanctioned time off for Ramadan.

The truth is, if Disney would let me live in It's a Small World, I'd be there. New York has always struck me as the next best thing—but Paramaribo started to make me reconsider.

My parting shot was of the massive Arya Dewaker Hindu temple, all red domes and white verandas. And as I beheld this seeming lovechild of the Mughal and Dutch Colonial empires—my belly full of Chinese Caribbean food and my ears tuned into an Urdu sidewalk debate—I left the city a very happy quester.

Mission C accomplished.

Alas, Mission D was another story. Though French Guiana is for all intents and purposes Caribbean, Expedia et al. clearly consider it Plutonian. (Fittingly, among the few outsiders who ever visit are astronauts and engineers bound for the French Space Station there.) So the average flight search will yield either a "no flights match your crazy fucking request"—or a $6,000 itinerary that goes something like:

> *New York, NY (JFK) San Juan, Puerto Rico (SJU)*
>
> *San Juan, Puerto Rico (SJU) Pointe-à-Pitre, Guadeloupe (PTP)*
>
> *Pointe-à-Pitre, Guadeloupe (PTP) Fort De France, Martinique (FDF)*
>
> *Fort De France, Martinique (FDF) Cayenne, French Guiana (CAY)*
>
> *Total duration: 28hr 5min*

And even *I* had my limits.

But on the twelve-year anniversary of the quest—and the verge of conceding defeat—I thought of something: What if I could redeem miles for a round-trip ticket to the Caribbean, then buy a separate ticket to French Guiana on a local carrier? Suddenly, $6,000 became $600—and I was off.

To pile on the gravitas—as one should when completing a journey of this magnitude—I arrived in Cayenne on my birthday. O.K., I really wanted to distract myself from the completely improbable idea that I was turning forty-three. And distracted I was. The place was a total enigma: an "Overseas Department" of France at the junction of the Amazon and the Caribbean, where—beyond the millions of imported French schoolteachers and nurses, plus the aforementioned astronauts—I was pretty much the only out-of-towner. Good thing, too, as the local tourism official could recommend nothing to do—and no way of doing it if I didn't have my own car, as I happened not to. Making clear I was keeping her from her afternoon siesta by insisting there must be *something* I could see on my own, she ushered me out of her leaflet-laden domain and back onto the sidewalk.

But no matter. I was determined to like this place in spite of itself and made my way to the eerily engrossing old French prisons of Saint Laurent du Maroni, the capybara-filled marshes of Kaw, the faded colonial glory of Cayenne—even the wildly incongruous space station at Kourou, where I happened upon a rocket launch. And while all of the above was duly impressive—not least, the fiery ghost tail of the Soyuz over the Caribbean—nothing was quest-satisfying.

Until I reached Cacao—which I did thanks to . . . well, a rent-a-friend. Having asked around Cayenne for a guide who would make the hour-long drive with me, hang around for a bit, then return me to my hotel, I was eventually sent to Gwyn. Never mind that this Parisian transplant wasn't actually a guide, but rather an event planner with a car. She was friendly, interesting, and my only recourse.

Picture, if you will, a Hmong village in the middle of the Amazon Basin where you can find not only the exact same dishes you would in, say, Luang Prabang—but eat them in the company of the Creoles, Caribs, Arawaks, and Parisians

(Gwyn was one of many) for whom the Laotian market is *the* thing to do on Sundays. In fact, if you don't get there by noon, chances are you'll forfeit your seat at the big communal tables—and even worse, your portion of pho.

Though probably not what the French had in mind when they plucked forty-five Laotians from a Thai refugee camp and deposited them here in the 1970s—because really, who could predict that traditionally clad Hmong-speaking women would one day be selling sticky rice and bubble tea to African slave descendants and various indigenous tribes (plus one crazy, self-appointed U.S. emissary) in the jungles of South America?—the scene is impossibly beautiful. And fragrant. And cacophonous. And yes, by God, quest-fulfilling.

Mission D accomplished.

On my return to New York, I found myself wandering once again into that fateful Midtown Barnes & Noble. As I instinctively headed for the travel section—its rows overflowing with possibilities (and of course, the corresponding guidebooks)—I froze in my tracks . . . and took a last-minute left toward New Fiction.

◊◊◊ ◊◊◊ ◊◊◊

Having had longstanding dual citizenship in the women's magazine world and the travel writing world—and having contributed to every publication from Cosmo to Condé Nast Traveler—Abbie Kozolchyk recently fused both identities to become beauty and travel editor at Every Day with Rachael Ray.

﹩ ﹩ ﹩

Dreams from My Father

She goes back in hopes of understanding her dad—
and herself.

*A*fter my last trip to Haiti, I didn't want to come home. I had gone to collect stories—from earthquake and cholera survivors, from childhood friends—and after a week of potholed roads, windswept, eroded mountains, and fresh-caught fish drizzled with lime, I felt alive and inspired. Once again, Haiti had mesmerized me with its all-contradictions-at-once insistence on life. I had interviewed peasant farmers and been out to sea with fishermen on cell phones; I had bargained in Kreyòl, cupped a fledgling parrot in my hands, laughed with friends, and cried at the stories of strangers. The last morning, I woke at 5 A.M. to a cacophony of roosters and cicadas and realized I wasn't ready to leave. When I confessed this to my sister, whom I had talked into coming with me, she laughed and said, "You've come a long way, baby."

At thirteen, when my parents informed me that they wanted to return to Haiti as missionaries, I was furious. It had been five years since we'd last lived there, and I was ensconced in an elite Southern California prep school that had given me a scholarship. I was loath to relinquish horseback-riding lessons, rock-climbing courses and trips to Catalina Island. In

Haiti, I would be consigned to a three-room school with two dozen other missionary kids. Instead of dances, we would have Bible dress-up days. Halloween, a pagan holiday, would go uncelebrated. To make matters worse, when I lived in Haiti, I always stood out: My red hair and pale, freckled skin marked me as a foreigner, and I hated the taunts of *"Blan! Blan!"* when my sisters and I left the compound. Poised on the edge of adolescence, I was deeply self-conscious. I wanted to blend invisibly into the crowd; in Haiti, this was impossible.

My father, on the other hand, seemed to thrive in that same spotlight. He was shy and awkward in the U.S.—he'd worked as an organic vegetable farmer and forest ranger before becoming a missionary—but in Haiti, he was in his element. Neighbors grinned and encouraged his fumbling Kreyòl. People laughed at his corny jokes. He was still awkward, but in Haiti no one seemed to mind. The improvisational nature of agricultural-development work, where everything was dependent on weather and politics, suited him fine. As a farmer, he understood that life was unpredictable.

Most important, Dad felt as if he could make a difference in Haiti. In the early 1980s, he had managed a tree nursery in Limbé that supplied 500,000 seedling trees a year to Pan-American Development Foundation projects in the north of Haiti. Planting trees was urgent work: Without roots to hold the soil in place and a canopy of leaves to slow the torren-tial tropical rainstorms, fertile topsoil washed away with each new storm, leaving the gardens sparser and the peasant farm-ers hungrier. In Haiti, Dad felt useful.

As a teenager, I couldn't have cared less. Whenever my father talked about reforestation, I rolled my eyes. I didn't understand why he had to be the one to save Haiti. I thought he suffered from an overactive ego and told him as much. My mother and sisters tried to play peacemaker, but Dad and I had little patience for each other.

Eventually, we took a family vote on whether or not to return. Dad reminded us of the things we'd loved about Haiti as kids: the beach trips, the green-throated lizard on the dining room wall, our friends in the missionary compound. I folded my arms and glared at him, unconvinced. My sisters wavered. Mom reminded Dad that the country had undergone a series of military coups and riots after the demise of the Duvalier dictatorship; in 1990, Haiti wasn't the safest place to take three young girls. The final vote was four to one against the move, yet somehow my father overruled us. Mom sighed and grumbled that she had married Atlas—he carried the whole world on his shoulders. "There goes my life," I scrawled bitterly in my journal.

The next few months were predictably volatile. To raise funds, my parents gave slideshows about deforestation at local churches, then called us girls up front to sing in Kreyòl. I sulked and pouted. At home, Dad and I fought like hell. Once, he threw a Bible through the window because I refused to participate in family devotions. When Mom came home that night, she accused me of provoking my father and called me "the devil's handmaiden."

A few days after my fourteenth birthday, I flew alone to Haiti. The rest of the family had arrived there two weeks earlier, while I was on a school trip to Baja. As the plane circled the sugarcane fields outside Cap-Haïtien, it all felt strangely familiar: the tiny, mud-walled houses; the white-sand beaches; the desolate hillsides empty of trees.

At the airport, my sisters threw their arms around me, their thin cotton dresses blowing in the wind. I noted, skeptically, that Mom and Dad seemed glad to see me. My father had a Haitian straw hat shoved over his ears and a faded backpack slung over one shoulder. He looked sunburned and relaxed. My long hoop earrings brushed against my shoulders as I straightened my skirt. Within minutes, I realized with disappointment that my carefully teased bangs were starting to wilt in the tropical humidity. But I was confident that anyone who observed my boldly squared shoulders, teal eyeliner, and world-weary half-smile would realize that I did not belong in this backward, unfashionable missionary family.

The airport was low and squalid. Incompetent ceiling fans, caked in a layer of greasy dust, rotated uselessly while customs officials rummaged through my luggage. The breeze from the sea smelled of rotting fish and garbage, confirmation that Dad had, in fact, brought us back to Haiti to ruin our lives.

As we drove toward the Limbé Valley through the soot and noise of Cap-Haïtien, bare-chested men strained against wooden carts piled high with discarded tires and sugarcane. Children shouted, "*Blan! Blan!*"

I sank deeper into my seat.

In the mornings—hot, humid, smelling of hibiscus and smoldering charcoal—my sisters and I dressed for school while Dad tromped off into the hills with a backpack full of seeds, a jug of water and a Kreyòl Bible to preach the gospel of trees. When strangers asked him what he carried in his *macoute,* he answered, "I'm carrying hope."

This time he had struck out on his own, leaving the tree nursery in the hands of another horticulturist. He was determined to work directly with the peasant farmers to solve the problem of deforestation. His goal was to persuade them to sow tree seeds in their gardens so that the roots would hold the soil in place. He introduced drought- and animal-resistant trees that coppiced readily; even when harvested for charcoal, the trunks would send up offshoots. It was a new paradigm: trees as a renewable resource. And at least initially, the peasant farmers seemed excited. The tiny seedlings began to unfurl tentative, green-fringed leaves. Hope was in the air.

My sentiments were less optimistic. "I never thought I'd live to see the day I'd hate weekends," I wrote in my journal, "but from here on out, they can kiss my ass. At least during the week I can keep busy with school and see other Americans, even if they despise me, but weekends are miserable in this deserted hellhole. Everyone is at a soccer match now. Talk about a dead sport."

Determined to punish my parents for dragging me to Haiti, I fought over the dress code (they had forbidden us to wear pants or short skirts in public), and at least once a week Dad and I had a standoff at the front door.

"You're not leaving the house wearing that," he insisted, the tendons in his neck straining, his shoulders hunched into a wrestler's stance, as if to hurl me to the floor if I tried to slip past him.

"Fine, then I'm not leaving," I retorted, my hands on my hips. When I felt the sting of salt in my eyes, I angrily flicked away the tears—careful so as not to smudge my mascara.

Eventually I'd slam my bedroom door and change clothes (though a few times I simply put a longer skirt over the miniskirt and removed it later). In the afternoons, I hid behind novels: *Anne of Green Gables, The Far Pavilions, The Clan of the Cave Bear.* I wrote long, heartbroken journal entries while my homesick sister cried herself to sleep across the hall.

As hard as the adjustment was on the rest of us, it was obvious that Dad felt at home in Haiti. When he shuffled in at the end of the day from some remote village, I tried to tune out his stories of Haitian poverty and resilience. I despised his unpredictable temper, his faded, rumpled clothes, and his dirt-stained fingernails. I avoided sitting next to him at dinner so I wouldn't have to hold his hand during the prayer. But a few months later, even I could tell that his enthusiasm had begun to falter.

After months without rain, the tiny seedling trees he'd handed out so hopefully had withered in the eviscerated soil. Farmers in the north called it the worst drought in seventeen years. Creeks slowed to a trickle, then evaporated. Dad spent weeks trying to pipe water into a cement cistern so he could save the gardens. But the cement was faulty, and in the middle of the night the walls collapsed. The farmers woke, terrified, to a shuddering explosion of water across the parched soil. It seemed to me that nothing we did mattered: Even with Dad's help, the farmers were still poor and hungry; the trees still died.

My father was able to hold it together until the funeral of Nosben, a promising young man whose death from sickle-cell anemia was more than he could bear. At the gravesite, mourners filed past a pile of decaying bones that had been dis-interred to make room for death's most recent victim. When Dad returned home, still agitated, to squabbling teenage girls, he lost it. He picked up a wooden statue of a Haitian peas-ant woman struggling under an impossibly heavy load and hurled it across the room. The statue shattered when it hit the wall, the basket splitting open along the wood grain, the woman's broken arm flying from her body.

My sisters hid behind Mom. I raised my eyebrows, my face cold. I just wanted to escape before Haiti destroyed the rest of us.

By the time we left, a year later, none of us knew how to talk about what we had just survived. We didn't talk about the time we were evacuated from the missionary compound for fear of riots or the time we watched a man burned alive inside a rubber tire. We didn't talk about the rural woman Dad had come close to having an affair with. For years Haiti was a sub-ject we avoided.

It wasn't until I was in my late twenties that I asked my father if I could read through our family letters from Haiti. He shrugged and pulled a stack of musty Chiquita-banana boxes from the barn. Sticky with tractor grease and coagulated fruit stains, the boxes had been hidden under outgrown baseball gloves and loose bales of hay. I waited until I was alone, then gingerly brushed aside the cobwebs to find translucent orange Roman Meal bread bags full of letters, bills, church bulletins, and missionary newsletters. As I sorted through the torn and separated pages, I discovered that my father had given me a gift I hadn't anticipated—his journals.

I sat back on my heels and opened the day planner Dad had filled with his jagged, left-handed scrawl.

"Beautiful sunset coming down the mountain," he noted just after we returned to Haiti for the last time.

A short while later he observed, "Girls forlorn tonight." I put my hand over my mouth and choked back a sob. I hadn't realized that he'd noticed.

As I read on, I was surprised by how deeply he had internalized the suffering of the Haitian farmers. As the drought worsened and his friends along the mountain paths grew weak from AIDS and tuberculosis, with no crops to sell to pay for their medical care, Dad gave out more and more loans—with no hope of repayment. One afternoon, when he learned that a six-month-old baby was about to die of AIDS, he hid in the thin shade of a guava bush and stared out over the denuded hills. Solitary mango trees stood over the clearings as smoldering charcoal fires drifted into lazy plumes. He could see all the way down the flood-scarred valley to the faint blue edge of the sea. He put his head in his hands and sobbed.

For the first time, I saw Haiti through his eyes. I no longer saw the country as my competition—only regretted that I had tried so hard to thwart his attempts to help. A man of few words, terrified by strong emotions, he didn't know then how to vocalize his despair. I knew him only by his anger and his high expectations. I didn't understand, as my mother later explained to me, that when the topsoil in Haiti washes away, part of my father goes with it.

In 2003, I returned to Haiti with my father, along with my mother and my husband. We hiked to the villages where Dad used to pass out tree seeds along with Bible verses translated into Kreyòl. Everyone along the path knew his name and came out to greet him with big grins and firm handshakes. A few farmers took us to see tree-covered ridges that had been reforested as a result of my father's persistent prodding. Far more hillsides were still barren and despoiled, but it was a beginning. It wasn't the rapid, recognizable result Dad had once hoped for, but it was incremental change—the kind that lasts.

My husband, who had never been to Haiti, had heard me confess how much I hated living there as a teenager, but he surprised me by noting how often I smiled in Haiti—far more often than when we were at home together in Oregon. Mom just laughed: "She's like her father. She feels at home here."

Over the past ten years, I have returned to Haiti several times. Each time I leave, I feel a sense of loss. Lush, verdant Oregon seems empty and quiet by comparison. Even after the earthquake, which I covered for Public Radio International's *This American Life*, I came home with a renewed sense of admiration for the Haitian people—their resilience, courage, and ability to laugh in the face of overwhelming odds.

On my most recent visit, I explored the country without my father, for the first time in thirty years. My Kreyòl is nowhere near as fluent as his, but as I fumbled my way through boat trips and motorcycle rides, ate smoky *kasav* and savored the sweet-sour tang of *abricot* fruit, I realized how much I had inherited. It was Dad who had taught me to care about the earth and to value the stories of those who tended the soil. And while I would never have believed it as a teenager, I was finally converted to the gospel of trees.

In Gonaïves, an arid region just over the mountains from where I grew up, I hiked for hours in the humid glare of the sun, past schoolchildren in matching uniforms, past old women with bundles of firewood balanced on their heads, to see a new soil-conservation site that Dad had insisted be planted with trees. The drought-and-animal-resistant seeds had been sown by peasant farmers less than a year earlier, but already the glossy, dark-green leaves were as high as my waist. Those trees, like the Haitian people, had defied the odds. In a land of mountains beyond mountains, in a country both devastated and proud, maddening and beautiful, squalid and unimaginably heroic, the trees were survivors. The branches trembled delicately as a wind blew down the mountains and stirred the dry soil.

ℬ ℬ ℬ

Apricot Anderson Irving is a missionary kid, farmer's daughter, writer, audio producer, occasional waitress and high school teacher, and mother of two wildly imaginative boys. Her work has appeared in MORE Magazine, Granta, *and* Oregon Humanities, *and she has reported from Haiti for* This American Life. *She is the founder and director of the Boise Voices Oral History Project, www.boisevoices.com, and a recipient of a 2011 Rona Jaffe Writer's Award and a 2012 Oregon Literary Arts Fellowship. Her memoir,* The Gospel of Trees, *is forthcoming from Simon & Schuster. She is capable, when pressed, of belting out a passable Irish ballad or a Kreyòl hymn.*

ॐ ॐ ॐ

Business or Pleasure?

Dream towns have nightmares too.

*I*t was a simple question. One I'd been asked a zillion times before. But this time, I couldn't reply. "Are you traveling for business or pleasure?" the customs agent asked.

I'd left that box unchecked on the declaration form. They always ask you again in person regardless. Still, I just didn't have an appropriate answer, and my mind wasn't working very quickly.

"Business or pleasure?" he demanded.

Silence. The man gave me an odd look.

"I . . . uh. . . ." I wondered if my hesitation would set off some sort of alarm. Kind of like the time I was accosted by sniffing dogs at the Auckland airport for failing to disclose that I had a banana in my backpack.

"Neither," I finally stammered.

In that moment, I was put off by the insensitivity of the question. Life isn't always so black or white. Business or pleasure! I wasn't in Vancouver for some corporate sales conference where I'd wear a nametag and schmooze with strangers in a hotel function room. Nor was I there to poke around Granville Island or traipse across the Capilano Suspension Bridge.

And neither were Rupert's parents. The thought of the customs agent confronting them with this same, seemingly routine question made me shudder. How could they possibly respond? I would learn later that, thank God, they never had to. That someone, somehow, had pre-arranged for them to skip customs. I thought no one was ever allowed to skip customs.

I have to say, for much of my adult life I have blithely checked that box. Pleasure! Pleasure! I am, always have been, a travel addict. Put me on a plane—to anywhere but say, Florida—and I'm happy. When I became a travel writer in my twenties, I secretly loved how I could, when I felt like it, check Business. Writing a story on surfing in Mexico? Business! Heli-hiking in the Bugaboos? Business! The two terms grew interchangeable. The mark of a Good Life, in my mind.

Later, working as a travel editor at a magazine, I loved that my job was to share that Good Life with millions of readers—to curate the very best experiences in the best places. To sell travel as pleasure. Picturesque. Pure fun.

Among the many areas I covered was British Columbia. I'd edit glowing stories that highlighted Vancouver's authentic ethnic food, its gorgeous gardens, easy access to the outdoors, and of course, a few years back, the Olympics! The mere mention of Vancouver would evoke cries of joy from people. "Oh, I looove Vancouver!" "Isn't it the most beautiful city in *the world*?" "Don't you want to just pick up and *move* there?"

Not really. *My* Vancouver isn't so idyllic. My memories of the city are foggy and surreal and disjointed.

I remember that the airport shuttle was there, waiting, when I stepped outside. That Men at Work's "Land Down Under" was playing on the radio as we pulled away from the curb, and that I found it simultaneously eerie and soothing. I'd always assumed real Aussies hated that song, but Rupert, who was born and bred on a farm near Melbourne, would proudly sing along.

I remember it rained. So much that I never got to wear the flowy knee-length skirt I'd bought the day before at Banana Republic, specifically for the occasion. Because as rugged as he was, Rupert always kind of liked it when I wore skirts.

As I arrived at the hotel, not knowing exactly who would be there or what I was supposed to do, I remember feeling relieved when I saw Aunt Toosie first. We hugged; her fleshy arms and extra rolls were suffocating, in a good way. She led me to the front desk and told me my room was under the name Stinson. Like I was part of the family. Like I always wanted to be.

I recall the hotel being surprisingly nice, right on the water with big windows and an airy, light-filled lobby and a lounge bar with couches, which is where we'd end up gathering that evening and the next, late into the night. Together, we felt safe there, sequestered, and we would order round after round of shots and beers. As if it was a wedding. We'd laugh and cry and swap hilarious stories, until the bartender cut us off and we'd have to return to our rooms to try to sleep.

And I remember that my bed was so comfortable, I was actually able to. I was swallowed by at least six pillows, which were soft and huggable and muffled not only my own sobs but also our friend Mike's, which I'd hear every so often throughout the night, coming from the bed beside mine.

I remember piling into two long tables on the second floor of a kitschy waterfront restaurant called The Boathouse. It was a fitting venue as The Boys were fishermen. They would have approved of the oversized laminated menu featuring local, sustainably caught steelhead and wild sockeye salmon. And the waiter, the poor waiter, who rattled off the specials—in what seemed like excruciating detail—to a group of people who would barely eat a bite that night. Didn't someone tell this guy? Stop! Stop! I wanted to say, as he languidly described the appetizer special, then the entrees, and the prices for each. *We don't care*, I wanted to tell him. But this was a restaurant, and we were just customers, and he was only doing his job.

I remember taking a squeaky-clean Greyhound bus with carpeted seats to a lush, wild park on the outskirts of the city. The rain poured down. The ground was squishy, and we climbed over logs slippery with moss. In lieu of my skirt, I wore a pair of velvety blue pants I'd brought as back up. But they were too long, and though I tried to roll up the bottoms, they trailed in the mud.

Apparently, the church that someone had scouted was too formal and stuffy and random. But this park, this small muddy clearing in the trees, next to a river rushing with salmon, was perfect. As if a mirage, a fisherman stood nearby, casting his line into the river. I wondered if he could hear the Ben Harper song playing softly in the background. Or the reading of Johnny Cash's "A Cowboy's Prayer." Or the funny story I spontaneously told about camping together in Yosemite. Thinking I could make people laugh. Or at least smile. And some did. But not Lou and Bobby, barely able to stand, holding umbrellas over their hanging heads, and thanking us for being there; telling us they would need us for the rest of their lives.

As we walked over a footbridge to a covering where we cracked beers and toasted The Boys' lives, I remember thinking: I didn't expect an urn to be this heavy.

Eventually, I managed to give the customs agent a response. "My boyfriend died," I said, out loud, for the first time since the accident. He paused, then stamped my passport and waved me through.

This was, actually, partially a lie. But the truth seemed too difficult. Was I going to tell a customs agent that Rupert was, technically, no longer my boyfriend when he and his brother Finn were killed in a car crash? That after three years together in San Francisco, he had broken my heart a few months earlier? *Before* The Boys veered off the Alaska Highway and into a ditch, somewhere near a tiny town in the Yukon named Whitehorse. (Yet another area travel writers would pitch me as a "must-do" story. Sorry, you'll have to sell that one to someone else.)

You see, Mr. Customs Agent, I wanted to say, ready now to ramble through the Plexiglas, I'm not even sure I should be *going* to this impromptu funeral in the first place. I mean, I'm not Rupert's Girlfriend anymore—though from all of the emails and voicemails and handwritten cards I've received, it's clear people still feel like I am. I *feel* like I am. It's almost as if death overrides a break-up. And maybe it does. A break-up! It sounds so trivial now.

But at the time, I felt like *I* had died. Pushing thirty, Rupert unraveled. In a matter of minutes, sitting in the same over-stuffed armchair we'd had sex in the night before, he reversed the grand, impractical travel plans that we'd excitedly hatched together. He said he loved me, but maybe not enough; and that, What If, when we finally made our way to Melbourne, his business didn't take off. And What If I couldn't find a job that would sponsor me. And then What If we had to get married. Then what.

Finn fell asleep at the wheel. After they'd fished hard, for ten days straight. Hooking trout as big as their smiles—which I later spent weeks staring at, in photos retrieved from the digital camera, documenting their good time.

They always had a good time, The Boys. Especially when they were together. And especially when they were fishing.

But I could tell, looking into their eyes—only just beginning to crinkle with age, alive and energized by a summer spent guiding in the wilderness—that this particular summer, this particular trip, was their very best.

Of course they hadn't wanted it to end—they never did. And so, they no doubt stayed a little too late, getting in every last delicate cast before they had to hightail it hundreds of miles back on a desolate, dangerous road to the Anchorage airport. And, eventually, home to Australia.

But Finn's narcoleptic tendencies and international red tape got in the way. Their once strong, now crumpled bodies couldn't be flown overseas. It was too tricky. Or too expensive.

All I knew was, there we were. A handful of people who loved them most—from Sydney to San Francisco to Scotland—convening in Vancouver, of all places. And I learned that while little checked boxes might make the customs line move slightly faster, ultimately, labels like business and pleasure—or boyfriend and girlfriend—are just that: convenient shorthand for something much more complicated. Like life.

♫ ♫ ♫

Rachel Levin is a San Francisco-based writer and editor. She is a frequent contributor to Sunset *magazine, where she formerly was a senior travel editor. Her work also appears in the* New York Times, Slate, Outside, Food & Wine, *and* San Francisco *magazine, where she is a contributing writer. She blames her spontaneous Orbitz-booking habit on her parents, who sent her off to Japan, solo, during seventh-grade summer. Her most recent trip was to Cuba with a busload of Jewish seniors from Boca, Florida. Visit her at www.byrachellevin.com.*

🪶 🪶 🪶

Connie Britton's Hair

Climb every mountain. Or maybe don't.

"How much longer?" I ask Eugene.

"We have a very long way," he says. "Also, it gets much steeper."

In our short acquaintance, I already know our guide isn't one for sweetening the news. In fact, he seems to relish his role as grim realist, the battlefield reporter with the cold hard facts. It's difficult to say which half of his response fills me with greater dread.

"Long way, like another hour?" I ask, panic leaking into my voice. "Steeper than this?"

With an upraised palm like a hostess at a car show, I indicate the vertical swathe of mud looming above me.

It's not yet 9 a.m., but an hour since we started up Mount Bisoke, a dormant volcano in the Virunga range, which straddles northwest Rwanda, southern Uganda and the eastern reaches of the DRC. My legs are trembling, periodically forcing me to lurch off the wet, shiny stones into clusters of stinging nettles and pools of black magmic sludge.

There are seven other climbers, and the Greek one won't shut up. Between his white noise and the realization that my body is already failing me, I know I need to make quick work of this mountain. The woman who booked my excursion assured me I'd be back at the hotel in time for lunch. The idea that I'd also be alive was implicit. Yet I already feel the heat of a fresh bruise spreading across the upper quadrant of my right thigh after one humiliating tumble. I have no idea for whom or what I am traipsing upstream of a landslide. And I kind of want to get back to *Nashville* and Connie Britton's hair.

When I arrived at the park earlier this morning, after registering and filling a mug with coffee, Pierre, my driver and companion for the week, directed me to the briefing with Eugene. The man was all business, laconic and unsmiling. From the outset, I tried to soften his bluntness with my usual attempt at charm. It was a cry for reassurance, the obvious ploy of the terminally insecure.

"I hear this is a snap," I said, my voice larded with cheer. "Couple hours up and back?"

"Oh no, not during the rainy season,"—which we were smack in the middle of—he said. "It is a strenuous climb. You must be very fit."

I scoped out the other climbers. Demetrius the Greek, already chattering pointlessly, was no David Beckham, nor were the Russians exactly Olympic decathletes. The rest I surmised were roughly on a par with me. Only Monica from Holland looked to be in fighting shape, but she was about twenty and, well, Dutch.

I took a spin class once in a while. I'd manage.

The air was laced with the smell of eucalyptus at the clearing beyond the entrance of Volcanoes National Park, the staging area for the day's excursions. The other tourists, most of whom were preparing (or at least hoping) to see the gorillas, milled about under a large gazebo sipping coffee and tea to ward off the chilly morning. I snickered at the safari folk tricked out in gadgetry and pricey adventure wear—gaiters, air-permeable layers, and high-performance hiking boots. I was awfully confident in my trail-running shoes and my teen-age daughter's surf hoodie.

Sunlight shot across the mountains and fields, rapidly eras-ing the shadows from the landscape. It was a gorgeous morn-ing for a trek, much like the one I'd enjoyed a year before when I set off with seven other people and two guides in search of gorillas. We'd been unusually lucky that morning; our group had barely broken a sweat when we got word that "our" family of primates, which included a set of newborn twins, was about to swing into view. On that trip—my first to Rwanda—I'd been captivated by the sight of the gorillas, but also by the vision of five volcanoes that formed a sensuous but formidable ridge cradling the forest. It didn't occur to me that I'd be back a year later to climb one.

I'm not much of a nature girl. But because I come from hardy immigrant stock—ship captains and quarrymen on one side, farmers on the other—I'm a bit ashamed of my predilection for pure linen sheets and finely tooled Italian pumps. It's always struck me as a weakness—a trait I should at least resist, if not someday overcome. When I was young, although I'd have preferred to spend summers perfecting my country club backhand, I nevertheless marched off to camp in Vermont every year with my three older sisters, outfitted in flame-retardant shorts and rubber boots that even then offended my fashion standards. I was certain (as was my mother, probably) that if I could rough it, even briefly, I would be a better and more selfless person. There were no tennis courts or bubble baths or even pillows on the flume slide trail of Mount Wash-ington, but the stew we slung up in our mess kits was tasty and the hardship temporary. I didn't exactly love the nights I spent shivering in my sleeping bag on a floor covered with grit and spiders and eleven other campers, but I did appreciate the camaraderie and shared purpose—at least in retrospect.

Many years later, when I could make the choice, I almost settled down with an Argentinian clotheshorse, but instead married the reincarnation of Ernest Shackleton—an outdoorsman who has bestowed his love of adventure and fresh air upon our children. And I appreciate this, because it takes the heat off me.

While my family sets out on summer mornings before dawn on twenty-mile hikes through the Adirondacks, I sleep in. Long after the sun comes up, I enjoy the view of the mountains from my perch across the lake over slices of toast with marmalade. I have taken on the role of Princess in our family narrative, and my children and husband play along, coddling me, but also needling me lovingly about my preference for the languorous lie-in over physical exertion of any kind. They fall short of calling me "lazy" but their knowing euphemisms speak their own truth, or so I imagine. After a hip replacement at forty-five (it was trashed by high school sports and faulty anatomy) I finally had the excuse I needed to basically never go outside again.

But now, a few years later and a few years older, I've begun to find this conceit tarnishing with age, and my adventure phobia turning into one of many oncoming regrets. When my family pushes off with their water bottles and trail mix, I still wave goodbye cheerfully, but with the nagging sense that by hanging back on solid ground, I'm missing—how many?—seminal moments, the gorgeously lit future memories that will, if I can only bring myself to participate, flood my mind when I am nearly done on earth, a day from dying. I have never seen my son run up ahead on antelope legs, nor have I ever extended my hand to my daughter over a steep patch of trail and seen determination flood her being.

And there's something else. Not since my summers trudging up the White Mountains have I experienced the singular do-or-die obstinacy it takes to make it up and down a tricky slope, heart and legs begging for mercy. Lately I've begun to envy the accomplishment my family feels after a day's climb and how honestly they have earned their fatigue. Several months ago, with a reporting trip to Rwanda on the calendar, I decided it was the perfect opportunity to tackle a mountain. And after some online research, I determined that Bisoke—"the easy one"—was the one for me.

Which is why, with the clock running out on opportunities to conquer things, I am inching up the side of a volcano this morning. Only now, an hour into the climb, I'm beginning to understand that Bisoke's reputation might be relative—like calling *Pulp Fiction* Quentin Tarantino's least violent movie. And I'm also realizing that people who climb volcanoes for fun apparently blog for *other people* who climb volcanoes for fun—not for people like me.

I frequently travel solo. Often this is because I'm on assignment, but the other truth is I'm someone who craves brief, solitary journeys. I live for these respites when I eat meals alone, answer to no one, keep my own counsel. It's only after dinner, during the hours of extreme quiet in my room while the single glass of wine drains from my system and I wait for sleep, that I get twinges of loneliness. I wonder where my kids are and begin to question what problem I'm trying to solve in my need to escape.

I've found that the best distraction from the torture of my misgivings and the attendant insomnia is entertainment. But twenty-five-watt bulbs, the bedside standard in a certain kind of hotel, offer my eyes little sustenance for reading. Nights on international assignments, therefore, have turned into an excuse to watch whatever TV series I've missed that everyone insists I should see. And this time, here in remote Rwanda, it's *Nashville*, a nighttime drama about generational rivalry in country music with gorgeous tunes, often sung by Connie Britton.

Who is this woman? In *Nashville*, she plays Rayna Jaymes, a woman roughly my age, give or take a couple years (O.K., ten), a beloved country singer facing challenges from an ambitious up-and-comer. I'm hooked after three episodes, and all because of her. It isn't just the pitch the actress strikes perfectly, portraying both celebrity and suburban hausfrau—it's her character's take on middle age. She never lapses into self-pity—she has too much going on to dwell on the inevitable downsides of aging. Instead, she keeps evolving by working harder than anyone else. And in so doing, she spares us the usual "Forty and Fabulous" bromides and cougar manifestos endemic in pop culture. It helps that—with wavy strawberry-blond hair coiffed with curling irons and volumizer, and a wardrobe that changes in the course of fifty minutes from jeans to a sheath dress to spangles and back again (along with her nail polish: navy blue, then aubergine, ending with flannel gray)—she is endlessly fascinating to watch. She is groomed and rich and desired by men of every age, and never wears the same pair of Louboutins twice.

And I confess, as I look down at my legs trudging up Mount Bisoke in these god-awful hiking pants, I hate her for all of it. But mostly I admire—and even envy—her. "Time is precious," her actions insist, as she braves one creative leap after another. Unlike me, the woman is afraid of nothing.

What I have never told my family, what they don't know, is that I am averse to nature writ large because, in fact, it terrifies me. I fear insects and unseen branches that could draw blood from my neck. As for mountains: I fear I won't make it up, and even more that I won't make it back down. What doesn't scare me are the four soldiers from the Rwandan

Armed Forces with AK-47s strapped to their torsos who are accompanying us on our climb. That's security, as far as I 'm concerned. We are spitting distance from the DRC, where a brutal war is in full swing and refugees and soldiers are rumored to be seeking cover in the dense forest. I don't care if some hopped-up Congolese rebel interrupts our peace, I'm not even afraid of the wild buffalo known to pose an even greater threat to tourists. I'm only afraid of confronting my own helplessness.

But at least I had the good sense this morning to hire Foster. Since I'd convinced myself the hike would be a snap, at first I balked at the idea of engaging a babysitter.

"Do I look like I need a porter?" I asked Eugene after the orientation.

He didn't laugh. As they had done on the gorilla trek, the young men lined up at the trailhead to be snapped up, rather like migrant laborers for the day, working only for tips. I caught Foster's eye and handed over my backpack filled with three bottles of water, some cashews, a Milka bar, and a raincoat. He smiled broadly, and later I wondered if he was just happy to be hired or if he knew he'd be saving my life that day.

There is little to see on the way up, and after two hours I stop looking. Eugene, Dr. Doom, keeps bearing bad news, but I ask for it, appealing desperately for word that we are almost there. We aren't. We don't even bother to veer off for the mile-long walk to Dian Fossey's grave. According to Eugene, we still have five kilometers until the crater lake at the top. It's treacherous going, and the temperature is dropping.

"And if it rains," he says, "we will really have a problem."

The sun is toasting my bare shoulders and I am drenched with sweat. There doesn't appear to be a cloud anywhere within a thousand miles of the African continent.

"It's not going to rain," I say.

"Yes, it will rain," Eugene says.

"You need to work on your delivery," I tell him.

There are three things on this hike. There is the ground in all its viney chaos, studded by rocks glazed with mud. Then there are the Greek guy's dire prognostications, delivered on a continuous loop but somewhat mirthfully.

"One of us is going to slide off this mountain!" Demetrios offers. "And our friends with the Kalashnikovs are not here to scare buffalo, I can tell you this."

Lastly, there is Foster's hand. I have friends who, when I am in a crisis, know better than I do what I need. This is Foster. He is pure instinct, like a farmer who knows from a scent threading the air that the weather will change. Sometimes when Foster reaches for me, I wave him off. "It's O.K. Fos, I'm fine," I say, and lose my footing anyway—it's a game of millimeters—while his hand appears from the ether to lock into mine and right me standing.

He reads my body, pointing to a spot in the mud where he intuits I can safely place my shoe so it will not veer sideways in the other direction of the rest of me. If he thinks I look completely idiotic to be on this march, he never lets on.

"Very good, very good," he says after sparing me a pirouette off a boulder or untangling me from the brush with one deft tug. They are the only words other than "thank you" he knows in English. If Foster were to ask me to help him hold up the Bank of England today, I would dutifully follow.

As I climb, I pray not to God but to Dr. Schutzer, the surgeon who installed a titanium rod where my hipbone had been. Even my good joints are giving out, my legs quake from exertion, and my lungs are tight and breath halting from the elevation: we are climbing to over twelve thousand feet.

I am appalled that as I bushwhack, vertically, through this supposed war zone, I'm not contemplating lofty geopolitical concerns, the kind I went to graduate school to ponder. No, as I slog ahead, I'm thinking about Connie Britton, seeking life lessons from ABC primetime entertainment. Take risks, her character tells me—but be true to yourself. It's all kind of boilerplate self-help stuff. But maybe boilerplate is what one needs when one has no business trying to summit a Rwandan volcano in flimsy footwear in January.

Just above the tree line, I hear a text message jingle inside my bag. I know my guide, Pierre, is worried about me. I've already been climbing for five hours and am meant to be back by now. Foster turns to let me fish the phone from my backpack. As my hand clutches it, I fall backwards into the basin of mud and roots I have just labored across. My skull grazes a stone that juts from the swamp like the head of a shark, and my knee smashes against another rock. Nausea pools in my stomach. I push the button with a mud-soaked finger. "Vodafone welcomes you to the DRC!" it says. Foster grabs my other hand and as he pulls me up, I fall against him and weep.

"Very good," he says.

I turn to Eugene. "I will not make it down," I sniffle. "There is no way I will make it down." As I utter the words, a horizontal wind slashes across my face, ushering in a dense curtain of sleet that paints the sky dark gray.

"We are really fucked now," says the Greek guy.

"Demetrios," I say, "Could you lighten up?"

"Do you think they could send a helicopter?" he says, turning and laughing. Maybe he isn't so bad.

An hour later, we summit. The crater lake sits under the weight of heavy clouds, with only brief slivers of water visible through the mist. As we stand together looking at absolutely nothing, hailstones the size of gumballs start pelting us, making hollow conking noises as they bounce off our heads and shoulders. Demetrios has no raincoat and I worry for him. But with a flourish, he yanks an umbrella out of his pack.

"Come seek refuge from the elements," he says.

I crouch with some of the others in a huddle. Even Monica, the strapping Dutchwoman, looks wretched. Demetrios's arms are still bare, now pink from the wind and chill. I reach for his arm and for a second rub it vigorously.

"Are you okay?" I ask.

"Of course," he says. "Never better." Somehow, I believe him.

The hail continues to pound us. Eugene is sheltered under a ficus tree with Foster, the soldiers, and the other porters. After a while he approaches our group.

"We'd better head down."

"What is the word for hail in Kinyarwanda?" I ask him.

"Hmmm," he says. He looks miserable too—or maybe just grave. "I've never seen this before up here."

"How long have you been climbing this mountain?"

"Thirteen years."

"Will we make it down?"

"Of course," he says.

I cannot move my hands. "What do you think is the temperature?" I ask.

"It is below freezing."

My fingers are frozen into claws. I think of the cocktail ring Connie Britton twirled on her index finger in the episode last night. I think of her manicured nails and smooth hair, no doubt scented with Parisian styling crème, the kind I might be massaging into my own waves if I weren't on this fucking mountain. I think of my children, this voyage and my self-inflicted misery, which when I recount to them, they will surely assume I'm exaggerating. I contemplate my need to triumph over something, anything, if only because I'm afraid that time is running out. And I think about how exhausting it is to do battle with your own character.

As sleet slips behind my neck, carving rivers of ice down my back, I consider an entirely new option: maybe I don't need to be ashamed that I like to be safe and warm and out of harm's way. What if I'm not fearful and lazy, but rather cautious and observant, with a preference to stand apart from adventure rather than be in the thick of it?

It takes three hours to get back down the mountain. Demetrios keeps me company on the descent, and I appreciate his optimism. When he falls silent on occasion for a minute or two, I worry that he is as scared as I am.

"Hey Dima," I yell, "how ya doing?"

"Good thing I know how to snowboard!" I watch him skid down the mud, now a foot deep.

The storm has sluiced cascades where the path used to be, and the trail is now a waterfall flowing with the same icy sludge that paints every inch of me and soaks clear through to the molecules in my pancreas. Foster keeps a permanent grip on my hand, and if I ask to be carried, he will surely toss me over his back like a sack of potatoes. For a moment I consider this option. I am utterly helpless—we all are—in the downpour. I fall hard and often, sometimes bringing Foster down on top of me, and I laugh to show I am still conscious and to prove that there is something pretty comical in almost-tragedy. And then, at the very end, I begin to enjoy myself a little. But only because I am almost off this mountain.

When we say goodbye, Demetrios and I exchange kisses but not e-mail addresses. I know he will remember me with a certain tenderness, as I will him.

"*Murakoze*," I say to Foster, hoping the Kinyarwanda word for "thank you" might also mean "I love you." I give him all of $40, four times the going rate.

I spot Pierre in the parking lot, and he doesn't recognize me as I approach. I collapse in his arms. "It was so scary," I say.

Eugene catches a ride with us back to the staging area.

"You did it," he says to me, grinning for the first time all day.

"I felt very safe with you," I admitted. "Was today an unusually tough climb?"

"It was normal," he says. I give him a look. "Actually a little tougher."

"Were you scared?" I ask.

"It's a mountain," he says. "They make their own rules. It's nice that people climb them, but maybe sometimes they shouldn't."

We head back to the hotel, where the staff scrapes the mountain off my walking shoes and polishes them clean. I de-cake myself of mud in a rose-scented bath, and my fingers defrost with the help of South African brandy. Later, a man appears out of the darkness to build a fire with eucalyptus logs in my bungalow.

"How was your climb?" he asks as he rearranges and lights the pile of logs.

"It was hard." I am aching and bruised but sweetly exhausted and a tiny bit lonely. "For me."

"It's a big mountain," he laughs. "You must be very strong."

As the flames grow in the fireplace and the room fills with the spicy smell of burning wood, I take in his words. Is it strength that brought me up that mountain? Or weakness? If I'd remained true to myself, I would have stayed on terra firma. Who exactly am I trying to be? My children aren't keen on changing me, so why am I? Maybe, I consider, *maybe*, not every fear is there for the conquering.

After the man leaves, I slip into the big warm bed and feel my body collapse from the day's strain. I relieve my loneliness by watching a nighttime soap opera from Hollywood via iTunes. Of course Connie Britton has a glorious head of hair throughout the episode, and in one scene she sports killer chocolate brown eye shadow with the perfect dash of shimmer. I don't envy her tonight, though. I finally understand for myself what her character already seems to know: time is unstoppable, but so am I. And I don't have to climb a volcano to prove it—not to anyone else, and especially not to myself.

$$\mathcal{S} \quad \mathcal{S} \quad \mathcal{S}$$

Marcia DeSanctis is a journalist and writer whose work has appeared in Vogue, Town & Country, O the Oprah Magazine, The New York Times, The New York Times Magazine, Tin House, Travel & Leisure, The Best Women's Travel Writing 2011 *and* 2012, *and* The Best Travel Writing 2011 *and* 2012. *In 2012, she was the recipient of three Lowell Thomas Awards for Excellence in Travel Journalism, including the Silver award for Travel Journalist of the Year. Visit her at www.marciadesanctis.com.*

ॐ ॐ ॐ

We Wait for the Sun

Fury is more tolerable than fear.

Everyone in the village is congregated at Bahar Dar's dirt airstrip, each of us dripping sweat in the hot afternoon sun. But not one of us is thinking about searching for shade. We've come out of respect to witness Flora's coffin as it is loaded onto an Ethiopian Airlines DC-3. Tropetas is leaving with her, and we don't know if he will ever return. The elderly Greek couple has run our village bakery for decades, and now Flora will be buried in the Greek cemetery in Addis Ababa.

Tropetas beats on his chest as if it's a drum. He's worked himself into a sweat that soaks the hair on his head, absorbs into his cotton shirt, and flies off his body with each successive strike of his powerful fists.

Four men dressed in Ethiopian Airlines khaki uniforms push a rolling luggage carrier across the bare red dirt. On it is the coffin, a simple, ordinary, plywood shipping crate bizarrely festooned with colorful airfreight tags—yellow, green, blue. The tags are in constant motion, cheerfully waving and bobbing about in the mid-afternoon wind coming off Lake Tana, as if celebrating a festive birthday party rather than solemnly mourning a tragic death.

We mill about the airfield, encircling the silver plane, until we move to open a pathway for the metal stairs being wheeled out to meet the plane's passenger door. Tropetas is oblivious to everything except Flora, who's dead and in her coffin, his deep voice locked in a continuous chant. "Flora! Flora! Aaaa-waaa-waaaa-waaaa, Flo-raaa! Flo-raaa!" Over and over, shouting in an anguished voice that booms as if through a megaphone, trying to call her back.

The uniformed men roll the luggage cart to the airplane, pause, and instead of lifting the shipping crate into the cargo hold, slowly, with the dignity of pallbearers, carry it up the stairs and into the passenger section. Tropetas follows close behind, still bellowing his calls to Flora, keeping a rhythm by thumping his chest, one fist after the other. I imagine his public grief must be mixed with fury at his helplessness and failure to protect his wife from attackers.

Early this morning, while the air was still cool and fresh, I first heard the news: Last night, two men invaded their home, assaulted and murdered Flora, and stole their savings. I felt my usual disconnect from yet another harsh village reality and even now, while everyone around me seems completely con-sumed with loud sobbing or funereal wailing—the traditional and respectful observance here of any death—I feel only plain and simple sorrow.

Living here as a Peace Corps Volunteer, I've seen how the Amhara people accept death in this grand, ceremonial way. They embrace loss with a rowdy ritual, for to resist suffer-ing is considered unnatural, against God's plan. Acting out today's sorrow makes it possible to wake tomorrow and to cel-ebrate life with gratitude for a new day.

Never before have I witnessed such dramatic grief, and seeing Tropetas in this state increases my sweaty discomfort under the oppressive sun. Soon the damp hair on my head will drip sweat onto my shoulders. I'm sticky with heat under my arms, between my breasts, and where my thighs touch beneath the hot tent of my skirt.

For me, it seems Flora's death was an aberrant burglary and murder. And since there is no way to make things right, my quiet, modest sorrow is all I can summon. I cannot behave as if I am an Amhara, and I don't want to.

On my walk home, I buy a box of powdered milk at Alem's *suq*, a convenient stop on the way from the airfield.

"These *shifta* are mercenaries. Eritrean mercenaries," Alem informs me from behind his service counter.

I know he's speaking of the robbery and murder. He says it as though something actually has been determined, but this is the first I'm hearing of it, and I'm skeptical. Living in this village, I've learned it is a place where an opinion is allowed to quickly become a fact, where too often nothing will stop conjecture from becoming a false truth.

"Uhmm, Alem," I say, "we're way far south of Eritrea. Why do you think Eritrean *shifta* would be down here in Goj-jam Province?"

He hands me the cardboard milk box and a few coins in change. I'm only half listening for the response, already contemplating my next task. This morning I boiled water and left it on the stove to cool. Right when I get home, I'll try once again to mix the powdered milk with that water, something I have to do at least once a week. But even though I use an eggbeater, I'm never able to eliminate lumps. I'm considering the wisdom of straining them out. But do Sue and I even have a strainer? Maybe we should just give up on the already-stale Kellogg's cornflakes we bring back from Addis Ababa. The cornflakes are no longer crisp, the powdered milk doesn't even taste like real milk, and the lumps are disgusting. Each morning, the only thing truly crunchy about our cornflakes is the sugar we sprinkle on top.

"They don't all stay north and fight in the border war," he says, returning me to the errand I came for. Now he emphasizes his words by loudly spitting a disgusting, thick wad of yellowish sputum onto the hard-packed dirt floor; generations of tribal hatred ooze from this Amharic man. "They raid homes here to pay for their secession movement. Disloyal Eritreans!" He speaks the last words in an obscene growl. "Be careful, *weizerit* Carol," he says, addressing me as Miss Carol for emphasis. "Tonight you must lock your doors and shutters tight."

His words walk with me on the path through the eucalyptus forest to our home. I ask myself: what does the battle for Eritrean secession have to do with me? And of course I lock up at night, but why "must" I tonight?

A widespread, fearful chatter had started at daylight and was soon enhanced by the throng at the airport. Everyone had heard something, seen something, or had suspicions. Was an item missing from someone's compound, or was it simply misplaced? Was a certain chicken taken, or had it merely not returned from its morning or afternoon scavenge? Fewer eggs in the nest—had someone helped himself? The stories got invented and reinvented, but always with one essential question—are the two *shifta* still here? By day's end, it seems suspicion and distrust provide our only defense against harm. This is why a stranger is noticed in this little village. And two strangers together might as well be a dozen.

It's taken until this evening for me to realize how naïve I've been. I should have understood earlier what everyone else already knew: The *shifta* are looking for cash money and American women not only have money, we are also defenseless. All day I've been able to keep the murder in some distant, comfortable perspective, but now I'm uneasy. Am I merely joining in the village hysteria? After all, I'm from someplace else, and I expect to go back there. Since I'm not really from here, I tell myself, I needn't and shouldn't fall into irrational fear.

But I know I will be lying awake tonight, listening for strange sounds. This is a village without telephones and, as far as I know, there's no one to call for help anyway. How ignorant, helpless, and ill-prepared I am. It's not something I grew up with, learning how to protect myself from the most basic of threats—assault and burglary. Would it have been too difficult for the Peace Corps to include the possibility of real dangers during our three-month training? Or did such things not occur to them, just as they had never occurred to me?

We ask the boys to move Sue's bed into my larger room. Neither of us wants to be alone this night. I decide to keep our one sharp kitchen knife in my bed, insisting that Sue arm herself with our scissors. And this is it; we have nothing else to serve as weapons. Sue wants to flip a coin for the knife, but I refuse. I don't believe she would be capable of inflicting a knife wound on anyone. Of myself, I have no doubt—I will. We agree not to turn off my bedroom's single light bulb hanging on a wire in the middle of the ceiling. She has never really stopped being afraid of the dark, and I have to admit, I do feel safer with the light on.

"Please do not worry, Madam," Alimaw says in his new, manly voice, which has thoroughly changed from the boy's voice he had when we took him into our home. He's the oldest and tallest of the three boys who live in our extra room. They're students at our school, all from poor families in distant villages; they do simple chores for us, and in return, they have a place to live and a small allowance. But only Alimaw—who is self-appointed—is the kindly caretaker of the American women Peace Corps teachers.

"But what if they come here?" I ask. "We're all alone out here in the forest."

"We will stay together in the house," he says.

"But what if they are out there?"

"We will know they are here if we hear stones thrown on the roof, Madam."

"What? Why?" This seems totally crazy. "What do stones on the roof mean?"

"*Shifta* make the noise to see if we are home, or if we have mean dogs."

"But we don't have dogs. What do we do?"

"Madam, we turn on all the lights."

"Huh? Why? To show them we are inside?"

"Yes, Madam. And we do not open doors or shutters until dawn."

I'm working hard to control a searing, hot fear as it rises from my gut and enters conscious thought. All my life I've hated feeling afraid or helpless. I don't know which feeling I hate more, but I do know that as this night wears on, I'm getting angry at the *shifta*. And fury is always more tolerable than fear.

We doze off finally and are awakened by *Bang*! *Rattle rattle rattle*. *Plop*! Sue and I both sit up straight in our beds and stare at the ceiling. *Bang*! *Rattle rattle rattle*. The tin roof announces our predators, no mistake. I grasp my knife and have not a shred of hesitancy to use it.

Now at 4 A.M., teeth clenched so hard and tight I fear cracking a tooth, I am determined that I will not die tonight. Not in this country. I refuse to die a victim here. *Bang*! *Rattle rattle rattle*. *Plop*! How many times must I hear this?

Alimaw is deliberately making noise as he moves through the house, turning the lights on, all bare bulbs hanging by wires from the ceiling in each room. There are few glass windows in Bahar Dar—thankfully, none in this house. For the first time, I see the wisdom of sturdy wooden shutters that lock or open only from the inside.

Now—sudden gunshots in the eucalyptus forest. How surprising that they sound like toy cap guns. *Pop pop*. Over and over. And no way to know what is actually happening. No voices. No authorities shouting commands or *shifta* begging for mercy. Suddenly it's quiet again, completely silent, and I know I'll spend the remaining hours of this dark night with teeth clenched in my dry mouth, tense, waiting. Am I safe? In danger? Can I stop being scared now?

"Madam," Alimaw says through my closed door. "The lights are on. Also the porch light."

"Were those gun shots, Alimaw?" I'm speaking so rapidly I fear he may not understand my words.

"Yes, Madam," he says in a calm, hushed voice.

"How do we know if they were *shifta* guns? How do we know if *shifta* are still out there?"

"We wait for the sun, Madam."

Not just this day, but every day, news travels with morning light. Alimaw learns first thing that two *shifta* were captured.

"Oh dear, dear," Sue says in the high-pitched tone she uses when she's frightened. I hear this voice frequently, because Sue is frightened of so many things here, even the bugs.

"Where were they captured, Alimaw?" I ask. I want more information, and quickly.

"Madam, they were very near." Alimaw is hanging his head. He does this when he doesn't want me to read his emotion.

"Oh dear! Oh my goodness!" Sue says in that tremulous soprano, while I say nothing.

Perhaps I should feel relieved by their capture, but a clot of hatred forms in my heart instead.

Alimaw leads us outside to the constantly growing group of neighbors, all heading together in the same direction, as if we're a herd being led to morning water. Walking within the group, I'm absorbed in thoughts of what happened in the little village. Flora's murder and Tropetas' hysterical grief affected each of us. Everyone was threatened, even we who intend to be in Bahar Dar only for our two-year stays.

The traveling mob of villagers, the women's heads covered with their white *shamma* to protect against the damp morning chill, begins to squeeze down into a narrow column of women. Sue and I step in with them, while the men stand apart, tall, slim, and barefoot with stick-thin calves below their once-white jodhpur trousers. The men have wrapped their shoulders and heads in thick, white, cotton *gabi*. Each man has a *doula*, and some lean on them, the tall poles grasped upright in one hand like a staff. Others hold *doula* across their shoulders with both wrists resting over the top, with hanging folds of *gabi* draping below their elbows like feathery white wings.

Even as the column lurches forward in stops and starts, each woman huddles against the women beside her, as well as the women ahead and behind. This tight, close group carries with it the familiar, rancid body odor of the provinces, a combination of the rank smell of *kibbay*, a culinary butter also used as a hairdressing and skin lotion, and the stale smoke of indoor cook fires. At last we reach a jail—the first time I become aware that there is one—a three-sided building, its fourth side open to the elements, enclosed only by iron bars and a locked iron door.

We feel righteously entitled to view our enemy, two despised *shifta*. Though they remain in the morning shadow, far back from the bars, we see their disdainful expressions. They seem arrogant, completely unrepentant, as they stare directly at Sue and me because, as usual, white *firengi*, foreigners, stand out anywhere. I pass along with the line and, never looking away, glare my hatred back at them. This hatred is new to me, rising easily from beneath my breastbone, a concentrated heat that stops and sticks in my throat. Our tormenters are caged like animals, and I want them punished. I want them to see me and my gloating, triumphant sneer.

* * *

The next morning, I'm walking to school early to prepare for another week of teaching and am surprised to see the village gathered again, this time on the bare, open land between the airstrip and our school. What they are looking at is too awful to believe. And in this instant I know what everyone must have known and understood would happen, even though I didn't.

Suddenly breathless, I can no longer silently bear the painful pounding in my chest. "Ahg. Uhg." It is all I can say, repeating in rhythm with my heart. My lungs stop. And then I'm panting, out of breath, and I want only to be able to move my feet, to run away as fast as I can and pretend I never saw this. At the same time, I truly cannot believe that what I am seeing is real. I try to take it in with small, quick glances—two *shifta*, a rope tight around each broken neck, heads off-kilter from their bodies, trousers soiled by the emptying of bowel and bladder.

But yes, it is real, and I understand exactly why they have been left to hang here for these hours since dawn, the time of execution. It is hard to do, but at last I am able to look at them, dangling from ropes attached to newly erected scaffolds. We stand together, all of us staring at the dead men, considering what each of us understands and feels about what has happened here. Happened to us, and to our village.

How is it I can feel glad? I wouldn't say happy, just glad, satisfied to see those men hanging by their necks, dead, knowing they cannot harm me. Primal revenge.

So much at once. Anger. Hate. Revenge. Satisfaction. Worse, I have learned two terrible things: I could kill to save myself; I could get over feeling bad about doing that.

So here we stand, we who lusted for revenge, and now we're avenged, satisfied that two men are dead. But for me, this bright satisfaction suddenly tarnishes, because I am also deeply, deeply ashamed.

🐾 🐾 🐾

Carol Beddo, a Peace Corps Volunteer in Ethiopia, 1964–1966, returned to her Peace Corps station in 2003. Flooded with memories, she began to wonder: Who was that young woman? While writing those memories, Carol is coming to understand how the Peace Corps experience provided a foundation for the rest of her life as a community activist and as a consultant in public policy, political campaigns, and elections. Numerous personal essays have been published in the San Jose Mercury News. Her Peace Corps stories have also appeared in anthologies: The Best Travel Writing *and* One Hand Does Not Catch a Buffalo: 50 Years Of Peace Corps Stories. *The Peace Corps anthology received the Silver IPPY (Independent Publisher Book Awards) for travel essays in 2011. "We Wait for the Sun" won a gold Solas Award in 2012 for Travel Memoir.*

❧ ❧ ❧

Half-Baked Decisions

Moments ride on currents. If you don't act,
you'll just be tossed along.

I awoke to the friendly chirping of my roommate, the gecko clinging to the flimsy wall of my palm-frond hut, and tossed on a bikini. No need to shower; the ocean was my bath, and salt and sand my natural exfoliants. My hut neighbor, the Dutch man, stopped by for a smoke. He was trying to quit, so he was having me hold his ciggies and ration accordingly. I didn't think he was smoking any less, but I was getting my fill of longwinded existential conversations for which I had no answers.

I ate breakfast on a sprawling wooden deck with swaying hammocks and boldly colored triangle cushions, overlooking the blue-green water of the Gulf of Thailand. I'd been staying in this island hut for a week now, waiting for my next teaching contract to begin, and my life was starting to resemble a photo-shopped screensaver. I listened to Bob Marley, sipped bitter coffee sweetened with thick condensed milk, munched slightly burnt toast, and contemplated how I'd spend the rest of my day in Paradise. And then I went to the Internet café, where Paradise fell apart.

There was the usual email:

Spam—Gran sends her love along with a coupon for penile implants!

Family—somewhat concerned inquiries as to where I am exactly?

Friends—Pam and Steve got engaged; Tim and Tina had a baby; Bobby and Jen bought a new home.

Skip, skip, skip, and then STOP. There it was sitting harmlessly in my inbox. From Him.

I alternated between a trigger-happy urge to fire open the letter and some sort of frozen but jerky paralysis. Like a video buffering. Finally, slowly, I clicked, and read, until the annoying pounding in my heart stopped at one sentence.

Allison and I got married.

Tears instantly welled in the corners of my eyes. Suddenly chilly, I pulled a ratty old gray sweatshirt from my beach bag and wrapped it around my body like a protective shield. Why was I reacting like this? It had been two years. I pulled the sweatshirt tighter.

Nigel was a handsome man. I could spout clichés for days about his lanky athletic frame, his hair soft like butter, eyes bluer than the Gulf of Thailand, voice smooth as warm honey. I won't. I also won't mention his skin—silky, or his teeth—gleaming, or his wickedly charismatic smile.

We'd spent a summer together in Korea. I met him on my second day there, he broke up with his girlfriend on the third day, and was my boyfriend by the fourth. By the end of the week we hadn't left his bed. Life was good. So good, in fact, that six months later I was meeting him in Thailand. He and his best friend were heading there as they traveled though China and other parts of Southeast Asia. It was unfortunate that we had to be separated for six weeks while I finished my teaching contract, but it would be O.K., we said—six weeks wasn't long at all.

Looking back, there were signs. There always are.

Sign One: He stopped writing. For which, of course, there could have been any number of plausible explanations. An elephant could have stepped on his laptop, or there might have been no Internet at the Kung Fu monastery. Then one day I got a bunch of emails all at once.

Sign Two: The emails weren't meant for me. They were addressed to three Swedish whores he'd met at a Shanghai McDonald's. (O.K., I don't actually know if they were whores, but it's my story, so whores it is.)

Sign Three: What was he doing at McDonald's? He hated McDonald's. Said it was bad for his skin. His silky skin.

I could have let these flashing neon signs of relationship failure get to me. Instead I boarded a plane as planned and landed six hours later in the steaming city of Bangkok.

Nigel was there to greet me. The next day we were on an island downing fresh mango smoothies and frolicking in the sand. On the third day he broke up with me in the shower. By the end of the week he was off to Vietnam to see about his Scandinavian sluts, and I was on an overnight train to Laos with his best friend Sean.

How did this happen? I'm sure Sean was thinking exactly that as he boarded the train with his friend's sobbing ex-girlfriend. We didn't know each other well, and I really should have just gone home. But home was too far from Nigel, who was at least still in the same time zone, give or take an hour.

I cried a lot in the beginning. Sometimes I sat by the Nam Song River and cried while naked children splashed in the water with their pet cows. Other times I cried on the porch of our guesthouse as Sean strummed his guitar and made up sad lyrics. He had a sweet voice, calm like a yogi. I was surprised. Sean had a reputation for being a bit of a ladies' man, yet here he was content to idly strum beside a sobbing mess. It wasn't fair that he got stuck with me in the breakup, especially when he could be out chasing Swedish tail. I told him as much.

"It's not fair that you got stuck with me in the breakup. You should be out chasing Swedish tail."

"Nah. I'm tired of that," he replied, then continued to hum and strum along.

We became inseparable. Our days were picnics of crusty baguette sandwiches and orange Fantas, hikes through rice paddies and dusty two-chicken towns, and idyllic floats down the river in big rubber inner tubes, stopping at times to grab a semi-cold beer from an industrious local who had set up shop where the current slowed. But I still thought of Nigel, and talked about him to the only person who would listen.

"He's just not baked yet," Sean said as we bobbed along in the water. "He's like a cookie. He looks ready. He's all crispy golden, smells delicious. But don't be fooled, he just needs more time in the oven. He's still gooey on the inside."

I smiled. *Sean must be baked himself*, I thought. *Only a guy baked out of his mind could come up with a hippie metaphor like that.* The joint hanging lazily out of his mouth was also a giveaway.

After about a week in the small town of Vang Vieng, it was time to move on. We'd heard of a gibbon refuge in the far northern corner of Laos near the border of China and Burma, where guests could sleep in a tree house. This little bit of backpacker folklore proved too enticing for us to ignore.

In every town we stopped, somebody knew something about the gibbons. An eighteen-year-old German girl escorting a bear to Cambodia pointed us in one direction. A local man selling warm soy milk in a plastic bag pointed us in another. Our passage through Laos resembled one of those old Family Circus comics, loop-the-loops and detours galore. Neither of us seemed to mind. We just liked going, so we went.

* * *

Transportation in Laos falls into one of three categories:

Option One: Bus. Usually donated from another country that deemed it no longer safe to operate. Holes in floorboards allow for breezy airflow! (A perk when your window won't open.) Prone to breaking down in the most inconvenient locations.

Option Two: Minivan. Always advertised with air-conditioning. Doesn't mention air-conditioning is broken. Plastic stools and chairs crammed in for extra seat space! Prone to breaking down in the most inconvenient locations.

Option Three: Pick-up truck. Popular with chickens and pigs. Sturdier livestock may be used as a footrest. Passenger participation required on muddy steep inclines—you can either jump out and push, or stand on the back bumper hopping up and down to create traction. I prefer the latter. When the pick-up does take off, however, if you don't leap back in quickly enough, you're walking. Prone to breaking down in the most inconvenient locations.

It had been a minivan day. Sean's plastic chair fell apart not long into the journey, and the minivan soon followed suit. We were exhausted when we finally arrived in a tiny one road town that began, I believe, with the letter D. (We'd been to so many by this point.) But it was there that we received our most promising news.

"Oh, yes. Of course. The gibbons! You are not far. Just go to Huay Xai. Ask for the French man," the owner of our guesthouse informed us, happy to have guests presenting such tourism quandaries.

"Wonderful news. How do we get there?" I asked.

"You can take a bus," he responded helpfully.

"Is there an actual road?" I had come to understand that roads were more like ideas.

"Of course. A very good road," he declared. Sean and I let out a collective sigh of relief.

"They are building it now!"

Sean and I opted for the slow boat up the Mekong. We sat on the deck watching the scenery: mostly jungle, with small pockets of fishing villages dotting the landscape. I desperately wanted to see an elephant emerge triumphantly from the dense tropical foliage. It didn't happen, so Sean wrote a song about it happening instead. We slept that night in a village lit entirely by candles. There was no electricity, but as I lay down beside him on a candle-lined road to gaze at stars, I felt a buzz.

We eventually made it to the gibbon tree house. The proprietor gave us a bottle of local hooch, two zip-line harnesses— the only way in and out of the tree—and a hearty, "See ya!" I loved Southeast Asia with its blatant disregard for pesky safety regulations.

Our companion in the tree house was a spirited primate named Willy. He was a baby black-crested gibbon with the face of a little old fuzzy man. He wore a blue cast on his leg because he'd recently fallen out of the tree and broken it. Willy liked to cuddle, and when he wasn't cuddling, he enjoyed taking my personal possessions and dropping them over the side for the rooting pigs far below. It was like having a really hairy toddler around. I could never get mad at the little guy, though. Poachers had killed his parents. Willy clung to me like a two-year-old, then stared longingly into the rainforest when he heard the cry of his fellow kind. He didn't know where he belonged.

That night Sean and I slept on a futon mattress in the master bedroom. The bedroom was perched in the tiptop of the tree, above the living room, kitchen, and bathroom. There were no walls, just 180 degrees of inky black jungle night and the occasional terrifying thud and scamper of creatures lurking amongst us. Then, suddenly, the sky filled with little bits of dancing light. I'd never seen anything like it—I didn't know what I was looking at.

Sean pulled me from the bed. "Fireflies," he explained. He walked me to the railing, and then wrapped his arms around me. I leaned back into him. A sprinkling of fairy lights filled the darkness all around. I can't recall how long we stood there in silence. Five minutes, forever.

Days later we arrived at the northern border crossing of Thailand and Laos. Already a month had passed, and by this time we had spent almost every moment together. Most people assumed we were a couple, and in the beginning I liked to joke that I was going to make a t-shirt that read: "I'm not with him, but he's a really great guy!" At some point in the month I stopped making that joke. And at some point in the month we also abandoned the pretense of making friends with fellow travelers, preferring our own company. We read together, played endless games of chess, sketched each other's faces, even held hands. We often shared a bed, sleeping in little more than our underwear. It was intimate, yet innocent.

At immigration I handed over my passport and prepared to board the narrow wooden boat that would take us to the Thai side. Sean fiddled in his backpack. Soon he had the entire contents emptied on the ground.

"What's the problem?" I asked.

"My passport. It's gone," he responded in his typically relaxed manner. "We'll just have to go back to Vientiane. To the embassy."

He said it so casually: *we'll*. He and I will both go together. It was an easy assumption to make. I froze. Hesitated. Just for an instant, but he sensed it.

"Nah, it's cool. I'll go back," he said, slowly zipping up his pack. "You go on."

He made it so easy for me. He knew about the email I'd gotten from Nigel. He knew Nigel would be in Bangkok for the next two days, and that I wanted to be there. There was no doubt in my mind that if I'd been the one to lose my passport, he would have stayed by my side.

I got in the boat, and Sean didn't. In the middle of the river, I was in the middle of nowhere. Halfway between Laos and Thailand. Halfway between Sean and Nigel—the very last moment where I could turn in any direction. But moments ride on currents. If you don't act, you'll just be tossed along.

I climbed out of the boat in Thailand, and looked back to Laos. Clinging to the idea of Nigel, yet longing for Sean. I didn't know where I belonged.

It was then that I remembered. I was still wearing his ratty gray sweatshirt.

ॐ ॐ ॐ

When she's not somewhere else, Sarah Katin can be found in her southern California office (the cushy chair by the window at the café du jour) where she writes for film and television. Her travel essays have been featured in The Best Women's Travel Writing *series,* Leave the Lipstick, Take the Iguana: Funny Travel Stories *and* Strange Packing Tips*, and various print and online magazines. She's currently in Borneo fulfilling her childhood dream of procuring an orangutan sidekick.*

❧ ❧ ❧

The Road to Wounded Knee

There is no question that American life is in the process
of changing, but, as always in human history, it carries
some of the past along with it.
— *John Steinbeck*

On our way into town we passed billboards offering $6.99
breakfast platters and genuine leather wrangling gloves.
Our sixteen-seat puddle jumper had landed not even an hour
before, but my mother was already well into her stories of
childhood on the prairie. Growing up not far from here, she
said, in a single gas station town named Murdo, she and my
grandparents had dreamt of thunderheads: black clouds that
divined themselves out of indigo and tore across the sky feeding thirsty crops, then disappearing only slightly slower than
they'd materialized. Like the work of an angry but loving
God.

I saw the eyes before the body: two reflective dots in the
dark, one on top of the other. *Bump*. My mother didn't see it
in time either. A deer.

"It was already dead," she said. She was sure of it.

We had arrived in Rapid City just as the wide sky faded
from purple to black and the tall blonde grass disappeared into
the night. After the soothing golden lights of San Francisco,

South Dakota felt isolated and cold. I had never been here, but I knew it—if only from the stories passed down from my mother, and its residue in my blood.

Our plan was to sleep in an original homestead in a prairie outside of town; we'd booked it through the owner, a corn farmer, thinking it would give us a sense of local history. But when we creaked the weighty door open, we took the unwelcoming stench of kerosene and dank wood, and the presence of a terrified mouse and a half-dead beetle twitching on the dirt floor, as omens. We checked into the nearest motel, where we sought refuge in stiff hotel sheets that smelled of chlorine while trains whistled in the distance throughout the night.

In the morning while we dressed, I drank weak coffee with powdered creamer—poor fuel for the day ahead. My mother slipped on a pair of dangly turquoise earrings she had bought from a Lakota man at a jewelry show in California, then twisted her long hair into a ponytail.

"South Dakotans don't wear dresses," she said, wagging her finger at me. She handed me a pair of jeans and a white shirt, and looked satisfied when I put them on. "Now you look like a local."

Then we loaded our rented nickel-colored Impala with the bulky suitcases we had hauled from San Francisco and headed into the prairie, unsure of exactly what to expect on our journey to Wounded Knee.

My mother first proposed this trip as a mother-daughter bonding pilgrimage to our homeland, to see the town where she was born and reconnect with our roots. But I knew her primary agenda was to face the horrors she'd heard about at Pine Ridge. Maybe to understand it better. Maybe to purge herself of the demons that plagued her.

Pine Ridge, the Indian reservation that encompasses Wounded Knee, sits in southwestern South Dakota, larger than the state of Delaware. I understood Pine Ridge in two ways: from my family's guilt-colored stories, and in extreme, almost impossible, mathematical figures: the poorest region in the U.S., eighty percent unemployment, ninety percent alcoholism (it's not unusual for kids to start drinking when they're six), and the highest suicide rate in the nation. There's no bank, there are almost no businesses, and aside from a new Subway, vegetables are basically nonexistent, resulting in a fifty percent incidence of diabetes.

In 1906, my great-grandparents homesteaded in Murdo, a two-hour drive east of Rapid City and three hours from Wounded Knee. It wasn't until my mother, aunt, and grand-parents moved to California in the 1960s that they realized homesteading in South Dakota had displaced the Native Americans who were living in the area, by forcing them onto the Pine Ridge Indian Reservation, which set them on a fast track to poverty, disease, and dysfunction.

As we rolled across the Pine Ridge reservation line, swollen gray clouds sagged in the sky, ready to break. We passed a billboard reading, CATCH THE WINNING SPIRIT AT PRAIRIE WIND CASINO! A thick purple bug splattered on the windshield, black skid marks veered off the road in front of us, then we hung a right on Snake Butte Road.

Occasional dirt driveways branched off the main path and disappeared into the prairie. Wooden crosses stood taller than any house in sight, and long-abandoned homesteads had been weathered down to splinters in the dirt. Other structures resembling homes with makeshift tin roofs appeared at random, and I would have wondered if anyone still lived in them if not for the old Ford pickups in the driveways.

The anti-drug signs that punctuated our path with astonishing volume and frequency—PLEASE DON'T BRING DRUGS INTO OUR TOWN! were more pleas than authoritative statements. We had yet to see a person.

As we passed Little Wound High School, my mother commented proudly that she donated money regularly. Oglala Lakota College, HOME OF THE BRAVEHEARTS, whipped by on our right. Five wild horses roamed the campus, but there wasn't a human in sight. Every few feet there was something to tug at our hearts and our fears—a dead cow on the side of the road, ribs protruding from a horse's thin side—and I saw that here, it was as bad as my mother thought it would be, if not worse. It was a place that knew it had been forgotten.

It was already noon, and the temperature hadn't broken 45 degrees. Moisture collected on the windshield and formed bead-sized drops against the wind as the clouds above turned from gray to livid. I was underdressed, wearing only jeans, a light jacket, and a thin scarf that was more accessory than function. My mother was better prepared in a heavy black cotton jacket, the collar inching up her neck. I surrendered my iPod for the randomness of the radio, and Johnny Cash's "Hang My Head" droned in and out. Then we turned into a town named Kyle. There were no fences around the houses. No flags. No welcome mats. Gaunt dogs flopped in yards next to rusty propane tanks. I saw clotheslines swinging loose and empty, an idle trampoline, an unoccupied wheelchair. A hulking black Suburban rumbled in a driveway and two men, not in uniform, escorted a cuffed man with a shiny black ponytail into the SUV.

"As a country," my mother said, turning down the radio, "we don't help them. Because in order to do so, we'd first have to look at ourselves and acknowledge what we've done. And we don't yet have the courage to do that."

I knew my mother was approaching her soapbox. I quickly glanced at her before staring back out the window. Though she was wearing her usual brown scrunchy and matching eye shadow, everything else about her seemed different. Back home, where she worked as a psychology professor, she was known for her disarming Midwestern sense of humor and her Zen outlook on life. Her intellectual curiosity and grace were the highlight of any dinner party she attended (that, and whatever decadent chocolate desert she'd baked). But here, she seemed tense, as if anticipating something I didn't know was coming. She wrung the steering wheel with her hands and repeatedly checked the rearview mirror. And on the topic of Native American reservations, she spoke with an evangelist's tongue.

Listening to her, I felt a sudden tinge of shame: I was a journalist—why had I never publicly acknowledged the situation here?

"The past is bad enough," she continued. "But what's worse is that we live based on a lie of people who are still here and living. My family didn't know they were taking away land from other people when they homesteaded, but the schools do now, and they still don't teach it that way." Then in her usual good-natured way, she joked, "O.K., that's my sermon for today," and veered back onto the main highway.

We pulled up to Wounded Knee with blood on our tires— evidence of the deer from the night before—and walked to the mound where two hundred Indians were killed and buried in 1890, in one of the bloodiest massacres in American history. That was sixteen years before my family homesteaded 150 miles away.

My mother's demeanor changed when we approached the entrance. She looked calm and present as we stood alone above the shallow mass grave. But it wasn't what I expected an important historical site to look like. There was no granite memorial wall or line of tourists taking photos—only plastic and moldy wooden crosses sprouting from loose dirt. Some tombstones bore names like TWO TWO, and RESPECTS NOTHING. Others were just uninscribed stones protruding from the dirt.

The ground was littered with fake plastic neon flowers, Sprite bottles, and Slim Jim wrappers, which had gently corroded over many harsh winters.

FAGS, DAVE EATS HAPPY OUT, and YOU'RE ALL LITTLE KIDS was scrawled on a post near the entrance.

Down the hill a Native American teenage girl with jet-black hair was hoofing it up the hill in our direction, stopping every few steps to rest her elbow on her knee and glance up at us. When she got to the top she approached my mother, who was carefully reading one of the tombstones.

I waded through the piles of stone and trash, heading toward them. The girl was wearing a black puffy FUBU jacket with flared jeans and Sketchers. When I reached them, she didn't turn to acknowledge my presence. Her clay-colored cheeks were flushed pink and she scrunched her jacket sleeves to her elbows, revealing two armfuls of tattoos. She was deeply engrossed in a story she was telling my mother, who was all ears. The girl didn't avert her eyes from my mother's once, not even as the wind lashed leaves and M&M wrappers around us.

"You see, I started college—I wanted to go to school and be smart, you know? Like, I wanna get outta this place. But my grandma—she had this foot infection my first semester. I mean, I was the first one to even graduate high school in my family—and then my grandma, she stepped on this piece of glass. She's diabetic, and the infection spread faster than they could treat it, so they amputated her leg at the knee. She survived, but how was she supposed to cook fry bread and sweep the house with one leg, right? So I had to drop out. To take care of the rest of the household, you know." My mother nodded.

In the girl's right hand was a Ziploc baggie filled with dream catchers and little beaded bracelets, and I noticed how beautiful and timeless her face looked. I knew my Mother would have emptied her wallet if given the chance, if the girl just asked.

But something felt off, and I was suddenly acutely aware of how far we were from anyone who would care if something happened to us. I tugged at her coat sleeve and told her we should go. When we turned around three men were standing behind us dressed in ponchos and dirt-splotched jeans. One said something to the girl, but I couldn't make out what. He was in a daze, his eyes vacant and his words crashing into his few teeth.

"Man, Buddy, not yet, man." She spat the words, then kicked the dirt.

I felt panicky. "Mom, we need to go," I said, but she shot me a glance like I was the rude guest at a dinner party, then turned back to the girl.

"As I was saying, I really just want to go back to school—" her words were now competing with faint droning and heavy breathing noises coming from behind us.

She pointed to a run-down wooden building at the bottom of the hill. Its planks splintered in different directions, and it was corroded like a decayed tooth on the north end. "We can give you a tour of our medicine house, in that building down there, get to see what real life is like in Pine Ridge, not the tourist draw of Wounded Knee. Don't you want to know what we Indians actually live like here?"

My mother's eyes lit up as she opened her mouth, undoubtedly to say, "yes."

I sensed that if we were about to be taken, financially or physically, on the mound of Wounded Knee, my mother would have welcomed it as a sacrifice, some kind of retribution.

"I'm sorry, we need to go, but thanks," I said, my voice trembling.

As we turned to leave, one of the men whispered after us, his voice coming from another dimension—deep and hollow with no trace of inflection—"Welcome to Wounded Knee," in a way I knew would haunt me.

My mother reluctantly headed for the car with me, but couldn't help glancing back at them.

As we left Wounded Knee and headed toward Murdo to see my mother's childhood home, we passed more signs: GOD SO LOVED YOU and WHY DIE?

Then on the border leaving Pine Ridge, we approached the biggest billboard yet: a picture of Mt. Rushmore and the headline, COME HEAR THE PATRIOTIC STORY OF AMERICA!!! I shifted uncomfortably in my seat.

We were silent, both staring at the road that stretched infinitely in front of us. In the distance, thunderheads rolled through the sky; the grass seemed to dance for the oncoming rain. I turned to my mother to comment on the weather, and maybe the sign, but something in her expression stopped me— she looked almost blissful. Her grip on the steering wheel loosened as she focused her gaze on the road ahead. I admired the way her turquoise earrings reflected the light and the faint but distinct smile that started to form on her face. I realized that we both had a new—if different—understanding of Wounded Knee. Then the sky opened and the rain started, and we drove on.

Jenna Scatena is a writer and editor based in San Francisco. She earned her B.A. in Nonfiction Writing from Ithaca College and is currently the Associate Editor at San Francisco magazine, where she covers travel and city life. She also leads journalism training seminars at California colleges through Campus Progress. Her work has appeared in San Francisco magazine, Sunset, Via, and The Huffington Post, among others. When she's not traveling to new places, she can be found exploring the nooks and crannies of San Francisco on her red scooter.

༚ ༚ ༚

The Saffron Rabbit

Nothing is too much trouble if it turns out
the way it should.
— *Julia Child*

"You are late," my landlady's granddaughter Ana announces as I top the stairs, my lungs on fire from sprinting through the streets of Madrid. Ana and her grandmother, Señora Valentina, hover near the door of my apartment. In her hand the elderly woman holds a raised polished black cane, which explains the insistent rapping I heard echoing through the stairwell during my five-flight climb.

"I'm so sorry," I reply in English between gasps. My hands fumble with the keys, tremors still coursing through me from the adrenaline of the past hour. That Señora has a key and could have opened the door herself is a thought I keep to myself.

The key slides in the lock; however, the door is old and opening it requires lifting the knob while twisting the handle and pushing. It's a skill my roommate Kaylie and I have mastered over the past several weeks—succeeding even after too much sangria—but today I can't seem to find the correct combination. The women watch my struggle in silence.

"I'm so sorry," I repeat, this time in Spanish. Behind me I hear Señora snort and tap her cane, the textured silver handle cupped in her blue-veined hands. Although no one has said it, I understand that my attempts at Castilian offend her. But I think my grip on the language has at least tightened a little, thanks in part to her weekly cooking lessons—which began against my will.

"You do not know how to cook," Ana said when I answered the door a few weeks ago, just as the last minutes before siesta slipped away. Señora Valentina, dressed all in black and looking just over me despite being almost a full head shorter, rattled something in Spanish that seemed directed at neither me nor Ana.

"She has come to teach you."

Señora gave a brisk nod of her head, using her cane to push open the door and shove past me. I jumped clear—my reflexes had sharpened after multiple encounters with well-aimed canes from elderly Madrid ladies who wanted my place in line, my seat in the park, or the payphone I was using. As she hobbled the few feet into the apartment's sliver of a kitchen, I looked to Ana for explanation.

"My father saw your frozen lunch yesterday," she offered before following her grandmother. The previous week Kaylie and I had discovered that we couldn't get the pilot to light and called the scrawled number on the bottom of our typewritten lease. A girl on the other end told Kaylie someone would fix it. A week of cold showers later, a middle-aged man arrived, a canvas satchel dangling from his willow-branch hands. The visit was brief, less than ten minutes. As he was leaving, he saw me preparing a tray of frozen empanadas, my go-to meal on the days I chose to stay home and read instead of sit for hours at lunch.

I followed Ana and her grandmother into the kitchen like a curious puppy, nosing into the edge of the room, unsure of where to stand or how things would proceed. Ana set a rough beige cloth bag on the counter, and Señora Valentina poked it with her cane, spitting her words in my direction for the first time.

"Unpack the groceries," Ana translated.

I spent the next hour with two other women in a one-person kitchen, standing just out of range of Señora's cane as she grumbled orders in Spanish, which Ana then translated, and I executed. Even with my cane-alert reflexes, I still felt it graze my hand when I made a movement that displeased her, such as attempting to crumble the stale bread she brought for the gazpacho base instead of cubing it as I'd been instructed. By hour's end, my back and hands ached from standing in the same position. But Ana's translation style, directive and never referencing that she was speaking for someone else, had ceased to feel strange, and the result of my labors—deep crimson and smelling of summer—filled a tall glass pitcher.

Señora nudged me aside with her cane and leaned close to the pitcher, one eye shut as she peered through the etched glass. Her finger stabbed the red liquid and brought it to her lips. Instead of placing the finger in her mouth, she darted her tongue out, as if fearing poison. Then finally she rubbed her gazpacho-coated finger against her thumb.

One sharp whack of the cane on the floor, one definitive nod of her salt-and-pepper wire-haired head.

"It is good," Ana confirmed, interpreter of gestures as well as words.

By then Señora was at the front door, her finger wiped clean on a cornflower handkerchief pulled from her sleeve. Ana followed behind, translating her grandmother's message: she would return for another lesson next week. Then they vanished into the hallway, leaving me staring bewildered at my messy kitchen, which was still and silent now, and somehow transformed. Curious, I dipped a finger into my gazpacho. It was fresh and bright, the sweet tomato mingling with spices and a subtle tang of vinegar. Without a doubt, it was the best thing I'd ever cooked. I had to stop myself from drinking it straight from the pitcher.

True to her word, Señora returned the following Wednesday with Ana at her side. And every Wednesday after that. Each lesson was a variation on the first—bag of groceries, grumbled Spanish instructions, Ana's flat translations, and a tasting. The tastings were like standing once again in front of my acting teacher after an emotional performance: my nerves alert in the desperate hope for praise while the nagging voice in my head braced for disappointment. Sometimes I would receive the nod of approval. Sometimes not.

"You season like an Englishman," Senora said one day after tasting my seafood stew. What that meant exactly I had no idea—but judging from her wrinkled nose and pursed lips, it wasn't something to which I should aspire. Asking for clarification, however, was unthinkable; I quickly learned during our second lesson not to question, chatter, make her repeat instructions, or argue.

When Señora arrived the next Wednesday, I saw pork in the shopping bag and balked.

"I'm sorry, but I don't eat meat," I told Ana. Because of my surprise at the first lesson and the absence of meat in gazpacho, I'd somehow forgotten to mention that crucial bit of information. As soon as the words left my mouth, I wished I could call them back like an ill-behaved dog.

Ana just looked at me like I'd announced I collect used toothbrushes.

"*Ella no come carne*," she whispered to her grandmother, holding her hand over her mouth like an aside from a Shakespearean comedy. Señora's expression was unchanged; instead, she spat out a string of machine-gun words that defied my meager translation skills. Then Ana did something that would become familiar in the coming weeks—edit Señora's tirades into a single sentence. As my Spanish improved, I was grateful to Ana for shielding me from the uncensored diatribes, as the few words I did catch terrified me.

"You don't have to eat it to cook it. Someday your husband will thank her."

The decision had been made that I would cook meat. This was something Kaylie (who found reasons to vacate during the lessons) came to appreciate when she returned to my creations every Wednesday. Soon our classmates, hearing of my cooking lessons, also started dropping by to sample the tortillas, *cocido madrileño*, *fabada*, and *torrijas*. Anchovies became a staple in our apartment after a smashing reception of the marinated *tapas* I made one afternoon; Kaylie kept replenishing our fresh anchovy stock, and friends who stopped by requested them by name. Though I was all alone when it came to boning and preparing them, I saw no end of volunteer tasters.

Back home in Texas, the women of my family were wonderful cooks. That gene seemed to have skipped me—I lacked intuition to follow even basic recipes like meatloaf. My mother and grandmother spent their evenings in the kitchen, transforming love into food without even the need for cookbooks. Once, they translated a generations-old recipe for Prince of Wales cake with instructions like "enough flour to make a cake" into a delectable masterpiece. I, on the other hand, had been known to serve boxed mac and cheese that had much in common with glue. My sophomore year, I almost set fire to my dorm room attempting ramen noodles.

But under the strict tutelage of Señora, my knife skills improved. I developed a hand for seasoning, a prejudice against any olive oil not Spanish, and a passion for saffron. My culinary intuition blossomed, as did my Spanish. Despite the apprehension I felt during each lesson and my fear of disappointing or angering Señora, Wednesdays became the highlight of my week. Outside the kitchen I was just an American student, an observer who participated in superficial ways. My academic class provided useless phrases to parrot in an attempt to refine my accent and teach conjugations. The school sponsored trips to museums and palaces to show us the history of Spain. It was all interesting and inspiring, but it also made me feel separate, like being shown pictures from a book.

Inside the kitchen, I was invited into Spanish life. Señora, while strict, was generous with her time and food—each week she brought a bag of groceries. When I offered to do the shopping for the next lesson, she waved me off.

"You buy frozen food—you know nothing about quality," Ana translated. When I asked to pay for the groceries, she stared at me for a long moment, thumped her cane, and turned to leave. Ana shook her head slightly, my cue to drop the subject.

And so it is with distress that I have raced from the Instituto Internacional to my apartment on this Wednesday, feeling with each passing minute, even at a distance, Señora's escalating agitation.

When the lock finally gives, I almost fall into the apartment, righting myself just before I tumble into the china cabinet at the edge of the living room.

As Ana and Señora head to the kitchen, I toss my black messenger bag on the bed in my box room, scoop up a towel Kaylie's left on the floor, pitch it into her bedroom, and shut the door. I don't need a repeat of the day Señora found a bra forgotten on the bathroom sink. ("This is not a brothel," Ana translated, avoiding my eyes.)

In the kitchen, I close the window to the airshaft, having learned my lesson during the fish stew tutorial—my clothes drying on the line outside stank of boiled ocean when I retrieved them later. Even with the window closed, I can hear a flurry of guitar from the aspiring *tocadores* across the way.

Señora's shopping bag today contains onions, garlic, a glass vial of saffron, herbs bundled in twine, a bottle of white wine, and something wrapped in brown paper. Even though over the weeks Kaylie and I have started stocking our once-bare kitchen with several of these items, Señora never asks if I have any of the required ingredients, and I don't want to insult her generosity by bringing it up.

"Today you will prepare rabbit," Ana says.

This is an ingredient I do not have on hand.

"Chop the onions."

My nerves are still jumping around, and the cleaver, one of three knives in our kitchen, wavers as I begin chopping. I soon find my rhythm, watching it rise and fall through the onion, thudding in time to the delicate guitar notes. But my mind replays the explosion of just a few hours ago, over and over, as if it's still ringing in my ears.

I was in Spanish class when I heard the detonation—the boom of lightning striking metal, razoring it into pieces, a knife into my eardrums. I immediately catalogued it in my brain as a new sound, like the first time I heard a tornado.

My classmates and I rushed to the windows, which always stayed open in lieu of central air conditioning—but all we saw were people rushing in two directions—both toward and away from the rumble. Soon we were herded by a flustered older man away from the windows, out the room, and into the windowless library that was already filling with students. We hadn't all gathered in one room since the orientation on our first day in Spain, and for an hour we flitted around like guests at a frantic cocktail party, seeking information. But no one had any, so all we could do was speculate.

Finally we were released. There was, said the administrators, a minor incident with a car blowing up: we shouldn't worry.

Kaylie fell into step with me on the staircase.

"It was a car bomb," she said in an undertone.

"What?" I replied, my stomach twisting.

"A car bomb, couple of miles from here. They think it was some Basque group, but they can't be sure."

I must have looked like I didn't believe her.

She gripped my arm. "My professor told me. They don't want us to know because they think we'll tell our parents."

"Are people dead?" As I said it—*dead*—I could feel my heartbeat in the tip of my tongue.

Kaylie shrugged. "I didn't think to ask."

In my kitchen, sautéing onions, I debate whether to ask Ana or Señora Valentina about it. Perhaps they can explain who, how, why. But I'm afraid to ask, in part because I'm afraid of the answers. Instead I powder the saffron between my fingers, watch as the tips become stained burnt orange, notice the color beneath my nails. The powder drifts into the hot water, tinting it a deep gold, and I stir.

In the brown paper is a rabbit: shiny, pink, and blessedly in pieces with no sign of a head. I can stomach fish heads by now, but I'm not ready for mammals. Arranging all the pieces of rabbit in the pan to fry, as I've been instructed, is more difficult than I anticipate, and the cane brushes my elbow.

Distracted, I glance over my shoulder at Señora. She isn't looking at me, focused instead on the pan. Her eyes, usually intense and all-seeing, lack their normal laser focus. It's as if she sees not the pan but through it. When she realizes I'm looking at her, the cane jerks into my arm, hard.

"Pay attention or you will burn it."

Ana stands, as always, just to Señora's right elbow, reciting. Her eyes don't stray; she never checks her watch, though I imagine there are a hundred places she'd rather be. Or maybe not. Out of the corner of my eye during last week's lesson, I glimpsed Señora's hand caressing one of her curls. Ana leaned her head just so, her cheek brushing her grandmother's fingers. I thought of my own grandmother, and our own relationship. We'd always been close, but somehow it would never have occurred to me to dedicate so much of my time to her needs, as Ana does with Señora.

Once the rabbit is covered, snug in its pan with thyme and wine and left to simmer, Señora heads to the back of the apartment to use the restroom, and Ana and I are alone for the third time in our short acquaintance. The first time I learned that she's a college student as well, studying art history, even though her family doesn't approve. The second time she advised I visit the Victor Hugo exhibit at the Thyssen-Bornemisza.

"That Hugo exhibit was amazing," I begin, my eyes trained on the pan, alert for any signs of over-boiling. "Thanks for telling me about it."

"You are welcome," she replies. Her voice changes when she speaks for herself; it's softer, more musical in cadence.

"The octopus sketch was my favorite." Aromas of thyme, saffron, and lemon waft up, and I inhale the spices, notice my breath for the first time in hours.

"It is very good. I also like the faces."

"Yes—really fantastic." Then, before I can stop myself, "There was a car bomb a few blocks from school. That's why I was late."

When Ana doesn't reply, I continue. "Someone said it might be related to the Basques?"

Silence.

"Sorry—I just didn't realize . . . things like that. . . ."

"They happen," Ana mumbles. "Not often, but they do. Every now and then the nationalists do something like this."

"Why?"

"They want to break away, be on their own. They do not think they should have to remain part of us. We do not like to talk about them much."

"I'm sorry," I stammer, though it's clear she isn't angry. On the contrary, her voice is calm. The tightness in my chest loosens but refuses to dissolve.

"Why should you be sorry?" Ana says. "I imagine it must be strange for you, all of this."

I look away from the simmering rabbit to find her watching me.

"Thank you for letting my grandmother teach you. Most of our tenants pretend they are not in when she comes."

I smile. "I'm grateful for her—both your—patience with me. I'm honored to learn from her."

Ana returns my smile, the first time since I've known her. Her face, pale and heart-shaped, glows. I realize how little I know about her life—who she is when she's not her grandmother's translator. She's like Spain, beautiful and complicated, revealed to me in glimpses like a face behind a fan. Captivating me even though I may never entirely understand.

"You must love your grandmother very much," I say. "To help her the way you do. With the tenants, I mean," I add, not wanting to offend her.

Ana thinks for a moment, scratching her nose. "She helped raise me when my mother left. It is hard sometimes . . . there are things I would like to do. But there will be time for it someday. Now my time belongs to her."

Her honesty disarms us both. She looks away, and I stare at my rabbit, realizing I've been stirring the same inch of sauce for several minutes. We're silent.

"You are a good cook," Ana finally says, smiling quickly again. A toilet flush from the back of the apartment indicates that our private exchange is nearing its end. "But your Spanish is terrible."

I smile back at her and keep stirring.

❧ ❧ ❧

Amber Kelly-Anderson remains a vegetarian and butcher of the Spanish language, a dangerous combination in her home state of Texas. When not succumbing to the charms of her husband (who does *wish to thank Señora Valentina), two children, and three animals, she is geeking out over literature to her students, writing, or dreaming of growing up to be Patti Smith. She is a 2013 contributing blogger for* Ploughshares *and has had her work featured in* The Best Women's Travel Writing Volume 8, Toasted Cheese Literary Journal, Sprout, *and* Brain, Child. *For more of her shenanigans (and some of Señora's recipes), visit her at www.generationcake.com.*

HELEN RUBINSTEIN

❧ ❧ ❧

Leaving Kishinev

Some treasures are never lost.

When Dad and I left Kishinev, Vladek was crying. It wasn't the first time—he'd cried twice a few nights earlier, once when we said goodbye after dinner, and once before dinner, at his apartment, when Dad handed him a hundred dollars in an envelope. "Oh no, no," he'd said then, and walked away toward the other room, making wheezy weeping sounds that were surprisingly high-pitched for a man. I watched his white-white hair bobbing above his scalp.

When he returned, he was honking into a dirty handkerchief. "Take it back," he said. "Please, I can't keep it. I can't."

He pleaded so urgently I thought there might be some reason he was literally unable to take the money—maybe it was illegal, maybe he'd recently recovered from an addiction that forbade him to keep any hard cash in the house. Maybe his having the American money would be dangerous, would lead to his getting kidnapped, or worse. "I can't, I can't," he kept saying—in Russian, but in words so simple, I understood—and he tried to force the envelope back into Dad's hands.

Never in America had I seen Dad act like this: generous without reservation, kind in a way that was solemn and direct. Back at the hotel he'd worried that a hundred wasn't

enough—but we still needed to keep some cash for the airport,
he'd reasoned—and then he worried that it wouldn't be nice
to give five twenties instead of a single one hundred-dollar
bill. Before that, he'd worried it would be insulting to offer
any money at all to his oldest family friend, but I'd insisted
that it would be equally insulting to not at least try. That was
another thing about being in Kishinev: Dad sometimes asked
for and took my advice.

"I can't keep it, I can't—"

"It's nothing," Dad said, brushing the envelope in Vladek's
hand away. "Really, it's not much. Did you look inside yet?
Did you see?"

"Please," said Vladek. He reminded me of a sickly old man
in a movie, with bright blue eyes that bored straight into you.
I'd seen those eyes go watery when he first saw us, and then
again, that first day, when he and Dad were talking, reminisc-
ing about old times. Dad had spoken to him over the phone,
and we'd gone to meet him at his building as planned—
though at first we had some difficulty getting in.

"Does Vladek live here?" Dad had asked a woman who
emerged from the front door. When she hesitated to answer,
he explained who we were: "Old friends; I'm an old, old
friend from America," said Dad. "I haven't seen him in thirty,
maybe forty years."

We crept up the stairs without speaking, and after Dad
knocked and yelled through the door—"*Vladek? Eto Osya.*
From a long, long time ago," he added, a reminder—and after
Vladek had responded in a voice that sounded, I thought,
appropriately pleased, it still took a long time for the door to
open. We listened to the rustling noises inside. Dad turned
and looked at me as if for a moment he'd forgotten I was
there, standing in my sandals just behind him, this thing that
had sprouted up, this person, over the last twenty years. The

lock disengaged, someone peered out ("It's you? Really? *Osya*, you?"), and we were finally waved in.

It stank, like mildew and urine and dog. For a second, my eyes adjusting, I felt afraid of what I saw—the old man in a stained undershirt; the tiny, darkened room; the dog barking, fast and loud and mean. Vladek was holding the animal by the skin on its neck. "Boosch!" he yelled—that was the dog's name, and he would continue to yell it over and over during that visit, "Boosch! Boosch!" At some point Dad tried to ask Vladek if it had anything to do with the American president—this was 2004—but Vladek didn't understand, didn't get the joke, and eventually Dad just waved it away, "Never mind."

Vladek apologized: he hadn't expected there to be a girl, and he buttoned another shirt over his undershirt, telling Dad I was lovely, congratulating him, asking where was his wife, and listening to the usual explanation of how Mom had stayed home to work and take care of the other daughter. Dad had stopped telling people I was trying to write a book. I'm not sure why—maybe I'd asked him to; maybe it had felt like a jinx, bad luck. Or maybe it just seemed too inviting of questions: Why a book about *Dad*? What would it say?

Vladek apologized, also, for the doorbell being broken, for having nothing to offer, no tea, no cakes—his refrigerator was broken, he told us, empty. The water he served came from the small second room in the apartment, which was the bathroom and, he said, the dog's room. It was lined with newspapers that indicated it was the dog's bathroom, too.

"So what, you don't eat?" Dad asked, and he said it as a joke, letting out a short laugh, but Vladek answered, too seriously, "Usually I have some crackers around. Actually, I think I have some here," and went rummaging behind a pile of magazines. The place was filled with newspapers and books and dust and, on top of it all, a not-insignificant film of dog hair. "Want some crackers? Here." Vladek dug out a box of crackers, then went off to find a plate. When he left the room the dog lurched at our legs, slobbering, its breath awful.

"No, no," said Dad. "It's okay. I was joking."

"You're sure? You're not hungry?"

"We already ate," Dad lied; as the afternoon wore on I willed my stomach not to rumble. Later Dad would ask to use the bathroom, and Vladek would show him that since the toilet was broken he'd been using a bucket. After, Dad would say to me quietly, "Do you have to go? Can you hold it? Better to wait."

But before that they just talked, talked for so long that I stopped trying to understand and got bored, sitting there on Vladek's bed—Dad was in the only chair and Vladek was standing, leaning against a table. ("You're sure? You don't want to sit?" Dad asked; we showed Vladek how he could sit beside me on the bed, or I could even stand—"She's young," Dad said, "Look how healthy, how strong." He'd pinched my calf to show it. But Vladek said no, no, his back hurt, it hurt all the time now, it was better for him to stand anyway.) They talked and talked, looking increasingly serious, and this was when I first saw Vladek choke up, his eyes watering. When I asked Dad why, later, he said they'd been remembering the good times.

"What good times?"

"You see," said Dad, "his father was also in jail. Our families were friends during that time. Our mothers were friends. And they were good times."

"While your father was in prison you had good times?" My voice sounded childish and high. I hated how little I understood about Dad's past.

"It's hard to explain. Financially it was very hard, my mother had to stretch everything because she was the only one working. There were many days she didn't eat, she would give everything she had to Fanya and me—"

"I know, Dad"—I'd heard this so many times.

"What I am saying is financially it was hard, but emotion-ally, in a way, sometimes it was good."

"Huh."

I must have sounded skeptical.

"Agh. You cannot understand, growing up like you did. It was tough, but good—they were very close, my mother and Vladek's mother. Our families spent a lot of time together. You see, in those days, if your husband was in prison, people didn't always—they weren't always nice, they didn't want to talk to you. My mother lost some friends in that time, but she got closer with other people too. Like this Vladek's family."

"You really remember it? Weren't you, like, five years old?"

"Of course I remember. I was five, and six and seven. We would go there, eat meals together—very simple meals, very simple; our mothers would drink tea and watch us play. You know what I remember? That their house, Vladek's house, had a dirt floor. Like in the old days, they still didn't have a real floor. I guess maybe they were even worse off than us, or maybe we were just lucky, because we had our house from before the war and somehow it didn't get taken away. I don't know how my parents were able to keep it. Anyway, Vladek's house had that dirt floor, and I thought it was so cool. I even asked my mother once, 'Why can't we have a dirt floor like that?' and she laughed and laughed. My mother thought that was so funny."

Dad laughed. "And, *doch*, you know what else I remember? One time—you see, Vladek is maybe six, ten years older than me, so I looked up to him, I liked to play with him, but he didn't always want to play with me, so when he did, I felt really cool—I remember one time, I don't know where he got it, but he had a little . . . a little pistol."

"A gun?"

"Not a real gun—you know, what is it called, this kind that shoots little—"

"A BB gun."

"Yeah. I don't know where he got it but it was the first time I ever saw a gun, and I was so excited. He was going to let me play with it, and he wanted me to ask my mother first, and I was trying to convince him not to. I was sure she would say no. But we asked her and she said since Vladek was older it was O.K. He was supposed to watch me. We went into the woods—"

"The woods? Here? In Kishinev?"

"Well, not forest, but you know, an area with lots of trees. And we shot at the trees and the rabbits . . . yeah."

"Then what happened?" I asked, thinking, *When you bring a gun into the story. . . .*

"What do you mean, what happened? Nothing happened. I think that was the most fun I ever had in my life. At least in those years it was the most fun. But I remember they were very good times, our mothers would drink their tea and play cards. You weren't really supposed to play cards in those days, but they didn't care. They had nothing to worry about anymore."

"Why?"

"Because, you silly, it couldn't get any worse. After my father came back, actually, we didn't see them that much. But he knew me right away, this Vladek. He knew me right away."

Dad put his hand around my ponytail. We were walking back to the trolleybus, back toward the center of town, past the train station, to where the hotel was. It was dusk, and the gray concrete and stone of the city, the buildings new and old—all of it glowed in a way I hadn't yet seen.

"That BB gun was cool," said Dad. "But you know what I have now?"

He pulled, and I jerked my head away, twisting my hair out of his fist. I knew what he was going to say, but I didn't want to hear it.

"You know what I have? *Dochka*. Now I have a real gun."

"I know," I said, and walked faster.

"You don't like that I have a gun?"

"What do you want me to say? Congratulations."

"It's okay," Dad said. "You don't have to be so politically correct all the time. It's good, if someone tries to get in. I am American! I need a gun."

We eventually convinced Vladek to keep the envelope of money, of course. "You know how much I get in pension?" he asked Dad. I couldn't understand the figure, couldn't do the conversion of Moldovan lei to dollars, but I could see that even Dad was surprised by how little it was. Later he told me: something like thirty-five dollars a year.

"What? Are you sure?" I said. "How can anyone live off that?" and Dad said, "You can't. Look at him, he's barely alive."

We took Vladek out to dinner after he accepted the gift, that second time we saw him. Dad had asked Vladek to suggest a place, but he'd resisted—he didn't often go out to eat, he said, and so didn't know what was good. Eventually we settled on the first-floor restaurant of the Hotel National, near the train station.

"Growing up," Dad told me, switching into English, "I always wanted to come inside this hotel, but I was sure I never would. I couldn't have imagined it. It seemed so fancy."

And Vladek, when Dad asked, said yes, of course, he'd heard it was nice, but no, he had never been there before.

By then I was annoyed with Dad for even asking.

I was tired that day, so I stopped trying to understand what he and Vladek were talking about during the meal. But there were long silences—lapses in their conversation—which made me feel sad for both of them: for Vladek because I wanted him to get some pleasure, some rare joy, from being with Dad; and for Dad because I wanted him to find something here, some connection to Vladek and so to the place and the past that he depended on so dearly. The past that—I thought—he needed badly, back in America, to be real.

We ate, and at some point it occurred to me that the yellow-brown color of the tablecloths and walls and carpet was meant to be perceived as gold. When the meal was over Vladek asked Dad to please let him pay, since he'd already given him so much. The meal cost something like fifteen dollars, but Dad refused. He was going to put it on a credit card anyway, he said. *Creditcheski cart. Creditni cartichka*—Dad could never remember how to say this in Russian. "You have one?" He showed Vladek the little magnifying lens embedded in his Discover card. By now, I'd watched my father do this at every other outing with an old friend: he would point it out, talk about how cool it was—what will they think of next?—then hand it over. Vladek turned the thing around in his hands. It wasn't clear if he knew that the magnifying lens was the part he was supposed to find impressive. Dad pointed again, but his finger was thicker than the lens itself, and Vladek's enthusiasm was only polite. When he asked again if he could pay, Dad let him leave a few coins for the tip.

That night, saying goodbye, then, was the third time Vladek cried, standing in the city evening on the sidewalk. It was well lit, because we were near the train station. As he and Dad hugged, Vladek hung on more tightly, and when they let go, the tears rolled freely down his face. He didn't move to wipe them away. Instead he began talking, fast. I imagined that he was saying how lonely he was, how difficult his life had become, how he was sick and sometimes hungry, or maybe how good it had been for him to see us; and when Dad responded I knew he was promising to keep in touch.

I wondered if he really would—Vladek didn't have a computer, and he'd told us his phone was often disconnected.

"Please," I could understand Vladek saying. "Please, let me meet you at the train tomorrow."

And though Dad said it wasn't necessary, I knew in another minute or two he'd give in and tell Vladek the time and the track. Because meeting us there, at the beginning of our trip out of Kishinev, seemed like a thing that Vladek needed to do.

And, I supposed, we needed him to meet us there too, or at least it felt that way when we left our hotel the next afternoon to go to the station. My suitcase, packed lightly so there would be room to bring things back if we wanted, was still light as I lifted it into the taxi. What I felt then was a mix of emptiness (unnerving emptiness, because, in the end, Kishinev was only a place, and it was a place that did not belong to me), sadness (because I was sorry to be leaving this sweet, green little city, cradle of my oldest and favorite imaginings), and relief (because the pressure was off: finally, we no longer needed to talk about Dad's past, and could just travel and hang out together). Beyond these feelings, though, I was aware that I wanted something else, something for Dad: I wanted the city to make some kind of gesture, some small overture to show it was sorry he was leaving. And so I looked forward to seeing Vladek at the station; I felt grateful that he, at least, would be there to say goodbye.

But we didn't see him when we arrived. We found the conductor and our car, lifted our suitcases onto the train, and then, once we'd examined our little room—it was an overnight train to Bucharest, and we were traveling first-class—went back outside with our luggage. Dad had been talking for months, since long before the trip began, about how dangerous this train ride would be—how certain it was that someone, some Romanian, he said, would try to rob us—so there was no way we'd be leaving our things out of sight.

We stood there with our suitcases, out on the platform in the August sun, and as I scanned the exits of the indoor part of the station, I tried not to let Dad see that I was anxious for Vladek to arrive. When he did finally come shuffling toward us, apologizing for being late, he carried a stuffed plastic shopping bag, some kind of gift.

"No, no, no," Dad protested, "I can't take this from you."

But Vladek insisted. "Please," he said. "These are some of my greatest treasures."

Still Dad resisted, told Vladek he should keep his own treasures, though I knew he'd relent. And after Vladek said that he had no one else to give them to, Dad finally accepted the bag.

They embraced. Vladek had dressed up, I realized, to come to the train station. He was wearing a collared shirt and slacks, and I wondered if he'd ever vacationed in his life, ever left this station on a train just for pleasure. He clung to Dad the same way he had the other night. I could hear him whimpering like a child; I could see that Dad was ready to let go, but that Vladek wasn't, was gripping Dad fiercely; and I felt bad for having wished up this kind of display.

Then a man in a coat and tie tapped Dad on the shoulder, forcing them to release each other. At first I thought the person was a conductor or a station attendant—was there something wrong with Vladek's being on the platform?—and then I saw it was Yuri.

Yuri: one of a group of high school classmates we'd shared a meal with earlier that week. He had never been a close friend, Dad told me, but since that dinner Yuri had called my father several times just to talk, arranged to meet us for coffee, and visited us at the hotel with a box of chocolates just for me. At first Dad seemed pleased—at the dinner, Yuri had asked if he might call, and when he did, Dad stretched out on the couch with his feet up, chatting for more than an hour, getting gossip, hearing old news: who was sick, who had died, how the city's geography had changed.

After the visit with the chocolates, though, when Yuri had lingered awkwardly in the doorway, coming up with more things to say while Dad tried to tell him goodbye, Dad told me, "I am worried he thinks I can help him get out of here. He keeps talking to me about some friend in Germany, saying he might try to go to Germany like he thinks I can do something."

"*Can* you do something?"

"I don't think so. Maybe for a good friend—for a really good friend I might try something, but even then . . . do you know how hard it was to work things out for Fanya and Anna?"

Now, at the train station, Yuri broke up Dad and Vladek's hug, and when Dad introduced the men to each other, I could tell from Vladek's demeanor that he would defer to Yuri, would let him direct the last-minute interactions of our little gang. God. I hoped Vladek knew we hadn't planned this—I could understand what Yuri was explaining to Dad: that he'd looked at the train schedule, knowing we'd be leaving today; that he'd come to see off the morning train to Bucharest and then, because he hadn't found us at that departure, had come again now. Vladek would understand this, too, of course, but he wasn't even really looking at them, maybe wasn't listening at all.

Of our entire month away, this moment on the platform was the one time that I really, deeply wished I could speak Russian. If I spoke Russian, I thought, I would say something to Vladek, would make something up to distract him from the awful scene playing out now between Yuri and Dad, in which Yuri chattered on, trying to force another two boxes of chocolate into Dad's hands, and Dad tried unsuccessfully, again and again, to turn away toward his older friend. Yuri's sport coat stank of sweat and bore a dusting of dandruff on its shoulders. He walked and stood in a broken way—one of his legs was much shorter than the other—and I should have felt sorry for him, but that day I despised him.

I met Vladek's eye and smiled, willing him to understand my meaning: *you and your gift are not secondary*, but he looked away without returning my grin. Because of the torrent of Yuri's words, the urgency of whatever he was saying to Dad, and the one pink and slightly dusty box of chocolates that Dad eventually accepted (he convinced Yuri to keep the other)— because of that, Vladek didn't get a chance to say much of anything else before the second whistle, the boarding whistle, blew.

We climbed aboard—Dad and Vladek hugged once more; Yuri kissed my hand with his dark, wet lips and then insisted on helping us carry our suitcases into the train—and once Yuri was finally gone from our room, once a conductor had shooed him out of the hall, we waved at them both through the window. Vladek had taken out his handkerchief, which he used both to wave and to wipe at his eyes: he was crying again. In front of him, slightly turned as if to block Vladek's view, stood Yuri, waving in wild desperation. The train pulled away, and I wondered if they would talk to each other after we were gone, if they would have anything to say.

We didn't open Vladek's bag of treasures until much later, sometime during the night, after we'd crossed into Romania, the wheels on the train noisily and laboriously changed to fit the narrower, non-Soviet tracks. By then we were both in our pajamas, side by side on two hard, narrow beds that folded out to cover our luggage. We'd met some of our neighbors in first-class—a couple of Peace Corps members from Wisconsin who offered me a pocket pack of Kleenex to carry to the bathroom so that I wouldn't have to use the provided toilet paper, which they told us was scratchy and brown; and a couple of Israelis from Kishinev who, it turned out, knew Fanya. They had all lived in the same neighborhood for years. "You're Fanya's brother?" they exclaimed. "Unbelievable! Well, maybe not; all of us Kishinev Jews know each other. Send her our regards—it's a small world."

In Vladek's plastic bag Dad and I could discern that some tightly packed papers—newspapers and pamphlets—surrounded a very used, very worn shoebox.

"Should I open it now?" Dad asked. "What do you think?"

When I said yes, he peeled off the tape that held the box closed. Inside, it seemed, was only more of the same: pamphlets; maps; some ancient travel guides for Soviet countries; ten or twenty small, unused photo calendars for years past. Dad began to sneeze—as we sifted through the papers, our hands grew dark with dust. "Shit. I am allergic to this crap," he said, but he continued to flip through what was there, searching, I think, for some sort of "treasure." At the bottom of the shoebox were a handful of Soviet pins, little medals.

"Crap."

"What?"

"I think these are his father's medals."

"Let me see," I said.

Dad held them up close to his face, squinting at the engravings on their surface. "Yeah. These are his father's medals from the army."

They were small but clean, not rusted. Looking at them, I tried to muster up some sense of awe and respect for what they meant, but I've never really cared much for army medals— I can never get them to move me.

"Shit, *doch*. What are we gonna do with these? Do you want them?"

I shrugged. I didn't feel like I had the right, the appropriate proximity to their original owner, to be their keeper.

"Phee." Dad waved his hands—his bed was covered in papers and dust. "Look at all this junk."

"Yeah."

"Wonder why he gave them to us."

"I don't know," I said, but I was thinking of what it meant to hand the stuff of your life over to another person like that—to need someone to hand your life over to. "I have no one else to give them to," Vladek had said. When we got to Bucharest, Dad considered throwing the whole sack away—it was bulky and heavy and smelled like Vladek's dog—and at first I was going to let him, was going to let him toss everything except the pins. But eventually we decided to keep some of the other stuff too. I don't know where any of it is now.

⁂

Helen Rubinstein's essays and fiction have appeared in The New York Times, Ninth Letter, Salon, Salt Hill, Witness, *and elsewhere, and her work on a book has been honored with fellowships from the MacDowell Colony, Yaddo, and the Elizabeth George Foundation. She is an MFA student in creative nonfiction at the University of Iowa.*

೫೧ ೫೧ ೫೧

Yanet's Vintage Emporium

What do you buy when you can't take it with you?

*I*t begins to pour while I'm at Yanet's apartment, packs of chubby raindrops in the tropical afternoon that make the dust in her Havana apartment feel even thicker, some-how, than it actually is. I'm trapped until the storm passes, and I don't mind at all. Every surface of Yanet's home is covered with objects waiting to be lifted, appraised, felt, perused. I browse the waist-high tables and rich wood armoires with rows of cut-crystal wine and port glasses, mod carafes with faded metallic polka-dots, kitschy ceramic table lamps painted with bright pastoral scenes, and patterned blown-glass globes that once held water and fish. Or maybe candles.

Technically, it's not legal for any of these objects to be sold. Only the Cuban government is allowed to buy and sell goods in Havana, but "Five-Cent Yanet," as she's known among the city's connoisseurs of inexpensive antiques, has been operating mostly illegally for over a decade.

There's no sign in front of Yanet's, nothing to indicate that hers isn't just another apartment in just another building. I lived in Havana for a year without visiting; the women I knew who shopped here never shared her address with me—they kept it closely guarded, equally to respect Yanet's need for discretion and because more shoppers meant more competition for her limited supplies. But I didn't press—my desire to visit waned once I learned I couldn't take any furniture or design objects with me when I left. In bureaucratese, officials call Cuba's affliction a "scarcity of objects." Anyone leaving the country can take only two suitcases and what fits inside them. It's far more than what was allowed in years past (twenty dollars and the clothes on your body), but still not much.

This both stunts and, of course, fosters Yanet's trade. Foreigners like me may leave accompanied only by what we brought in and, if we get the right permits, contemporary art. Locals must divest of the accumulation of lifetimes, giving it to family and neighbors or discreetly selling it off in the years before leaving. So Cubans with plans to head into The Rest Of The World arrive at Yanet's door cradling cardboard boxes, generations of tasteful domestic items sold to raise money for what waits on the other side of an exit visa. They trade the thin porcelain teacups inherited from grandparents, the ice cream sundae dishes from the Hotel Riviera, and their 1950s martini glasses for a one-way plane ticket. To live in Havana is to know that this bargain may one day take place.

I'm back in Havana for a short visit now, and my friend Aimara has finally brought me shopping. Yanet trots through her apartment as we browse, lifting her flip-flops high off the red and green tile floor as she navigates the bare paths between encroaching cliffs of carafes and lamps on either side of the hallway. She is the duchess in her domain, and based on what you select, she can point you instinctively toward another item you might like, which is usually buried behind a mountain of mismatched plates—if, that is, she is paying attention, which is infrequent. After she shows us into the apartment, she sits right back down on the stiff sofa just inside the front door. She gossips with a neighbor who has stopped by and smokes cigarette after cigarette, her short brown ponytail bouncing every time she laughs. Then she's in the dining room wrapping just-purchased breakables in scraps of *Granma*, the Communist Party newspaper. Once the sale is completed, she's on the phone in the kitchen, leaning into the doorframe and twisting the cord around her pinkie as she murmurs, "*no me digas*, that can't be, I saw him just last week and he said. . . ." She doesn't check on us once, only waves us toward a back closet where we can paw through a box of old purses once we've inspected the wares in her main rooms. Aimara dashes off—she's been coveting a particular black clutch since her last visit.

Yanet's covert customers are Havana's aesthetes. Owners of upscale *paladares*—in-home restaurants—pop in for stylish two-dollar daiquiri glasses. Artists and musicians, the cultural elite, pick up birthday gifts for friends. Foreign diplomats arrive in cars with telltale black license plates but park a few blocks away and approach Yanet's on foot. Government functionaries do the same—their cars also have distinct plates, and they don't want to endanger Yanet, whose job, apartment, and everything in it relies on discretion. She hides behind a sheen of legality, since she has a state license to work as a set designer, for which she pays a monthly tax of ten dollars.

"I just design with old things," she tells me with a shrug.

But Yanet hasn't worked on a play in years—and if her real occupation is ever deemed a problem by the authorities, she will lose everything. Attachment to the material and the beautiful is fleeting in Havana, breakable.

Nearly everyone who visits Yanet's apartment is a person who actually chooses to live in Havana. Her customers are locals who use similar tactics as she to eke out the privileges that make staying preferable to leaving; they're musicians who have returned home after playing piano on a cruise ship for six months, restaurateurs who serve double the number of

customers they're licensed to feed, artists who use hotel internet connections to arrange studio visits with vacationing art
collectors. They're Cubans whose Spanish friends stiffen in
shock when their offers to help procure permanent exit visas
are gently rebuffed. These people, locals and a handful of foreigners who don't want to live anywhere else, who fled European and American homelands for the weightless feeling of
Havana, entertain in their homes and have found peace with
the shortcomings, risks, and hypocrisies of making a life in
post-Soviet Cuba. They'll deal with getting their objects out
of the country if and when they must leave, or they'll sell them
back to Yanet.

I never found that peace, though at one time I wanted
to. I wanted to stay for the beguiling sense that nothing was
more important than the moment that wrapped me, and for
the paradox of a system that's at once collapsed and unyield-
ing, that both constrains and haphazardly looks the other
way. I wanted to stay to become part of the communities
that thwart the apparent monolith of the Cuban government and economy, like weeds that grow through cracked
sidewalks.

But the place is not mine. That I never really tried to go
to Yanet's while I lived in Havana to look at all the things I
couldn't have was symptomatic. Instead, I moved back to the
States, where I vote for my elected officials and shop at stores
with signs outside of them and feel fairly confident that I can
keep anything I buy for as long as I want.

Yanet's apartment feels swollen with both what I miss and
was glad to leave behind in Havana. Its faded, contradictory
glamour makes it a little hard to breathe. Or maybe it's the
dust. The ceilings are high and her chandeliers are caked
with salty grit, the combined consequences of clutter and
a nearby ocean. A dozen hutches encircling the enormous

dining room display rotund teapots with faded flowers on their bellies, teacups, and saucers piled in snowdrifts of delicate porcelain. Two armoires in the hallway hold glasses that I imagine were once filled with champagne and held by men in linen suits and women in stiff silk dresses. I lift an art deco martini glass with an opaque, star-shaped, fluorescent yellow stem. It would look great on my coffee table, but I can't see getting it home intact. At the bottom of a snake's nest of costume jewelry I find a locket shaped like a book. Inside, a woman wearing a bathing costume and a man in a three-piece suit wink out at me. I'll take it home and put it on a chain.

Aimara wanders over holding a four-dollar black envelope clutch and a few sturdy coffee cups.

"Ready to go?" she asks.

"Not really," I say. "Yes."

Yanet has hung up the phone and is now flitting around, her flip-flops smacking as she roams. She puts on an eggshell wool cape and models it, turning her hands out like a Barbie doll's. A couple walks in, a portly man and a younger woman, and sit in a pair of chairs at the dining table. Their closed umbrellas spit small puddles on the floor beside them. They light cigarettes and admire Yanet's cape, then ask after her teenaged daughter. The rain has nearly stopped, but the moist afternoon is just as warm as it was before it fell. Yanet twirls to show them the circular hem of the jacket and then stops.

"Isn't it beautiful? If only it were colder here," she says with a wistful sigh. She smoothes her hands down the front of the cape, shakes her head as if to press reset, picks up her cigarette, and smiles.

*Julia Cooke's writing on Cuba—including an account of acciden-
tally purchasing fifteen pounds of black market ham—has been
featured in* Condé Nast Traveler, The Atlantic, Guernica, *and
the* Virginia Quarterly Review. *Her first book,* All the Young
Punks: Grandchildren of the Cuban Revolution in Post-
Fidel Havana, *is scheduled to be published next year.*

SARAH MENKEDICK

✍ ✍ ✍

The Revolution

On the connections born in times of upheaval.

There was an art opening at the Centro Fotográfico the
Friday the federal troops came. Before it began I went
to the Hotel Victoria for piña coladas with a few friends. The
hotel was empty and we had the terrace to ourselves. Below
us, the city was an oceanic blue-green at twilight, studded
with glinting orange lights. I arrived at the opening slightly
tipsy and chicly late, did a round of greetings, and noticed
something was off.

"What's going on?" I asked my friend Carlos. At that time
in Oaxaca people's instincts were fine-tuned to slight changes
in vibration.

The week before I'd run a 12k through lingering tear gas
after a street battle. The fighting had begun during the pre-
race meeting, and the runners had scattered out the side and
back doors of the building. I'd called Carlos to come pick me
up from the corner of a block that was being taken over by
protesters on one side and an advancing wall of riot police on
the other. The police had used so much tear gas that it hung
in the air the following morning around the city, snug as one
of the Sierra Norte's low-hanging clouds. We still ran: people
still gathered and laughed and warmed up for the race, and

afterwards the runners ate tamales atop the Zapotec archeo-
logical site of Monte Albán, looking out on the crisp October
morning and the lachrymal fog shrouding the city.

I was accustomed to running past the barricades in the
morning, giving subtle nods of thanks to the protesters who
allowed me to slip by as they huddled around the smoldering remains of fires, eating *tortas* for breakfast. I'd grown
used to covering my mouth as I walked past smoking buses
on the way to work, their metal reduced to paper-like wisps
that swirled in clouds of ashy snow. I greeted the octogenarian señoras and hard-faced men and tired five-year-olds who
slept under tarps, guarding the radio tower. This was all part
of a daily routine, one in which it seemed possible that the
established order might be overturned at any moment.

Holding a sweating Corona, I readied myself for the latest
news.

"They killed an American in Santa Lucia," said Carlos.

I was silent. For a moment, the bustle of the opening
seemed to pause, replaced by white noise.

"They say the APPO killed him," he added. I scoffed. It
was a predictable spin from the state government.

"But it's pretty obvious," he went on, "that it was the PRI."
The Institutional Revolutionary Party, infamous for its sev-
enty years of dictatorial control over Mexico and its inveterate
corruption, controlled Oaxaca with a mixture of extrale-
gal violence, shabby clientelism (government hacks offering
bricks and cement, or a couple hundred pesos a head, for
votes), and nepotistic alliances with both the business community and the party heads in the capital.

Carlos recounted what he'd heard at that point: plain-
clothes officers with guns had jumped from a van near the
barricades in Santa Lucia and come running at the protesters.
American Indymedia journalist Brad Will had been filming
the officers when he was shot in the stomach.

This was going to be Bush on the phone with Fox in a matter of hours. This was going to be the end of the long nights and tentative mornings of protesters fighting and planning and waiting, the end of a period in which significant change seemed palpable in the discussions around the barricades and the sudden eruptions of angry, hopeful energy.

And indeed, as we said our goodbyes that night, the obligatory kisses on the cheek lingering a second or two longer than usual, hushed negotiations were taking place between suited men.

The next morning we woke to the buzz of helicopters. I walked to my Saturday morning class through deserted streets and felt the city taut with the type of nausea that precedes intense grief. The teachers had a meeting before classes with James, the school's leftist director, whose face was saggy and blotchy from staying up all night at the barricades.

"Whatever you do," he said, "avoid Santa Lucia." I kept mum about my plans to head straight to Jorge's apartment in Santa Lucia after class.

"Do NOT let the kids leave unless they have a parent waiting, understood?"

We nodded.

"Do NOT walk the streets today. Go home. Stay inside. You'll be fine." We nodded. The kids arrived, class began; we watched *Harry Potter* since no one had the energy to concentrate on much else. I defined "falcon" and "wand" for my teenaged students as the whir of helicopters and low-flying planes rose from outside.

Jorge called and I answered, breaking the strict rule about not answering cell phones in class.

"Go straight home," he ordered.

"Are they coming? Are they here?"

"They say the tanks are already here, in the Sierra," he replied. "It's going to happen soon."

We hung up. James came in a few moments later and told me to end the class an hour early, at noon. When *Harry Potter* was over, the students and I attempted to have a pointless, grammatically doomed conversation as I waited for their parents to arrive. One mother was late, so I sat with the student in the empty classroom, piecing together broken sentences about our favorite ice cream flavors until her mother finally picked her up and whisked her off to the city's wealthy Colonia Reforma.

When I finally left work, the sense of invasion was imminent. The whirring of the helicopters seemed to rattle the streets. Back on Jorge's concrete terrace, under swaying wet laundry, I tried to eat a sandwich and thought about this *restoration of order*, this *stabilizing of unrest*, feeling the cord of justified, authorized violence, the net of institutions and their power, being pulled tighter and tighter around the city.

By mid-afternoon I began to see columns of black smoke rising from the city center. The round front window of Jorge's apartment felt like the porthole of a tiny ship—a ship floating on a strange, uncertain sea. The quiet of the streets added to this feeling. No ice cream man passing, no shouts of "Tamales, tamales, tamales!" from down the block, no kids laughing and playing soccer. I saw the same things I always saw from the windowsill: the haphazard roofs of Santa Lucia, made of scruffy concrete and aluminum, cluttered here and there with bottles and metal rods to deter lightning; the crisscrossed laundry lines and pacing Rottweilers; the domes of churches; the jagged backs of the mountains framing the valley. But this time plumes of thick black smoke rose from the middle of the picture. The smell of burning rubber drifted across the city.

I called Jorge.

"The press is going to the Zócalo, *está cabrón, está cabrón*!" he shouted. There was a clamor of voices and metallic clangs and shouts and scuffling noises in the background. He hung up.

At 5 p.m. the electricity went out. I had been listening to the radio when suddenly, nothing. I weighed the possibility of going out to look for batteries and flashlights, but most stores were closed and the streets were beginning to feel too eerie for me to comfortably wander around, particularly in Santa Lucia. I foraged around the apartment and came up with two little white candles that would illuminate all of about half an inch of the counter. Then I waited for it to get dark.

It did, quickly. The smoke went the faintest blue-black before it mingled with the night. Downtown, things were happening. Windows were being broken; protesters were being beaten and thrown into vans; soldiers were marching; groups of people high on adrenaline, unaware that they were bleeding, were hurling Molotov cocktails and running through the streets. I waited in the silence, pacing between the terrace and the one-room apartment, lighting and relighting the candles.

When Jorge finally walked through the door it smelled as if a car had caught fire. He reeked of smoke, oil, burnt rubber, tear gas, smoldering plastic, and sweat. We met in a messy embrace and talked in a flurry back and forth.

"The army cut the power because the APPO has a radio station near Santa Lucia," he explained. "We should get flashlights or more candles."

"Can we go out?" I asked.

"Yeah, I think so."

I pulled on a hooded sweatshirt for a flimsy sense of protection and we shuffled downstairs and out of the house onto the street. There was a couple just outside, pressed together against a car. As we headed for Avenida Ferrocarril, a major thoroughfare that passed near the apartment, the man said loudly from behind us,

"I wouldn't go that way."

We stopped.

"Why not?" asked Jorge, turning around.

"They just raped a girl on Ferrocarril," he said. The woman snuggled against him, resting her forehead on his chin.

"Thank you," I said, and we turned the other direction. Jorge put his arms around me and squeezed, but I was too numb, too horrified to respond. Up ahead the protesters at the barricades were starting fires, and in flickers of orange light we could see the ragged edges of stones, tires and scrap metal, and a few dusky faces peering down intently at the flames.

A dog raced at us, barking and baring its teeth. I let out a scream and Jorge shouted in response, "*Cállate, cállate!*" And then, "Shhh, *está bien, callados.*"

We didn't make it any farther; I insisted we turn back. We passed the couple again, still holding each other in the street, and climbed the stairs to the apartment. On the couch, in the dark, we shared a *caguama* of beer and a bag of croissants, the only edibles we could ransack from the kitchen. Neither of us spoke.

We must have gone to bed around eight, still very early, but between the smoke and lack of power, the night was dense as 3 A.M.

Our relationship deepened that night. We did not embrace; we did not talk. We simply lay in the heavy darkness with the reality of the moment hanging over us, each thinking our own thoughts, feeling the other's warmth.

The next morning the sun was bright and the sky was a brilliant blue. The city was electric with unleashed power. We tried the lights, the radio: nothing.

I decided to try and make it back to my apartment on the other side of the city, and Jorge and I set out walking together. Near the Merced market, someone in a car passing about fifty meters behind us started firing randomly into the street. The few pedestrians on the sidewalks halted, shocked. *Señoras* in long, colorful aprons came out of the market to stare.

"*Porros*," said Jorge. *Porros* are unemployed teenaged or twenty-something boys from impoverished villages in the mountains and valleys around Oaxaca. Their lack of education and boredom are easily catalyzed into violence. The government gives them some small token from its coffers—five hundred, maybe a thousand pesos—to infiltrate protests and turn them into bloody confrontations, or to shout APPO slogans while going on vandalism sprees throughout the city, which the government can later point to with a *tsk-tsk* to show the international media the sort of destructive threat to order and justice they're facing.

We ate our empanadas in the market in silence. Normally La Merced was bustling and the throng of pedestrians entering and exiting would push against our backs, but today it was just us and a few lone men.

As we entered the city center, we began to see debris everywhere: twisted metal parts strewn on sidewalks and millions of glass shards like a sprinkling of light snow on the ground. Cars were overturned and charred buses lay on their sides. Tanks and fences of tightly coiled concertina wire blocked off major streets and all entrances to the Zócalo. Few people were out, and there were no cars; we walked down the center of ruined streets, between the shouts of fresh graffiti covering the walls: "*viva el pueblo de Oaxaca*," "*estamos en pie de lucha*," "go home turista we are not capitalists," "the twenty-first century revolution will surge in Oaxaca."

The air stung. We passed six-deep rows of troops, standing at attention behind opaque plastic shields and wire thick as swarms of bees. They were not actually the army but rather the PFP (Policía Federal Preventiva), an elite section of the federal police that fights insurgency via torture, kidnapping, strikebreaking and the violent repression of protests. They had entered the city around midnight and taken the Zócalo around 5 A.M.

They had not managed to wipe out the movement in a single blow. The protesters fought back and fortified a position around Santo Domingo, the majestic sixteenth-century

church on the city's main street. We passed those who had
fought through the night, sitting on the steps before the soar-
ing, stiffly wealthy church, bathed in the warm morning sun.
Beaten, bloody, covered in soot and dirt, they talked anima-
tedly among themselves.

I found my roommates in a candy-and-pillow-strewn bunker.

"You made it!" they shouted, and we embraced.

"We've been using junk food as comfort!" they offered as
an explanation for the litter of *dientes* and *gomitas* and *sabritas*
wrappers that cluttered the kitchen table and fluttered around
the pillows on the living room floor, where everyone had
slept. They explained that they'd raided the *miscelánea* before
it closed and then sat on the apartment's terrace, watching the
invasion while nervously clawing open bags of gummy frogs.

The apartment stank of sweat and stress. Jorge hurriedly
bid his farewells, and my roommates and I sat at the kitchen
table drinking coffee. After awhile, the fervent recounting
of events churned our fear into adrenaline, and we headed
downtown to investigate the damage.

There were hundreds of people in the streets now: protesters with blackened faces and bandages, dazed but
curious bystanders and citizens. University kids and middle-
aged shopkeepers and photographers assessed the ravaged
and remade city. As the day settled into itself, the air grew
strangely jovial. Bands of people began roaming the streets
as if this were the morning after. As if life as we knew it had
been extinguished, leaving behind this surreal, wide gulf in its
wake. People took pictures of overturned cars, fractured windows, graffiti. I climbed on a ledge and posed beside a broken,
twisted traffic light, feeling exuberant, then uneasy.

Where the PFP blocked off streets, the protesters formed
groups and antagonized them with songs, offers of food, and
questions. Seventy-year-old women harangued them: "Why

are you doing this to our pueblo? Don't you have shame? Why are you hurting your own people?" Others were less serious: "Don't you want a taco, *policía*? How about a kiss?" The policemen, many of whom looked barely eighteen, betrayed nothing beyond the occasional quivering eyebrow. They mostly stared ahead, unfazed.

This lasted several days, then stretched into weeks and slowly assumed the guise of normality. I grew accustomed to living and working in an occupied city in which revolutionaries gathered and plotted and federal troops guarded the sacred institutions. I stepped again around sleeping bags—now bundling the bodies of federal policemen—in the Zócalo; I shimmied around fences to cross barricaded streets, nodded respectful hellos to the protesters in their huddled discussions and rallies outside Santo Domingo.

I wondered then if I should have joined the battle. Grabbed a stone and thrown myself into breaking the spell of a corrupt, brutal government. At first I came up with analyses and rationalizations of why I didn't. I would have been deported. Quite possibly raped. And wouldn't I have been co-opting the movement, trying to claim a bit of revolutionary drama in a battle that wasn't mine, and perhaps even endangering other people's lives in the process?

But none of those reasons stuck. I continued to feel guilty until the day a student came to talk to me after class. He was a big high-schooler with long curly hair, dressed in heavy black boots and baggy clothes, obsessed with Pink Floyd and devoted to the revolution. His English was excellent, and he used it to criticize the U.S. I liked him because he could hold his own in a debate, and he liked me for the same reason.

"Why did you stay?" he asked. It was the first time I'd had to answer that question.

It took me a moment to pull the words together.

"Because I care about Oaxaca," I said. I could have added, because I met someone; because this city struck a chord of belonging and connection I haven't found anywhere else; because what happens here feels vital to me, lacking the sheen of distance and abstraction of so many travel experiences. But this only occurred to me years later, after I moved from Oaxaca and realized I'd left part of myself there.

In the weeks before the final repression began, before the walls were whitewashed, before hundreds of people were "disappeared" into vans and prisons, before the APPO's leaders made strategic last-minute deals with the government and left their followers to be crushed, I fell in love with the Oaxacan man who would become my husband. In the weeks before Oaxaca was opened to the tourists again and the Zócalo was renovated and planted with poinsettias at the cost of several million pesos, I met the group of Oaxacan friends who years later, when I moved away, would hold me in long embraces and tell me, "*Te vamos a extrañar, Sarita.*" *We're going to miss you*. Oaxaca became home like no foreign place had ever been.

Now, Oaxaca is once again a city of sun-dappled plazas and pretty cobblestone streets and courtyards lush with bougainvillea, and it's easy for people to understand why I hold such fondness for it, why it is the touchstone I return to after all these years of traveling.

"It's beautiful," they say. "The cafés in the Zócalo, the juices, the hike along the Cerro Fortín," and I agree. But my love for it stems not from this bright beauty but from a time that was uncertain and choked with smoke, when the revolution opened pathways of emotion and connection that might otherwise have taken years to establish. A time when the city was raw, and burning, and hopeful, and I stayed.

❦ ❦ ❦

Sarah Menkedick recently completed her MFA at the University of Pittsburgh. Before returning to the U.S. for graduate school, she spent six years living, teaching, and traveling abroad. Her work has been published on Amazon's Kindle Singles, World Hum, *and* Perceptive Travel, *among other online and print publications. She is the founder of* Vela, *an online magazine of creative nonfiction inspired by travel and written by women. She is currently at work on a book of narrative nonfiction about Mexico's returning migrants.*

☙ ☙ ☙

City of Beginnings

It's never too late to grant a child's wish.

"Would you push five for me?" asks the woman. "I'm having trouble with my hands today."

I poke the black button next to the cutout number and my knees plié at the jerk of the taut cables. I stare at the numbered panel of the elevator, waiting for the digits to light and extinguish, but eventually my eyes shift to the woman next to me.

I notice her crutches right away. They're not the type you buy at the drugstore after a twisted ankle then toss into the attic after a weekend of use. These have no padded ledges beneath her armpits on which to rest. Instead there are two rigid, four-inch cuffs, each locked over the long black sleeves covering her slight arms. Her hands, I presume, normally clench the foam grips that protrude from the metal sticks and hit her at the hips. Now, however, they fumble with the zipper of a brown saddle-shaped purse slung across her chest. Ignoring her is an option; avoiding her is impossible.

Not much bigger than a wine barrel, the elevator we're squeezed into is one of those cage-style carriages, typical in old Parisian buildings, embellished on three sides with delicate gold swirls and flourishes, and an industrial crisscross gate for a door that collapses and expands in graceless clacks.

The space is barely big enough for one, romantic for a couple, but for two sets of unfamiliar eyes, awkward. The elevator ascends sluggishly, as if being hand-heaved by two men in the basement.

"Can I help you with that?" I ask, nodding toward the woman's purse.

"Yes, thank you," she says.

I reach over and slide the zipper open.

She interlaces her fingers and caresses the length of each, then says again, "I'm having *so* much trouble with my hands."

Her statement is an inverted invitation; the equivalent of "I had the *best* meal last night"—only I get the feeling her answer won't lead me to a new bistro in the seventh arrondissement. I stare at my feet, the carpet, the rubber tips of her crutches. Out of the corner of my eye I see the number two button blink.

Asking the question was no problem in high school, when my friend Cyndi appeared on crutches one morning in a cast that stretched from her ankle to upper thigh. By the time the afternoon dismissal bell rang, her white plaster canvas had been transformed into a purple-penned, heart-dotted-"I" masterpiece. Cyndi made swinging like a pendulum on one foot appear flirtatious, and for the next six weeks girls carried her books, and football players carried her crutches—and her—up the stairs to her second-floor classroom. I laughed until my cheeks hurt when she dropped a pencil between the cast and her skin while trying to scratch an itch, and when she was finally cast-free, Cyndi ceremoniously chucked her crutches, and the rogue pencil, into the school dumpster to the cheers of about a dozen classmates. To this day, I don't remember the answer to the question of how she actually broke her leg; all I know is that Cyndi grew more popular because of her injury. She had somehow made it seem cool to be impaired.

But I can see this woman's crutches aren't about popularity. Nor are they temporary scaffolding to protect the underlying anatomy while it heals. They're permanent buttresses that prop her erect and tether her feet to steady ground.

Truth be told, I've never stood this close to a disabled person. Even with our backs against the farthest edges of the elevator, we are close enough to touch. I'm ignorantly uneasy, as if the crutches will infect me with the malady if I look her in the eye. Pity and curiosity swirl in my head, along with the crass assumption that nothing I say will make a difference. I don't like the sound of the word disabled, but don't know if *handicapped* is politically correct. Saying nothing doesn't feel right either, but is it O.K. to ask her what's wrong with her hands, or is it wrong to use the word *wrong*?

"So, what's going on there?" I ask, adding a quick jerk of my chin.

"I've been diagnosed with A.L.S.," she says.

I'm surprised by her candor. I've heard of A.L.S. but don't know enough to respond, so I just shake my head.

"Lou Gehrig's disease?" she prompts.

"I'm sorry," I say. "I don't know what that is."

"It's okay," she says. "I guess I've been talking about it for so long I expect everyone to know."

With academic succinctness she explains that A.L.S. is the acronym for Amyotrophic Lateral Sclerosis, a neuromuscular disease that attacks and degrades muscles and motor skills, like those in her hands and legs, until they atrophy and die.

The word "die" is the one I'm afraid of, and it lingers in the air with the hum of the elevator motor that has now lifted us almost to the fourth floor. A lump clogs my throat. I grapple with what to say next.

"How long ago were you diagnosed?" I ask.

"Nine months," she says.

Nine months. The time it takes to grow a life, I think; the time it took me to grow my daughter.

"And you've had a second opinion?" I murmur.

She gives a half laugh. "A second. A third. A fourth."

A weighty silence caws between us.

"Is this your first trip to Paris?" I finally ask.

She nods.

I think about the first time I saw Paris, nearly twenty years ago. It was covered in snow. Along the cement banks of the steely river; on the branches of squat, leafless trees; in the curves and crevices of filigreed balconies, and on the stone wings of angels, winter had dressed Paris in gray and white. It was nothing like the movies I saw in French class with canoodling lovers clinking wine glasses in the sunshine beneath the Eiffel Tower while a nearby accordion played Edith Piaf's *La Vie En Rose*.

For the first few days, I wandered the numbered neighborhoods and checked off the clichés. I traced the steps of former royal denizens and imagined them waltzing in taffeta gowns with gents who plucked gold coins from velvet pouches. I loitered in cafés where legendary writers once scribbled novels as cigarette smoke circled their heads. But the unexpected boon of being alone in the City of Lights was the self-scrutiny and liberation that anonymity brought. In a place rife with foreign tongues, where no one knew my name or my biography, I could be whatever I wanted. Paris became a patron of endless possibility. From the grand boulevards that shot across the city like arrows aimed at distant compass points, to the elderly couples who strolled the avenues arm-in-arm and held hands on park benches, to the zealous performers who rendered their opuses in the windowless underbelly, I saw my reflection. In the quest to reinvent myself, I found myself.

*   *   *

"I remember my first visit," I say, smiling.

"I've always dreamed of coming here," she says. "And I wanted to see it before I couldn't."

Tears sting and well in my eyes. For the first time in the few minutes we've been together, I really look at her face. Under the halo of a small overhead light, and with the golden elevator trimming the backdrop, she looks posed like a portrait in a gilded frame. She's older than me by about ten years, fiftyish. Her black hair parts in the middle and ripples against cheekbones that chisel sharp edges below her brown eyes and shade the hollows of her cheeks. Her skin gathers like a cinched sack at the outline of her rose-tinted lips, which hint at both a smile and something else I can't quite decipher. Maybe sadness; or is it acceptance, or surrender?

Stretching out my right hand instinctively, I introduce myself. She squeezes it harder than I expect and says her name is Leigh.

A cell phone rings from inside her purse. She maneuvers around the bag's small opening and I offer to help, this time without pondering proper etiquette. I flip the phone open and place it against her open palm. It's her mother; she has accompanied Leigh on the trip and is waiting in their room.

"She's always so worried about me now," Leigh tells me when she hangs up. "I just wanted to be by myself for a while."

I nod. As a mother, I empathize with the fear of losing a child, whether to the fever of a foreign city or to a fated malady. As a daughter, I understand the desire to find yourself by veering off a course that was planned for you and charting one that is meant for you.

I'd chosen to take my first trip to Paris for reasons spawned by quixotic stories and a poster of the Eiffel Tower pinned to the closet door of my childhood bedroom. But my journey was more than just a trip. It was emancipation from the rules and standards I was raised to follow. For years I'd listened to my mother dream aloud of going to Hawaii, Maine, Greece, and other far-flung places. When the foggy June mornings arrived in southern California each year, she'd tell me it was her favorite time to be at the beach. But she never went. Not to Hawaii, or Maine, or Greece, or to the beach that was twenty miles from our house. Her dreams were checked behind pretexts of time, money, and fear. "Maybe someday," was her response whenever I asked why she didn't just take the easy drive to the shore.

The shrug of her shoulders told me "someday" would never become today. As a kid, I was disappointed that we never took these grand trips. But as a young adult, disappointment turned to determination. I found the idea of *wishing* one's life instead of *living* it sad, and without a moment's hesitation, I seized my first opportunity to travel abroad.

When I became a mother, I vowed to myself that I would encourage all reasonable whims. And thanks to Ludwig Bemelmans' Parisian-themed *Madeline* books, it didn't take long to fulfill the promise. My daughter Chloé, who read each book until the pages creased, asked me if I'd show her the Eiffel Tower one day. When she turned six I took her to Paris, and as we rounded a corner and crossed the Pont d'Alma, the celebrated landmark came into view. It was night and the lights quivered like a million fireflies. Chloé gasped. I could see the curiosity and wonder in her eyes as she tried to reconcile the cartoonish sketches from her bedtime stories with the shimmering, larger-than-life monument she'd wanted to see.

"It's so big!" she said.

I hoped that somehow I had made her world a little bigger, too—and that I'd planted a seed of wanderlust. But mostly, in the flickering glow, I wanted Chloé to recognize a wish fulfilled and see her mother as the devoted granter.

*   *   *

When Leigh and I finally reach the fifth floor, the gate bangs open and I hold it while she shuffles toward her mother, whose smiling face and halo of white hair beckon her into outstretched arms. I step out behind her and let the elevator gate slam shut behind me.

Though I've spent only a few minutes and five floors with Leigh, the intimate details she's shared make me feel more like a trusted friend than an outsider, and I ask them if they'd like to have dinner one night. They say no; they only have a few nights left, and they'd prefer it be just the two of them. I say goodbye and watch as Leigh's mother places one hand on the small of her daughter's back and cups the other over the rigid cuff clamped on her daughter's arm.

"I can do it, Mom," Leigh says, pushing ahead.

But her mom doesn't waver, instead pulling her daughter a little closer. Leigh lets her. This mother's strength overwhelms me. It's something I both revere and hope never to have to summon.

Watching them, I understand the only way they can conceivably bear their grief is by doing it together.

Before she enters her room, Leigh turns back toward me.

"What's your favorite place in Paris?"

I've just spent the morning revisiting the familiar cobblestone streets that awakened me years ago. Paris is my favorite place in Paris.

But Leigh's searching eyes tell me that's not the answer she's looking for.

I suggest Notre Dame Cathedral—admired for its hovering demons and flying buttresses. "There's a bronze star in front, set in the cobblestones," I say. "It's from there that all road distances in France are measured. The star is point zero, the starting point."

As I say the words aloud to Leigh they sound callous barely off my tongue. I'd stood there first as an expectant young adult, and then decades later had returned to place my daughter's feet on the same spot. Paris had been my genesis, and I'd hoped Chloé's too—the beginning of a life unaltered by time and fate.

The door of Leigh's room shuts and I climb the final steps up to the sixth floor. Outside my window I see the peaks of ancient rooftops pierced by attic rooms, where lights flick on and off and occupants ebb and flow. And I see the crown of Notre Dame, below which I picture a mother placing her daughter's feet on a star, fulfilling a child's wish at the starting point of a different kind of road.

࿐ ࿐ ࿐

Kimberley Lovato is an award-winning author and journalist whose articles about travel, lifestyle, and food have appeared in print and online media including National Geographic Traveler, Executive Travel, AFAR, Delta Sky, Condé Nast Traveller (UK), EasyJet Traveller, American Way, Wine Enthusiast, frommers.com, leitesculinaria.com *and more. Her culinary travel book,* Walnut Wine & Truffle Groves, *won the 2012 Gold Lowell Thomas Award, and her essay, "Lost and Liberated," won the 2012 Bronze Lowell Thomas Award, and also appears in* The Best Women's Travel Writing. *She is a co-founder of Weekday Wanderlust, a monthly travel writer reading series. Visit her at www.kimberleylovato.com.*

ℬ ℬ ℬ

Discovery

They came to the land down under.

The British navy vessel commanded by Lieutenant James Cook on his first voyage around the world was the *HMS Endeavour*. She had a broad, flat brow; a square stern; and a boxy body with a deep hold. At 97 feet 8 inches long, 29 feet 2 inches wide, she weighed 366 tons.

The Boeing 747–400 I took was called Qantas Flight 23. She was a wide-body airliner with four Rolls Royce engines. Her wingspan was 213 feet, her length 231.8 feet, and her vertical fin height 62.2 feet. Maximum take-off weight was 875,000 pounds.

It took Cook, sailing from England in 1768, eight months to reach Tahiti and a few more to find New Zealand. He finally located Australia some twenty months later. He and his men would have felt every inch of the ocean they crossed, every wave breaking directly into their sea-weary bodies.

I arrived in Australia from Los Angeles in 2003. The entire trip took eighteen hours, and somewhere over the ocean, I lost a day. We hit a bit of turbulence when the credits were rolling on my third in-flight movie, and I instinctively death-gripped the armrests and began counting all the babies and priests and soldiers on board.

The standard meal on the *Endeavour* was salted pork and a biscuit. It was served for days on end and often had weevils crawling inside.

I like to order the kosher meal on long flights even though I don't keep kosher. When you order a special meal, they serve you first, and this makes the other passengers jealous.

During his voyage, Cook lost forty men. Three drowned. Two froze. One deserted, and another was discharged. Most died of malaria and dysentery, caught on their way home through the East Indies.

We lost no men, women or children on my flight to Australia, though some looked mighty pale after the dinner service.

Why am I comparing myself to Cook? I am not British. I am not a man. I am not a discoverer of faraway lands. But, you see, actually I am. Well, not the first two things—mind you, I'm not delusional—but the last one, certainly. Why should it be thought that I discovered Australia any less than Cook? When he arrived, others were already inhabiting the place. Same goes for me. When he disembarked, he was confounded by a foreign tongue. Have you ever heard a thick Aussie accent? Or tried to make your point known in an American one? Ninety percent of the people I met in Sydney still think my name is Rita.

Cook's mission was to find the unseen Southern Continent haunting the restless minds of kings and explorers or, if he could not, to confirm once and for all that it did not exist.

I was searching for something, too. I was twenty-one years old and had recently graduated from college. The only savings to my name were $4,000 earned waitressing at an Irish pub in Philadelphia, where I had been having a grand old time performing the type of physical labor my parents wished me to forego now that my degree was in hand. They wanted me to be a professor or lawyer—something financially sound—and I was thoroughly sick of hearing about the importance of embarking on a stable career path. I found it depressing how important money had become all of a sudden, how quickly my friends dropped their Bohemian airs once they encountered the skyscraper-high rent in Manhattan. I had planned to be a musician until my college's music school disabused me of that notion, leaving me with an artist's soul and a middle-class Jewish kid's sense of duty. Were Cook's parents pleased that their son discovered countries for a living in the service of England? Sure, it sounds impressive now, but it must have been inconsistent work. Maybe his mom comforted herself with the idea that, at least, he had a steady employer, not like that freelancer Columbus, who would sail for any old country that paid his way.

I set off for Australia a poor but privileged backpacker. (There is really no way around describing yourself as "privileged" if you're able to run away for four months to find yourself.) I chose Oz because a convincing Australian friend I had met as a student invited me there. Carly told me the best way to figure out what you wanted to do with your life was just to live it, and the best way to live it was to do something unconventional, like pick up and move to Australia.

Australia loomed in my imagination as one great expanse of dust, spotted with kangaroos and koalas and lizards, animals I pictured motorists stopping for the same way we brake for deer in upstate New York. Other images I had of Australia: the Sydney Opera House, surfers, shrimp on the barbie. That was pretty much it, but it seemed as good a place as any to escape to.

From Cook's journal, the day he reached Australia:

[April 1770.] THURSDAY, 19th. In the P.M. had fresh Gales at South-South-West and Cloudy Squally weather, with a large Southerly Sea; at 6 took in the Topsails, and at 1 A.M. brought too and Sounded, but had no ground with 130 fathoms of line. At 5, set the Topsails close reef'd, and 6, saw land extending from North-East to West, distance 5 or 6 Leagues, having 80 fathoms, fine sandy bottom. We continued standing to the Westward with the Wind at South-South-West until 8, at which time we got Topgallant Yards a Cross, made all sail, and bore away along shore North-East for the Eastermost land we had in sight, being at this time in the Latitude of 37 degrees 58 minutes South, and Longitude of 210 degrees 39 minutes West.

It goes and on and on like this. Dreadfully boring stuff, right? It only picks up a little at the end of the entry, when Cook finally describes Australia: "What we have as yet seen of this land appears rather low, and not very hilly, the face of the Country green and Woody, but the Sea shore is all a white Sand."

From Friedman's journal, the day I reached Australia.

[Oct. 11, 2003] Day 1: Or should I say—the flight over. Seeing as how I'm a somewhat neurotic flyer these post-9/11 days, fourteen hours straight on a plane—all over water—is pretty much my idea of torture. I somehow made friends with the elderly man sitting next to me, and by the end of the flight, I had heard his family's entire history. How his ancestors moved from Norway back in the day because the U.S. was advertising cheap land. I took a sleeping pill in the hopes I would be unconscious for the first half of the flight at least, but only passed out for five hours or so. Long flight! Enough said.

I am sorry to tell you it doesn't pick up any, even at the end.

When Cook arrived in Australia, he soon spotted darkskinned inhabitants dotting the shoreline; they quickly receded into the woods. I wish I knew what greeted the indigenous Australians when they first came upon the country, but there are no accounts of that expedition, which took place (depending on whom you ask) between 40,000 and 125,000 years ago.

When I arrived in Australia, I went straight to immigration. The agent inquired where I was staying. "Sydney," I responded. Where in Sydney? I realized I had not written down my friend's address and had no idea where she lived. "In Bondi Beach?" the beautifully bronzed official offered, citing the typical landing point for young backpackers. I nodded meekly. My friend lived nowhere near Bondi Beach, but I had no sense of geography back then (and not much more of it now). I should have charted my course more carefully, as Cook would have, or, at the very least, brought a pocket map. For remember, friends: My journey took place way back in 2003, before Google Earth discovered Australia.

Cook was a seasoned explorer. If he was scared of anything during his stay on this overheated continent, no evidence of it exists in his journal.

My first month in Australia I was scared of everything, even though there was no question, as there was for Cook, of whether darts shot at me were poisonous, because there were no darts shot at me. Snakes, I convinced myself, were no threat in the suburbs where I was staying with Carly's family, but spiders were another story. I took to shaking out my clothing every morning, peeking inside my shoes. I had dreams about redback spiders crawling into my mouth.

Cook could not understand a word the indigenous Australians said. Neither could Tupia, the high priest he had taken aboard in Tahiti, who was able to translate successfully for the crew in New Zealand but whose language did not overlap with this newly encountered one. Cook's journal includes a list of translated words, among them: Head: "Whageegee." Hair of the head: "Morye" or "More." Teeth: "Mulere" or "Moile." Chin: "Jaeal." Beard: "Waller." Scrotum: "Coonal" or "Kunnol."

Today, Australians shorten any and every word, even if it is already quite brief. A mosquito is a "mozzie," afternoon is "arvo," thanks is "ta," Christmas is "Chrissy," garbage is "garbo," sick day is "sickie," bad guy is "baddie," and football is "footy." In Sydney, I worked in a downtown coffee shop where "cap" sounded like "flat," and "flat" I mistook for "mach." Order after order was royally screwed up until finally Joey, the beloved, becurled barista, would stop the line to scold me in front of all the finance hotshots.

"Come on, Rita," he'd say. "Pull it together."

No one would dare speak this way to Cook, I thought to myself. No one would dare.

As if discovering an entire continent was not thrilling enough, each day offered Cook new bits of the unfamiliar. He had, for instance, seen canoes before, but not Australian canoes, which were "made of one peice [sic] of the Bark of Trees about twelve or fourteen feet long, drawn or Tied together at one end." Other encounters were so foreign he hadn't yet the language to describe them. In May, the men came across the "Dung of an Animal," which they only later realized belonged to the native kangaroo, a marsupial no one in the expedition had ever before laid eyes on.

The most ordinary things became extraordinary in my new land: Carly's mom cupping the bougainvilleas in her garden, Carly's dad washing his old car on the grass to conserve water. Even the quotidian task of riding the bus was an opportunity for anthropology. In Sydney, did you know, the friendly bus drivers wear shorts with striped knee socks? Knee socks!

Cook and his crew spent four long months in Australia. I picture him taking off in the early morning hours to explore at his leisure, compass in hand, perhaps a small snack in case hunger overtook him. Even Cook had to eat, after all.

I stayed four months in Australia, too. I spent entire blissful mornings carefully negotiating with a mango for my breakfast, whereas at home, I ate toast standing up, scrolling through e-mails with one hand while listening to NPR. The mango is occupied by a flat, oblong pit, so you want to slice off the sides first. I took the first half and cut tiny crisscross patterns into the yellow flesh with a paring knife. I held this slice of mango with both hands and used my thumbs to press it inside out. Now, I had my very own mango hedgehog, and sometimes, I set this up on the counter and examined it amusedly for a few luxurious seconds. Then, I bit off the squares, slowly, one cube at a time, working my way through the fruit at a glacial pace.

Some of the wildlife Cook and his crew encountered in Australia:

> Bustards, Eagles, Hawks, Crows, Pidgeons, Doves, Quails, and several sorts of smaller birds. Herons, Boobies, Noddies, Guls, Curlews, Ducks, Pelicans, etc., Sharks, Dog-fish, Rockfish, Mullets, Breams, Cavallies, Mack'rel, old wives, Leather Jackets, Five Fingers, Sting rays, Whip rays, etc., Oysters of three or four sorts, viz., Cockles and Clams of several sorts, many of those that are found upon the Reefs are of a prodigious size, Craw fish, Crabs, Muscles, and a variety of other sorts.

Some of the wildlife I encountered in Australia at the Featherdale Wildlife Park, where I proudly stamped my park-provided "passport" at each stop: koalas lazing on gum trees like portly old men, scruffy kangaroos and wallabies, kookaburras perched like professors, Tasmanian devils running in endless loping circles, goannas (like lizards but uglier), rainbow-colored lorikeets, pugnacious Cape Barren geese and cassowaries, whose nails might easily sever a limb or eviscerate an unlucky abdomen.

Enough of these endless lists, you're saying to yourself. What about the man behind the lists? Well, in truth, I can't find Cook's emotions anywhere on the page, except for some initial disappointment that the locals won't come close enough for him to get a good look at them. I suppose it wasn't Cook's job to record feelings, but, lucky for you, it happens to be mine.

Emotions experienced while staying in Australia: excitement, fear, joy, ecstasy, gratitude, melancholy, curiosity, bliss, comfort, surprise, optimism.

There. Now you're satisfied, I imagine.

Cook was already an adventurer when he discovered Australia, but I had to wait until I discovered Australia to become one.

I traveled all over the continent on my own—up the east coast and over to Darwin and into the outback. I lived in hostels, among strangers (some stranger than others), finding odd jobs around the place to pay my way. I circled Uluru, the great red rock, in heat so sweltering I thought it would drown me. I swam in croc-inhabited waters up north in Kakadu. Friends: I. Ate. Vegemite. And if that is not bravery, I don't know what is. Near the end of my trip, I bungee jumped and skydived in the same adrenaline-filled day. Back home, my life was predictable, and I was a skittish, sheltered girl. But in Australia, I discovered I was a wild thing.

None of this would impress the stoic Cook, I'm sure. What would he think of how easy his hard-won voyage has become? Now, Oprah and John Travolta fly entire audiences to Sydney. Now, we have the Outback Steakhouse and can order a Bloomin' Onion any time we damn well please. The external dangers of traveling have lessened considerably over the centuries, but the internal ones remain. I nearly disappeared altogether in Australia. I didn't want to go home. I had no use for this "real world" everyone kept invoking as the place where a reasonable person lives. I tell you, I was a whisper away from letting the place swallow me whole.

There are no more lands left to discover. Even Cook himself, who most call to mind as the first European to set foot in

Australia, was merely one of a number of explorers to have sighted and landed on the continent prior to English settlement, and he did so 164 years after the first such documented encounter.

The only truly virgin territory left is within us, and I located a small patch of untapped self in Australia—what I realize, in retrospect, was my nascent traveler self. She was a surprising revelation, this girl who thrived in the unfamiliar and did not let fear rule the day, this lady who moved more slowly through the world: observing, exploring, absorbing. In 1770, Cook planted the Union Jack on Australian soil and declared the land part of the British Empire. In 2003, in Australia, I declared my future life uncolonized. I would make my own way in the world, treacherous though it might be.

ॐ ॐ ॐ

Rachel Friedman is the author of The Good Girl's Guide to Getting Lost: A Memoir of Three Continents, Two Friends, and One Unexpected Adventure. *It was chosen as a Target Breakout Book and selected by Goodreads' readers as one of the best travel books of 2011. She has written for* The New York Times, National Geographic Traveler, New York, BUST, Bitch, Creative Nonfiction, The Chronicle of Higher Education, *and* Nerve, *among others. In addition to these literary accomplishments, she also makes a killer loaf of pumpkin bread.* "Discovery" *is the winner of lit magazine* Creative Nonfiction's *2012 Down Under Essay Contest.*

༃ ༃ ༃

The Black Bitch

'Twas off the bonnie banks of Linlithgow Loch, some
350 years ago, the king had sentenced a thief to starve
to death, ordering him chained to an oak tree on a
floating islet. The captive's faithful companion, a black
greyhound, treaded through icy waters with food in her
mouth attempting to save her master's life. When the
palace caught onto the canine's caper she was shackled to
a different tree on a nearby islet, leaving both prisoner and
pooch to perish. From that day forward the townspeople
of Linlithgow were so touched by the dog's loyalty that
they started referring to themselves as "black bitches."
— *Scottish legend*

fter watching an episode of "Who Do You Think You
Are?" a TV show that documents celebrities' searches
for their family roots, I enthusiastically joined Ancestry.com.
Since I'm not an Academy Award-winning actress, though,
my only option was hands-on investigation (as opposed to
having an expert do it for me), which turned into hours upon
days spent hunched over my laptop, dry-eyed and jacked up
on coffee, slowly comprehending all the mind-numbing background labor that television hadn't revealed.

During this online hunt for my family tree I'd gape at the screen and wait for green leaves to sprout, signaling new revelations of long-departed relatives; in truth, of course, they were complete strangers. But because these unknown souls were blood relations, it started to get interesting. My familial branches grew longer and longer, and beneath the Paris surname sprouted several individuals from a place I'd never heard of, Linlithgow. It was a tiny town, research revealed, located twenty miles west of Edinburgh. Finally, my penchant for plaid and bitter ale was explained!

Over the following weeks I researched Scotland and its history. One book detailed the magnitude of the country's diaspora and singled out a man in New York whose heritage began in Scotland. For years he'd accumulated Scottish memorabilia rivaling a museum collection. (I could just picture this guy decked out in full kilt regalia wielding an axe.) Asked when he planned to visit the Homeland, the man replied that he would never make the journey for fear of being "too disappointed."

Despite this, and fully realizing that the backdrop of Linlithgow would not resemble a scene from *Braveheart*, I longed to go—especially after looking up the town's website and reading the fable of the brave black bitch. Luckily, I'd be attending a conference over the summer in Wales and could easily travel to the royal burgh historically noted as the birthplace of James V and Mary, Queen of Scots. (Honestly, forget the nobility, I was dying to see if the townspeople, *my people*, were still living up to the legend.)

I'd arranged to stay at a bed and breakfast called Glenavon House situated on the outskirts of town. The owner, Sue Lindsay, insisted on meeting me at the train station. There was something all too familiar about her. My second sentence after "Thanks for picking me up," was "I've got a hideous hangover."

"Ha! No problem," she scoffed. "I've got one, too."

If "chatty" is a common Scottish trait, then I'd found the leader of my kind. Sue and I sat crossed-legged on a pale yellow divan flipping through her family albums, and our meeting took on the urgency of a high school reunion's mission—how fast can you cram your life's history into one evening. Her quick fill-of-the-wine-glass action never faltered or once stirred the resident cat asleep by my side. As nighttime finally fell on the land of lingering daylight, I climbed the stairs to my room and noticed a full crystal decanter of Sherry on the nightstand.

"Drink it all," Sue encouraged. "That's what it's there for!"

My people, indeed, I thought.

So I did—and then slept motionless beneath the diaphanous white drapery of a four-poster bed for what seemed like seventeen centuries.

The next morning I hopped a bus into the heart of the town of 12,000 residents, then veered straight into the building that housed public records. I might have been naive to believe I'd dig up actual evidence of my great-great-great-great-great-great-great-great-grandfather, John Paris, born there in 1660—but I did. For a couple of pounds, a kindly employee helped access the original page online, which showed proof of marriage between John and Issobel Aitken on November 19, 1682. Not only were John and I born exactly 300 years apart, but his wedding was on my birthday (a fact probably momentous to no one other than myself).

Still, I would never get to meet him, or even glimpse an old photograph. We'd never share a hymnal during services at the medieval kirk, or stroll together around the grassy lawn beside the castle ruin known as The Peel, tossing breadcrumbs to the swans. A sense of disenchantment choked me like a triple-knotted scarf. The only scrap to possess was a signature scrawled into a footnote of history?

There had to be more I could take with me. I decided to recreate John Paris's footsteps around the square known as The Cross, which was completely vacant. As I passed a stony wall near the church, the atmosphere grew eerily quiet. My pace slowed as I spied the tops of ashen tombs.

I wandered into St. Michael's Parish (once used to stable Oliver Cromwell's horses during a battle) to glimpse the altar where my ancestors had most likely worshipped. Only months before, their names had been as unfamiliar as characters in a novel. But now, as I stood proudly on Scottish soil, they somehow became genuine, dear, *people to remember*. As I was leaving, I noticed a collection of inspirational cards available for a small donation. Instantly, my hand reached for a lavender-colored offering titled "What is Dying" by someone named Bishop Brent. I dropped a few coins in the collection box and was tucking it away when a woman asked if I needed further assistance. I did, I answered gratefully: Would it be possible to see the burial plot locations? I asked, giving her the year of my relative's existence. The woman informed me that unfortunately, due to "lack of space," my ancestor was probably buried beneath the newer dead people—which meant there would be no visible indicator.

But I ventured out to the cemetery grounds anyway, traipsing atop crumbled bits of illegible markers. Time had erased almost every name etched onto the headstones, many broken and scattered below cypress trees. The only other living creature within the gates was a petrified hare with a sideways glare. Kneeling down, I peered into a rabbit hole underneath what may or may not have been anywhere close to John Paris's final resting place. Staring into blackness, I thought, *herein lies a fragment of my family, a piece of me*. A warm sun shone down and lit the churchyard like a thousand sacred candles.

Later that same Monday afternoon, I sipped on a beer as my eyes surveyed the dark-wooded interior of The Black Bitch, one of the oldest pubs in Scotland. Within minutes a man named Archie asked if he could buy me another pint.

"Sure," I said, wiping froth from my upper lip. "That's so sweet of you."

We'd only just met inside the empty haunt, and after my solitary morning it was a relief to see that the town's motto, "St. Michael is kinde to straingers," rang true.

"Ya know, when ya ordered dat," he said, pointing at my drained glass, "I t'ought it was fer somebody else . . . that you were waitin' fer someone," Archie chuckled. "Ya don't usually see a woman drinkin' Guinness."

I had to laugh, because in a way I *had* been waiting for someone. Someone who couldn't possibly ever turn up. I shrugged jovially at the gray-haired charmer and wondered in between chimes from a corner slot machine and his friendly banter if I dared tell why I'd come. Fumbling inside my bag, I removed the little card I'd purchased at the church. Its message seemed to preach directly at me:

A ship sails and I stand watching till she fades on the horizon and someone at my side says, "She is gone." Gone where? Gone from my sight, that is all; she is just as large as when I saw her. The diminished size and total loss of sight is in me, not her, and just at that moment when someone at my side says, "She is gone," there are others who are watching her coming, and other voices take up a glad shout, "There she comes!" and that is dying.

I took it as a sign that somewhere up there my ancestors had just acknowledged me. I began explaining to Archie, the bartender, and one other man about traveling all the way to Linlithgow from America to raise a glass in my eight times great grandfather's honor.

"Doesn't that . . . make me a . . . black bitch descendant?" I questioned in a lame stutter, praying I hadn't committed some secret breach of bitch ethics.

They all quit talking and looked at me. The pub's heart seemed to stop beating for a couple of seconds.

All of a sudden, the gentleman at the end of the bar wanted to buy me a pint as well. Together we lifted our glasses in unison—the townspeople and me—and continued our discussion about nothing much at all.

After about an hour, I announced it was my turn to treat.

"No, no, no!" Archie barked. "Always remember, Jillay," he advised paternally, "it's nice to be nice."

I felt like knitting him a sweater or something, but then remembered I didn't know how.

On my untelevised walk back to Sue's I felt sorry for that man in New York, so far detached, admiring his trinkets and treasures (presumably some too valuable to touch). If only he'd visit the Homeland and meet some of his people. Perhaps he might discover that the worthiest possessions in Scotland are stored within the living legends and cannot be bought.

જી જી જી

Jill Paris is a writer living in Los Angeles. Her essays have been published in The Best Travel Writing 2009 *and* Leave the Lipstick, Take the Iguana. *Her feature stories have appeared in* The Saturday Evening Post, Travel Africa, Gadling, *and others. She holds an M.A. in Humanities and a Master of Professional Writing degree from USC. She travels for the inexplicable human connection.*

෯ ෯ ෯

Trust

Sometimes it's simply the kinder way.

I stared out the airport window. Dusk was approaching, rain exploded on the ground, and hunched, glistening figures lurched through the downpour as if under attack. The sky was steely and raked with wind, and the thought of being caught in this hostile city alone with no cash for a decent hotel struck me with paralyzing dread.

For three long days I had been traversing Africa, trying to get from Niger to Kenya where I was to meet a friend and depart on safari. The bulk of those days had been spent bribing sour officials, battling malarial mosquitoes, and sitting wretchedly in filthy, stifling-hot airports. I had come from three tough but rewarding weeks in the Sahara, and the great beauty and monstrous insouciance of the desert had left me with a feeling of serene detachment. It was the closest I had ever come to achieving a Zen-like state of mind.

But by the time I reached the Congo, that hard-earned peaceful detachment had gone, replaced by a sudden loathing of travel. Now, nineteen hours behind schedule, all tolerance had fled.

Arriving in South Africa, I had twenty-five minutes to catch my fourth and final flight to Nairobi. But when I dashed off the plane at Johannesburg's airport, I was greeted by an obscenely lengthy queue snaking toward a line of passport control booths.

South Africa, a crucible of long-quashed anger and a now-flailing backlash, was in turmoil. World press had seized on the stories of crime, violence, and internationally linked corruption. In response, South Africa's authorities were forcing all visitors, even those in transit, to undergo document inspections. This delay rang a resounding death knell to my safari plans.

When I turned from the dreary airport window back to the crowded room, a young man was lingering beside me. I stared at him stonily, in no mood for small talk.

"Hullo," he said cheerfully. "Can I help you? You look in need of some assistance."

I judged him to be in his mid-twenties, possibly ten years my junior. Short, slight, and brown skinned, with a South African accent. He was dressed in jeans and a beer emblem t-shirt, with a well-used backpack slung over one shoulder—the global uniform of a traveling student.

"I doubt you can help," I replied dismissively. "I was supposed to be in Nairobi tonight. I *had* to be in Nairobi tonight. However, my plane is about to leave without me."

"Oh dear," he said. His eyes showed genuine sympathy. "Right, well then, let's see if there's anything we can do about that. Come with me."

The young backpacker moved off briskly but I remained where I was, confused, embarrassed, and reluctant to lose my place in line. He stopped and gestured for me to follow. This time I did, although hesitantly. He cut to the head of the line, approached an official, and spoke to her in Afrikaans. She regarded me coldly but said nothing as I walked past without showing any documentation.

"Wait here," he instructed, indicating a row of seats. "Which airline were you on? Right then, let me see if I can hold that flight for you. Won't be a mo'."

As I sat there waiting for him to return, I struggled to imagine who this youngster was that he could circumvent immigration officials and stop airplanes.

He returned shaking his head. "Sorry," he said, "it's gone. It was the last one out tonight and all the flights tomorrow are solidly booked."

I obviously looked stricken.

"Don't worry," he said. "We'll get you on a plane. I'm Ron, by the way." He stuck out his hand.

Who was this "we" that could get me on a flight? I looked him in the eye. "Ron, I was wondering . . . how did you know I needed help back there? Do you work here? What is it you do?"

"FBI," he replied, as casually as if he'd said "janitorial staff."

He was on loan, he explained, to the South African government by the United States. "Illegal immigration, drug smuggling, terrorism, that sort of thing. We're here to train their authorities. My job is to mingle with crowds and look for anxious people—suspects, in fact. And you looked rather anxious."

"You thought I was smuggling drugs?" I said, horrified.

"No, no," he answered earnestly, smiling. "I just thought you looked like a fellow American in need of assistance. But you're not American after all, are you? You must've lived there quite a while now, although you weren't born there. New Zealand, right? You fooled me, I had you pegged for American."

I was shocked. He hadn't seen my passport, nor was I wearing running shoes, baseball cap, designer labels, or a collegiate sweatshirt—all dead giveaways of Americanism. He was correct and yet had gleaned all this by the few words I'd spoken. I suddenly felt exposed and defensive.

"But you're not American either," I accused him. His English was thick with Afrikaans. Even his vernacular was Southern African.

"I am. I'm from El Paso, Texas. Been here four months now. Languages are sort of my thing. Afrikaans most recently."

Observing him more closely, it occurred to me that Ron was the perfect undercover agent, if that's what he could be called. With his mocha skin, brown eyes, and brown hair he could have been African, Arab, Mexican, sub-continental, or South American. How extraordinary it must be, I thought, to be able to fit in anywhere. Being blond, pale, and tall, my entire being shrieks "foreigner" in most parts of the world. Ron, on the other hand, would be unremarkable in pretty much any crowd.

"Look," he said kindly, "you're probably tired. Do you have somewhere you can go? I know a hotel. It's not too expensive, and it's clean, safe, relatively close. I could drop you off there, it's on my way home. We'll pick up your luggage—they'll send it through now that you missed the flight."

I was at the point where I had to decide whether to trust him or not. Women traveling alone are persistently faced with this dilemma. Rather than be paralyzed by suspicion, we learn to rely on the murmurings of instinct, calculate the risk, and then in the end hope like hell those instincts are correct.

"Do you happen to have any ID on you?" I asked. "I don't doubt you, but, you know, it's just smart. . . ."

He pulled out a plastic card with FBI printed in block letters, his name, and a photo. I peered at the photo. He looked completely different—he was, indeed, a true human chameleon. The situation suddenly seemed surreal and I resisted the urge to laugh. I knew people like Ron existed, but only on television or in movies—never in a reality of my own.

"I can take you to the hotel," he said, "but there's one thing I have to do before we leave. You can come along if you like."

I had nothing better to do—and by now I was extremely curious. I followed.

We stopped at an airport restaurant where Ron purchased pizza in large quantities, explaining the situation as he took the money out of his wallet.

"We arrested some Pakistanis this morning. They were trying to get up to Nairobi on fake passports. We're deporting them tomorrow. Just thought I'd drop by and deliver this to them. The police can't afford food for deportees here."

I was surprised by how much he was telling me, and even more so as I followed him behind the security doors and through the inner workings of the airport. No one bothered to ask who I was or why I was there. People nodded at Ron but asked no questions about me. Perhaps they assumed I was a suspect.

We entered a barren concrete building adjoining the airport. A long, narrow corridor was lit with fluorescent light and littered with cans and cigarette butts. There were no windows, only opposing rows of closed doors. I began to feel uneasy; how quickly I had turned from blithe traveler to a character in the gritty, behind-the-scenes realm of crime and law enforcement. I was unnerved.

A policeman stood guard outside the Pakistanis' room. He unlocked the door as Ron approached, and we entered. Through a serpentine haze of cigarette smoke I saw three men crouched on a narrow bed and another two on the floor. They were in their thirties, dressed in dark Western clothing. Their eyes were as black as onyx and hard with anger and defeat. Ron set the food on a table, speaking a language I did not recognize, probably Urdu. The men muttered. One said something and Ron dug into his pocket and tossed him a pack of cigarettes. The man inclined his head in grudging thanks. We left the building in silence.

"You must be hungry, too," Ron said cheerfully as we re-entered the airport to get my luggage. "Come on, we'll stop on the way to your hotel."

Over dinner at a local restaurant, we talked mostly about Ron's job. I could tell he was trying to impress me, but he did it in such an open way it was rather endearing. He spoke twenty-three languages, could tell time by the sun, was an expert in martial arts, and had never been seriously attached to a girl. He had been posted to cities all over the world, but he was tired of airport work. What he really wanted to do, he told me, was be an air marshal on international flights. Profession-als, he explained, were hired to sit in the center of the plane with a loaded gun in case of hijacking or other disturbances. "It rarely happens, and you get paid quite well."

Despite my insistence, he refused to let me buy dinner, tell-ing me to save my money in case I should be stranded again. Later, he dropped me off at a modest hotel somewhere on the outskirts of the city. He had been every bit the gentleman.

As I left the car he leaned over and said, "As far as tomor-row, I checked on flights and there's one leaving at eight in the morning. It's full, but I can arrange to get you on. I'll pick you up at six."

"No, no, no," I protested. "You've done enough. I won't get you out of bed at such an ungodly hour. You really are too kind, Ron."

"I insist," he said. "I'd rather know you got there safely, and anyway, you'll need me to get you on the flight. Sleep well."

He was there at six, as promised, armed with the same cheerful smile.

At the airport Ron disappeared, returning with a boarding pass. "Got you on. The airline thinks we're deporting you, but you shouldn't care so long as you get there. There won't be any record of it, don't worry."

I wasn't sure how to thank him adequately for all he had done. He'd undoubtedly broken rules for me, or most certainly bent them. I wondered if he'd bumped some other traveler from the flight, and I felt momentary guilt.

As he walked me to the gate I asked him something I'd wondered the night before.

"Why did you feed those men? You paid with your own money, didn't you? I mean, they looked terribly shady. Are they terrorists? Pakistanis hate us right now, don't they? Are they even Pakistanis?"

Ron sighed, and his chin dropped. I felt as if I'd said something dreadful, something terribly disappointing. He stopped walking. "This job," he said, "has taught me that our presumptions about people are rarely true. We have so many preconceptions, especially about foreigners, but they are nothing more than fear of the unknown. We quite comfortably make sweeping generalizations about entire nations of people. These people we suspect of being evil, most are just students and deadbeat dreamers and artists and teachers and greedy businessmen—the same characters that populate *all* societies. And then some of them, a *tiny* portion of them, are actually individuals with intent to harm others. But we foolishly judge them all by the few who are bad."

Ron was becoming heated, staring vacantly ahead. "I bought those men food," he said, "because in all likelihood they are simply seeking an improved life. And even if those five individuals aren't innocents like most of the folk I encounter, even if they are real criminals, then a show of kindness may help, just a little, to debunk their preconceptions about us. Until we can prove them as bad people it is simply *kinder* to trust their intentions."

"Besides," he added, "everyone has to eat."

I gave Ron a quick, awkward hug and was escorted down the gangway by the airport police. Although they believed they were deporting me, they treated me gently. There was no public scene with handcuffs, as I'd dreaded, nor any strong-arming. They simply carried my bag and escorted me to my seat, whispering something to the flight attendant, who looked at me with surprise. It was raining hard outside, and the wind still gusted, but the city no longer felt hostile. It hadn't changed since yesterday, but I had.

☙ ☙ ☙

Amanda Jones is a travel writer and photographer living in the San Francisco Bay Area. Her stories have appeared in Town & Country, Travel & Leisure, Condé Nast Traveller, *the* Los Angeles Times, The Sunday Times, Salon.com, *the* San Francisco Chronicle, Brides, Food & Wine *and* Vogue Australia, *among others. Her short stories have been published in several anthologies, including* Wanderlust *and* The Kindness of Strangers. *Amanda has also done story development for* National Geographic *television, and her photography series "Timeless," black and white photographs of African tribal peoples, was exhibited at the United Nations film festival. She has worked on staff at* Vogue *magazine and was formerly the editor-in-chief of* Antiques and Fine Art. *She was born and educated in Auckland, New Zealand.*

Acknowledgments

I'm grateful to everyone who helped this book come together, starting with the hundreds of women who traveled the world and sent us stories—without you, *The Best Women's Travel Writing* could never exist. To James O'Reilly, Larry Habegger, and Sean O'Reilly: you are smart and kind and generous and so damn fun to work with, and I thank you for your boundless trust and guidance, and for the important work you do. (James: coffee this week? Next week?) Endless thanks to Travelers' Tales Director of Production Natalie Baszile: Your personal house calls! Your saintly patience! Your attention to detail! Your wicked sense of humor! You're truly the best. A million thanks to my talented intern, Kareem Yasin, whose voluntary hard work, candor, and keen editorial insight contributed enormously to the quality of this book. And my eternal love and gratitude to Dan Prothero: without your steadfast support and enthusiasm, wise feedback, and tolerance for the countless columns of paper populating our home, I would be all kinds of lost. Many thanks to Jen Castle, Dolly Spalding, Marcia DeSanctis, Erica Hilton, Lynn Bruni, Marianne Rogoff, and Zahra Noorbakhsh for editorial support. And to all my wonderful friends and family who provided moral support—too many to name—I feel outrageously fortunate to have you in my corner. Thanks also to everyone who helped circulate the call for submissions, nominating stories and sharing and posting and tweeting and retweeting—this was a banner year for submissions. Special thanks in that department go to Stephanie Elizondo Griest, Jen Leo, Susan Orlean, Andrew McCarthy, Grant Martin, Don George, Rolf Potts, Erin Byrne, Ayesha Mattu, and Caren Osten Gerszberg.

Thanks also to the Writers' Grotto for providing a sweet, supportive work environment. And finally, thanks to all of you reading this book. It is my immeasurable honor to bring you these stories.

"The Risky Path" by Holly Morris first appeared in *MORE* magazine 2012. Published with permission from the author. Copyright © 2012 by Holly Morris.

"Chasing Tornadoes" by Kirsten Koza published with permission from the author. Copyright © 2013 by Kirsten Koza.

"The Women's Sitting Room" by Angie Chuang first appeared in "Women and War: A Tribute to Adrienne Rich" in *Adanna,* Winter 2013. Published with permission from the author. Copyright © 2013 by Angie Chuang.

"The Mighty Big Love Test" by Suzanne Roberts first published on *Matadornetwork.com* 2013. Published with permission from the author. Copyright © 2013 by Suzanne Roberts.

"Who Made this Grave?" by Molly Beer first appeared in *Vela,* October 29, 2012. Published with permission from the author. Copyright © 2012 by Molly Beer.

"Fill in the Blanks" by Abbie Kozolchyk published with permission from the author. Copyright © 2013 by Abbie Kozolchyk.

"Dreams from My Father" by Apricot Anderson Irving first appeared in *MORE* magazine 2012. Published with permission from the author. Copyright © 2012 by Apricot Anderson Irving.

"Business or Pleasure?" by Rachel Levin published with permission from the author. Copyright © 2013 by Rachel Levin.

"Connie Britton's Hair" by Marcia DeSanctis published with permission from the author. Copyright © 2013 by Marcia DeSanctis.

"We Wait for the Sun" by Carol Beddo published with permission from the author. Copyright © 2013 by Carol Beddo.

"Half-Baked Decisions" by Sarah Katin published with permission from the author. Copyright © 2013 by Sarah Katin.

"The Road to Wounded Knee" by Jenna Scatena published with permission from the author. Copyright © 2013 by Jenna Scatena.

"The Saffron Rabbit" by Amber Kelly-Anderson published with permission from the author. Copyright © 2013 by Amber Kelly-Anderson.

"Leaving Kishinev" by Helen Rubinstein first appeared in *Witness* Vol. XXV No. 2 (Summer 2012). Published with permission from the author. Copyright © 2012 by Helen Rubinstein.

About the Editor

Lavinia Spalding also edited the 2011 and 2012 editions of *The Best Women's Travel Writing*. She is the author of *Writing Away: A Creative Guide to Awakening the Journal-Writing Traveler* (named one of the best travel books of 2009 by the *Los Angeles Times*) and coauthor of *With a Measure of Grace: The Story and Recipes of a Small Town Restaurant*. She's a regular contributor to *Yoga Journal*, and her work has appeared in numerous print and online publications, including *Sunset*, the *San Francisco Chronicle*, *Gadling*, *Post Road*, *Tin House*, *Inkwell*, and *The Best Travel Writing Volume 9*. She lives in San Francisco, where she's a resident at the Writers' Grotto and a co-founder of the monthly travel reading series Weekday Wanderlust. She teaches writing and journaling workshops around the world, spends most of her money on coffee and airplane tickets, and can mispronounce "I love you" in thirty languages. Visit her at www.laviniaspalding.com.